Make Computers Speak Your Language

Computing in Your Own Language

Barun Kumar Sahu

UNICORN BOOKS

UNICORN BOOKS

E-mail: unicornbooks@vsnl.com
Website: www.unicornbooks.in • www.kidscorner.in

Distributors
Pustak Mahal, Delhi
J-3/16 , Daryaganj, New Delhi-110002
☎ 23276539, 23272783, 23272784 • *Fax:* 011-23260518
E-mail: info@pustakmahal.com • *Website:* www.pustakmahal.com

London Office
5, Roddell Court, Bath Road, Slough SL3 OQJ, England
E-mail: pustakmahaluk@pustakmahal.com

Sales Centre
10-B, Netaji Subhash Marg, Daryaganj, New Delhi-110002
☎ 23268292, 23268293, 23279900 • *Fax:* 011-23280567
E-mail: rapidexdelhi@indiatimes.com

Branch Offices
Bangalore: ☎ 22234025
E-mail: pmblr@sancharnet.in • pustak@sancharnet.in
Mumbai: ☎ 22010941
E-mail: rapidex@bom5.vsnl.net.in
Patna: ☎ 3294193 • *Telefax:* 0612-2302719
E-mail: rapidexptn@rediffmail.com
Hyderabad: *Telefax:* 040-24737290
E-mail: pustakmahalhyd@yahoo.co.in

ISBN 978-81-7806-121-4

Edition : 2007

Printed at : Param Offsetters, Okhla, New Delhi-110020

Dedico
este libro
a mi Sonu.

Preface

You are a housewife, and want to search the Internet for Bangladeshi recipes written in Bengali language. You are a Hindi poet, and want to key in the Hindi poems in your laptop by yourself. You are a Tibetan monk, and want to design a website in Tibetan language on Buddhist philosophy. You are a Tamil buff, and want to computerize Tamil literature. You have received an e-mail in Arabic, which you cannot figure out. You are a government servant, and want to implement the three-language formula in this age of e-governance. You are a priest in India, and want to send the Vedic texts to your client in the USA by e-mail. You are a plumber, and want to send SMS in Hindi to your customer. You are a …

Well, this book is meant for really ordinary computer users. You are a lay computer user, know little bit of typing, and can send email, browse the Internet and fine-tune the settings[1] on your computer, ergo you have all the prerequisites to understand and use the concepts illustrated in this book. Of course, if you are a serious computer user, you can still benefit from the book. Maybe you have collected data in an Indian language, which you want to process.

Today, computer is used by not only computer geeks and whiz kids, but also by ordinary people who use it in their homes and cybercafés. As computer enters more and more offices, homes, laps, palms and pockets, and becomes the ubiquitous means of data storage, data processing and data communication, the users are increasingly lay and non-technical. Some computer users today are barely literate. English is not the language of most countries. Even in the Indian subcontinent, English is used and understood by only a miniscule fraction of the population. Localization of the language is inevitable in this age of information technology. And it has already happened! The purpose of the book is to spread the awareness and knowledge of the use of local languages in computers. Some years down the line, maybe if you cannot encode a language in electronic form, the language will be only as good as bitmap pictures![2]

---

[1] In case "fine-tune the settings" sounds too discouraging, it is clarified that what you will be required to do is nothing more than clicking/double-clicking some icons, selecting from menus, checking boxes, and clicking the command buttons "OK," "Apply" or "Cancel". That is all! No writing of programs!

[2] Indeed, some websites show Indic/Arabic texts as bitmap/GIF pictures, and not as a sequence of characters.

- A few decades ago, you could write only in English language in computers. You struggled to type even English words with ligatures and diacritical marks such as: façade, Cæsar, naïve, cliché, El Niño, château, Rōntgen, à la, etc. Gradually, many European languages were included in the operating system. Now, even most major Indian languages have been included. And you can almost banish English from your computer because it knows many Indian (and other) languages![3]

The book starts with the non-standard methods of typing in computer in Indian languages widely used in the Indian subcontinent. Such methods only give visual appearance of being in Indian languages, even though internally everything is in English, more specifically maybe in English(US). This method is suitable primarily for taking printouts: you cannot process the data, nor can you communicate in it electronically. Unfortunately, such non-standard methods have done more harm than good to the popularization of Indian languages in the cyberspace. The book reveals the correct way of using Indian and other languages in computers and on the Internet: in ways that is technically correct and legally sound, and is the worldwide standard.

You can search the Internet in Indian languages. You can write email in Indian languages. You can sort text, and search it. Hindi text will no longer appear sheer garbage full of unintelligible characters like ^t@wß‡ËhÿT. One letter in one font will not become another letter/symbol/sign in another font. And when you send your document as e-mail attachment, you need not send the font as you might be doing now: because your document will not just look like being in an Indian language visually, but will be in the language and, nobody can misinterpret it. The word processor will not apply English spell checking or auto-corrections on Hindi texts. Your Hindi e-mail will appear in Hindi in your mobile phone. And yes, you do not need any software. Your existing Microsoft Windows operating system and the Microsoft Office suite are enough.

After reading the book, you should be able to write, store, print and transmit texts, data and documents in many languages: Hindi, Bengali, Tamil, Telugu, Gujarati, Punjabi, Urdu, Kashmiri, Kannada, Malayalam, Sanskrit, Sindhi, Nepali, Marathi, Oriya, Assamese, and Konkani. You can also write in French, Spanish, Russian, Italian, German, Arabic and Portuguese. You can even write in Thai, Persian, Tibetan, Myanmarese, Maldivian, Sinhalese, Catalan, Greek, Pashto and Hebrew. And in any combination of these languages! That is, one document may contain sentences in several languages. (However, the complicated East-Asian scripts have been left largely uncovered in this book.)

[3] It is not recommended that you banish English from your computer, at least for the time being!

Many concepts have been illustrated in Hindi, or in another Indic language. However, these concepts may be valid for other similar languages also. The illustrations have not been given in all languages for want of space. Those who do typing in computer will find *Annexure (E)* especially useful. It explains how to key in complex ligatures and conjuncts in Indic and Arabic scripts.

Information technology is a rapidly changing field. This is especially true for implementation of Indic languages where several far-reaching changes have taken place in recent years. Changes have taken place (and may still take place!) in the fonts and rendering of complex scripts. Moreover, general and technical features of Microsoft Windows, Office, Linux and OpenOffice have not been discussed in this book, for which you may refer to specific books.

I gratefully acknowledge the contribution my daughter Sangh Mitra Sahu in writing this book. I also acknowledge the contribution my younger daughter Shruti Sahu: I could not have completed the book without her non-interference.

Barun Kumar Sahu

barun_sahu@yahoo.com
barun_sahu@rediffmail.com

Contents

An Introduction

Information technology has facilitated and accelerated the pace of globalization. It has bridged the gap between the people, and made distance irrelevant. Interestingly, the same information technology is also facilitating localization. Until a few decades ago, one could write only in English with one's computer. ASCII[1] was the popular standard code.[2] One could grudge at not being able to work in one's language in computer—but there was nothing that could be done about it. It was one-size/language-fits-all situation.

The increasing popularization of computers the world over has encouraged the development of software environments in local languages. Today, computers process texts not just in English, but in most other languages of the world. More and more languages are being added to the repertoire. For example, texts in the following categories of languages can be used in computer:

1. European languages such as English, French, Spanish, Portuguese, Russian, German, and Greek etc,
2. East Asian languages such as Chinese, Japanese, and Korean etc,
3. Right to left languages: Arabic, Hebrew, Syriac, Divehi/Maldivian, Kharoshthi (script), Persian, Urdu, Kashmiri(Arabic), and Sindhi(Arabic) etc,
4. Indic languages of Brahmi family and similar languages such as Hindi, Sanskrit, Punjabi, Bengali, Assamese, Oriya, Gujarati, Nepali, Marathi, Tamil, Telugu, Malayalam, Kannada, Sinhalese, Myanmarese, Tibetan, Bodo, Romani and Thai etc,
5. Languages written in a different script: Mizo and Vietnamese languages in Latin script etc.

It is worth noting that many languages have more than one variant. For example, British and American are the two major flavors of English language, and 'Spain' and 'Latin America' are that of Spanish language.

While the handwritten forms of most languages are cursive, for the purpose of text processing in computer, the following scripts are not treated as cursive: Latin, Cyrillic, Greek, Hebrew, Divehi etc. Letters in cursive or complex scripts form different ligatures depending on the context. Indic and Arabic scripts are complex scripts. The following scripts are complex scripts: Arabic, Devanagari, Bengali, Gurmukhi, Gujarati, Oriya, Telugu, Tamil, Kannada, Malayalam, Sinhala, Burmese, Tibetan, Thai etc.

---

[1] American Standard Code for Information Interchange (ASCII) has 128 codes: 0 through 127. Letters of English alphabet (26 lowercase and 26 uppercase letters), ten decimal digits, some punctuation marks, and a few other signs—apart from certain control characters—were encoded in 128 codes.

[2] Fundamentally, computers work with numbers: binary numbers comprising zeros and ones, to be more exact. To a computer, every thing is a number or a numeric code—even English letters are just codes to computers.

This book explains how to write electronically in a variety of languages, with special reference to Indic, Arabic and European languages. As a prerequisite, it is assumed that one is well conversant with typing in English languages in an office suite, one can fiddle with the control panel/control center and property settings of the operating system, and one is comfortable with menu bar, keyboard and mouse. Under these assumptions, the book goes on to explain the implementation of Indic and other languages.

This book describes three ways of implementation of languages and scripts[3]:

i. Non-standard font method, with or without overlaying software,

ii. ISCII and similar standard methods having limited scope, and

iii. Unicode method.

However, the book recommends the last method only. (The first two methods have been included for historical and evolutionary reasons.) The Government of India is associated with the Unicode Consortium, and has been engaged in a dialog for additional characters in the Indic blocks and improvements to the textual descriptions and annotations in Unicode standard. Also, governments and other institutions in the region are members of the Unicode Consortium or are engaged in dialog for improvements in the Unicode standards. Unicode character set is used in short messaging service (SMS) in Indic languages.

Some concepts explained in this book may not be available in older versions of Microsoft Windows. The features not supported in the older versions of Microsoft Windows have been noted in the book at appropriate places. The features on which help is easily available in Microsoft Office have not been explained in this book. One may have to refer to the help available in Microsoft Windows and Microsoft Office.

It is expected that as one reads through the chapters, one will go on practicing on computer the ideas and methods described in the chapters. Hands-on experience should give better insights. Moreover, the following should be noted:-

1. In some situations, Left-Alt and Right-Alt keys produce different results. Wherever Left-Alt key has specifically been suggested, Right-Alt key should not be used and vice versa. If Left-Alt or Right-Alt key has been recommended in conjunction with another key(s), then Left-Alt or Right-Alt key may be pressed first, and may be released only after the 'another' key has/other keys have been pressed and released.

2. Entering decimal digits while keeping the Alt key pressed produces different results depending on whether the digits are inputted from the numeric keypad (where numeric keys are laid out compactly like that in a calculator) with NumLock in ON position, or from the main keyboard (where digit keys are in a row below the function keys).

3. The characters that are inputted on pressing of the keys of the keyboard depends on the keyboard layout/Input Method Editor (IME) selected at operating system level, as explained later in this book.

---

[3] There was also a fourth way, in which GIST card was used under DOS operating system for Indic and Arabic scripts. This was a hardware implementation of language, rather than software implementation.

4. If a language is not supported by the software then one may see (i) characters like □ □ □ □ , (ii) question marks (?), or (iii) incorrect ligatures and placement of accents and vowel signs such as व◌िर in place of वरि, अक्‌ष in place of अ{k etc.

5. Microsoft updates and upgrades features of Microsoft Windows and Microsoft Office. Same is the case with other operating system and office suites. It is recommended that system be kept updated.

Numeric codes in Unicode are conventionally written in hexadecimal number system, and not in decimal number system. As such, preliminary knowledge of the hexadecimal number system is helpful. A brief note on binary and hexadecimal number systems is given in *Annexure (A)*. It should be noted that "12 hex" or "10B2 hex" means that the number "12" or "10B2" is in hexadecimal number system, and is not in decimal number system.

Typists may find *Annexure (E)* very useful, which explains formation of complex ligatures in Indic and Arabic scripts.

Unicode

Unicode provides a unique number for every character: no matter what the platform, no matter what the program, and no matter what the language. Fundamentally, computers deal with numbers. They store letters and other characters by assigning a numeric code to each one. Before Unicode was invented, there were hundreds of different encoding systems for assigning the numeric codes. No single encoding could contain enough characters. For example, the European Union alone requires several different encodings to cover all its languages. Even for a single language like English, no single encoding was adequate for all the letters, punctuation and technical symbols in common use. These encoding systems also conflicted with one another. That is, two encodings could use the same numeric code for two different characters, or use different numbers for encoding the same character. Any given computer (especially servers) needed to support many different encodings; whenever data was passed between different encodings or platforms, that data always ran the risk of corruption.

The Unicode Standard has been adopted by most industry leaders as Apple, HP, IBM, JustSystem, Microsoft, Oracle, SAP, Sun, Sybase, Unisys and many others. Government of India is actively involved in the Unicode Consortium. Unicode is required by modern standards such as XML, Java, ECMAScript (JavaScript), LDAP, CORBA 3.0, WML, etc. It is supported in many operating systems, all modern browsers, and many other products. The emergence of the Unicode Standard and the availability of tools supporting it are among the most significant trends in recent global software technology.

The Unicode Consortium develops, extends and promotes use of the Unicode Standard, which specifies the representation of text in modern software products and standards. The scripts of the region supported by Unicode are:

Arabic, Bengali, Devanagari, Gujarati, Gurmukhi, Kannada, Kharoshthi, Latin, Limbu, Malayalam, Myanmar, Old Persian, Oriya, Siloti Nagari, Sinhala, Tamil, Telugu, Thaana, and Tibetan.

The following scripts of the region may be eventually supported by Unicode:

Avestan, Chakma, Lepcha, Meitei Mayek, Ol Chiki, Pahlavi, Saurashtra, Sorang Sompeng, and Varang Kshiti

The range of the codes for the above languages are given in *Annexure D*.

Unicode has 17 Planes (Plane 0 through Plane 16), and each plane has 65,536 code points (0000 through FFFF hex). Historical languages are included in the Supplementary Multilingual Plane (i.e., Plane 1). The historical languages of the subcontinent being considered for inclusion in the plane are:

Script	**Start code**		**End code**	
	In decimal	**In hexadecimal**	**In decimal**	**In hexadecimal**
Balti	*67680*	10860	*67711*	1087F
Brahmi	*69632*	11000	*69711*	1104F
Kaithi	*69760*	11080	*69839*	110CF
Ahom	*69952*	11140	*70015*	1117F
Sharada	*70016*	11180	*70111*	111DF
Tulu	*70144*	11200	*70223*	1124F
Turkestani	*70272*	11280	*70367*	112DF
Grantha	*70400*	11300	*70527*	1137F
Siddham	*70528*	11380	*70623*	113DF
Maithili	*70784*	11480	*70879*	114DF
Chalukya	*70912*	11500	*71007*	1155F
Chola	*71040*	11580	*71135*	115DF
Satavahana	*71168*	11600	*71263*	1165F
Takri	*71296*	11680	*71391*	116DF
Landa	*71424*	11700	*71519*	1175F
Modi	*71552*	11780	*71647*	117DF
Indus Valley	*76400*	12A70	*76799*	12BFF

1. Non-standard Implementation of Indic and other Scripts

Implementation through fonts

Fundamentally, computers deal with numbers—binary numbers[1] comprising zeros and ones to be more exact. Not only data, sound, video and pictures are in numeric codes, even letters of alphabets, symbols and other characters are just numeric codes to a computer. For example, in the popular ASCII code, the uppercase letter *A* is encoded as 65, uppercase letter *B* as 66, lowercase letter *a* as 97, lowercase letter *b* as 98 etc. So, when *ABCD* is typed in a computer, the computer understands it as four numeric codes: 65, 66, 67 and 68 in that sequence—the numeric codes for uppercase letters *A*, *B*, *C* and *D* respectively. There is nothing like *A*, *B*, *C*, *D*, …, *अ*, *आ*, *इ*, …, ا، ب، ت to a computer: these letters are just code numbers to a computer.

> ***ASCII code***: American Standard Code for Information Interchange (ASCII) code set comprises 128 codes: numbers 0 through 127. Lower 32 numeric codes (i.e., code numbers 0 through 31) and code number 127 are control characters, and code number 32 is blank-space character. The remaining codes represent uppercase letters, lowercase letters, decimal digits, punctuation marks etc. The first 128 codes of Unicode appearing in *Annexure (D)* are ASCII codes. That is, ASCII is a subset of the Unicode. For example, the text '*Barun*' is the sequence of five hexadecimal numeric codes 42, 61, 72, 75 and 6E in ASCII to a computer.
>
> Both ANSI and Unicode are supersets of ASCII. ANSI is almost a subset of Unicode, but is superset of ASCII. ANSI comprises codes 0 through 255, and a single byte memory space is sufficient to encode a character in ANSI. Unicode comprises codes 0 through 10FFFF hex, which needs more storage space per character. As such, if a text-file in English language is encoded in Unicode, it will take more bytes of memory than it would take if encoded in ASCII or ANSI. Of course, ANSI is insufficient for Cyrillic, Indic, Arabic texts.

The 1990s witnessed phenomenal growth of fonts[2] in "Indian" languages. Virtually anybody who had access to font creator software,[3] had a little interest in computer, and knowledge of Indic scripts were writing fonts for Indic scripts. Fonts were written for all Indian languages. Since one could key in text in computer in Latin script (also called English script and Roman script), one

---

[1] See *Annexure (A)* for binary and hexadecimal number systems.

[2] Font determines whether the English text *ABCD* will look like this ABCD, like this *ABCD*, like this 𝔄𝔅ℭ𝔇, or like something else. Change of font changes the look of the text. There are innumerable fonts for Latin script in which English is written.

[3] Font creator program is used to design fonts. For example, High-Logic Font Creator is a font creator program.

did printing of text in "Devanagari" script by deforming Latin letters. That is, one typed in one's computer using English keyboard, and the codes were for English letters, but what appeared on the screen was apparently text in Devanagari or other Indic scripts.

Fonts in Devanagari and other Indic languages were created by changing the glyph of Latin letters in the ASCII code. Let us explain it by considering a specific font, called Shusha by its creators. Shusha font was created by deforming the glyph for code 65 in ASCII (reserved for Latin uppercase letter '*A*') to give it the deceptive look of Devanagari letter '*अ*'. Similarly, the glyph for code 114 in ASCII (reserved for the Latin lowercase letter '*r*') was changed to 'र' etc. So as one typed *Ar* (that is, codes 65 and 114), what appeared on the screen and in the print was not '*Ar*' but '*अर*', provided of course that Shusha font was installed,[4] the application software permitted selecting the font, Shusha font was selected, and AutoCorrect etc did not play havoc (explained later in the chapter).

Non-standard methods have been quite popular in India even in early 2000s. With the help of font creator programs, one may redefine the way various English letters in a font look like on the screen and in the print. Font creator programs are supposed to allow users to decide how the various characters will look like. For example, whether the letter '*A*' should look like: '*a*', '*A*', '@', or 'A'. But the English letters can also be made to look like—though unauthorizedly—Devanagari letters or letters in other scripts. For example, in the popular font, usually called Shusha, the glyph of the Latin letter '*A*' is changed to look like '*अ*', a letter in an altogether different language and script! However, the code remains that of '*A*', i.e., 65, even though it adopts a deceptive appearance of '*अ*'. '*A*' looks like '*अ*', '*B*' looks like '*क्*', '*C*' looks like '*छ*' etc. The complete mapping between Latin letters/symbols and "Devanagari" glyphs is shown in Figure 1.

Figure 1: Latin to Devanagari glyph mapping in Shusha font in ASCII codes

[4] Existence of a font file on your computer is not enough. The fonts are to be installed so that applications like Microsoft Word etc may use the font. Installation of font has been explained later in the chapter.

When viewed in Shusha font, '*Aaz*' looks like 'आठ'. This is because *A* looks like अ, *a* looks like ा and *z* looks like ठ. However, internally to the computer and data processing programs, आठ in Shusha font is still an English word in Latin script: '*Aaz*', the codes being 65, 97 and 122 respectively.

It may be noted that Shusha font is not a worldwide standard font. It is not even a standard font recognized by any authorized body. There is plethora of differently coded similar fonts. For example, there is another very popular font DV-TTYogeshEN, so is Kruti-Dev and perhaps thousands of others. In different fonts, the same '*Aaz*', which looks like 'आठ' when viewed in Shusha font, will look quite different. For example, one can make '*Aaz*' look like 'एक', 'दो', 'तीन', 'नौ', 'दस', or whatever by simply changing the glyphs by font creator programs! So, the problem with this approach is immediately evident: What looks like a perfect Hindi document in one's computer may appear quite differently in one's friend's computer. It may even look like in a different language altogether: for example, something typed in "Bengali" may appear complete gobbledygook in another language on another computer! What looks like 'हाँ' (yes) in one font may look like 'नहीं' (no) in another font—or may look like कथ, હળ, घड्ड, or anything!

The non-standard fonts were used primarily for printing in Indian languages, or visual appearance on the screen. This method is not at all suitable for data processing and, data communication etc because of absence of standardization and non-recognition of the standard by any authorized or technical body.

Warning: The non-standard method is both technically incorrect and legally invalid. It is technically incorrect because the codes reserved for one character cannot be used to represent quite another character—that too in quite a different script and language! If a code is reserved for the Latin letter '*A*', one is not allowed to make it look like '*B*' or any other letter. If it is done so, then there will be utter confusion, and meaningful communication will be next to impossible. Moreover, it is legally invalid because such methods cannot be legally valid. Different people will interpret the data differently (possibly even contradictorily). There can be no universally acceptable agreement or communication in electronic form.

Note: Devanagari, Bengali, Oriya, Telugu etc scripts have so many ligatures that it may not even be possible to encode all the letters, ligatures, numerals and signs of these scripts in just 94 codes available in ASCII.[5]

The following are the salient features of such English fonts with deformed Indic script glyphs:

1. These fonts were not accepted as standard by any authorized organization. Fonts were designed and encoded in an uncoordinated way as per the whims and predilections of the font designers.

[5] ASCII uses 128 codes, but lower 32 codes and code number 127 are control characters, and code number 32 is space character. So effectively 128 - 32 - 1 - 1, i.e., 94 codes are available for encoding.

2. Even though tens of thousands of fonts were written, only a few fonts gained in popularity. For example, Kruti-Dev and Shusha series of fonts were among the popular fonts for Devanagari script.
3. Whatever was typed apparently in Indic scripts was encoded using the codes reserved for Latin letters. For example, the code 65 is reserved for the uppercase letter '*A*' in ASCII; but in Shusha font the code 65 was used for the Devanagari letter '*अ*' without any authorization. Notwithstanding the deceptive look of being in Indian language, these texts were in Latin script, and possibly in English (US) language as understood by Microsoft Office suite!
4. On the positive side, these fonts were immensely popular for printing, publishing and even webpage designing in Indic languages.
5. Still on the positive side, the user needed only font, and no software or other support for printing in Indian languages.
6. Still on the positive side, there was a time when operating systems did not support Indic scripts. Indic languages could be implemented only this way. Some software did not support Indic scripts; Adobe PageMaker being an example. One could write in Indic script only by using non-standard fonts.

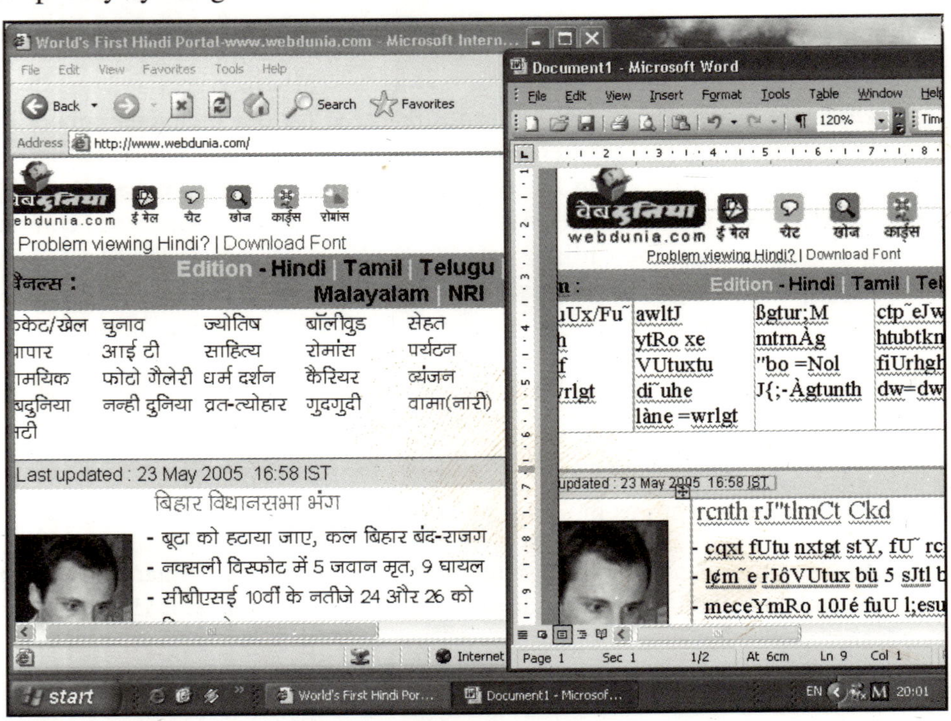

Figure 2: Faulty copying in non-standard fonts

If the font were changed then what looked like a perfect sentence in Hindi would appear a gibberish text in English. For example, in the illustration at Figure 2, the contents of a "Hindi" website using such a font was copied and pasted in a Microsoft Word document. What one gets to read in the default font of Microsoft Word is completely unintelligible garbage text.

Note: Some websites in Indian languages used "dynamic font" to depict Indic texts. The dynamic font makes the Indian language content accessible as English content to the visitor of the webpage. The technologies used may be "Portable Font Resource" or "Embedded Open Type."

Tips: If Figure 2 is analyzed, it will be evident that **rcnth rJ"tlmCt Ckd** has been made to look as बिहार विधानसभा भंग. That is, the following mapping has been used for transformation from Latin to Devanagari script:

Table 1: Latin to Devanagari glyph mapping used in the illustration

Character	Deceptive look
r	ि
c	ब
n	ह
t	ा
h	र
J	व
"	ध
l	न
m	स
C	भ
k	ं
d	ग

Even though this method is not recommended by this book, if it is desired to use this method, then the following will have to be done:

1. Get the font from some source; say in a CD, memory drive or on the network.
2. Install the font on your computer (see below on how to install font).
3. In the Microsoft Office application software (such as Word), select the desired font. This may be done either from the formatting tool bar, or the menu bar (say, Format → Font). See Figure 4.
4. Disable all language specific features such as autocorrect, spelling check, grammar check, smart tag etc. These features will give you only trouble. Spell-check and grammar check may show innumerable errors, as the text will be marked in English, even though it is apparently in a different language. You may do the disabling by going to Tool → Options, or by Tools → AutoCorrect Options, etc.

Figure 3 illustrates the use of non-standard KrutiDev series of font for typing in Hindi in Adobe PageMaker. This was the popular way of desktop publishing in Hindi.

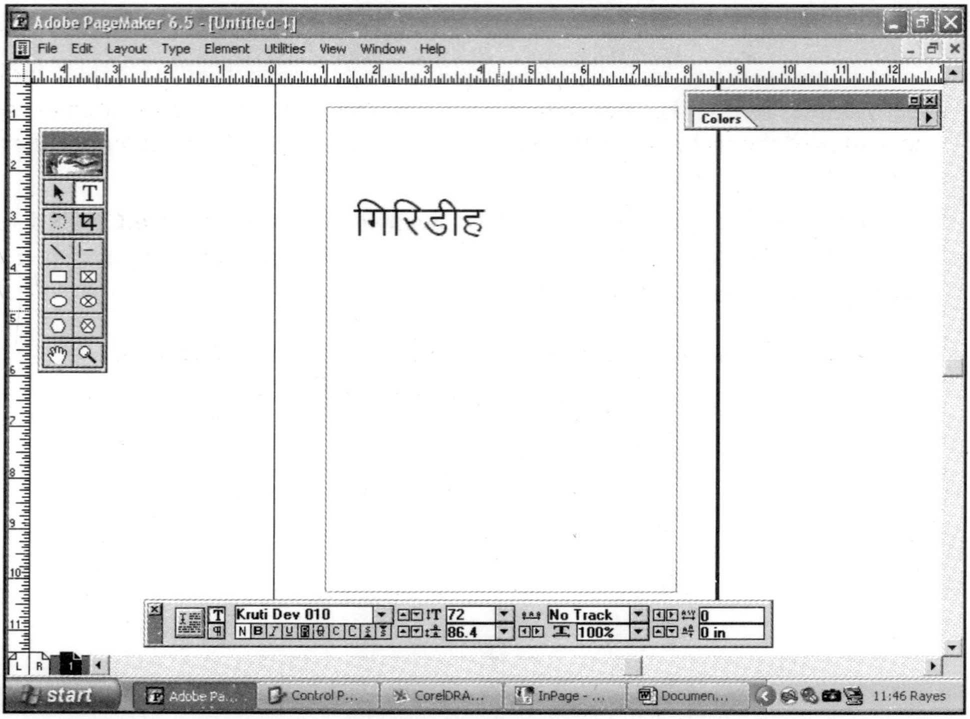

Figure 3: Typing in Hindi in Adobe PageMaker

Warning: This method cannot be used where the font cannot be selected. For example, the names of files and folders cannot be typed in Devanagari script by this method.

Tips: If a script is not supported by the operating system (explained in Chapter 3), then this is the only way to implement the script. For example, Chakma script (of Bangladesh and far-eastern India) was not supported by Microsoft Windows. So, DTP in Chakma script could be done only by this method. With font creator program, one may create the glyphs for one's yet-to-be-supported language, including a secret (or, new) script.

Warning: If AutoCorrect options are not disabled, the text may change unpredictably. AutoCorrect options are used in English: (i) to change case of the letter (for example, changing the case of the first letter of the sentence to uppercase), (ii) to correct specified common typing errors (for example, correcting *taht* to *that* automatically), and (iii) to replace one word/sequence of characters by another. For example, if ताहत is typed in Shusha font, it will automatically change to टहात. This is because *ताहत* is coded as '*taht*', which autocorrects (i.e., first letter capitalization and spelling correction) to '*That*', which looks like टहात in Shusha font.

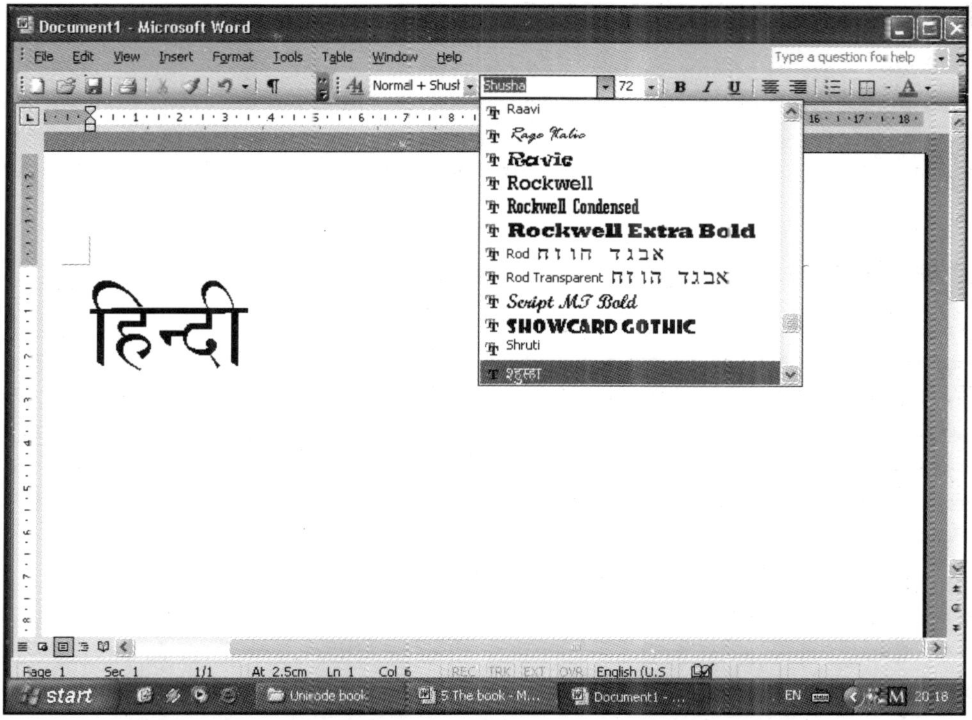

Figure 4: Selecting font in Microsoft Word

How to install a font under Microsoft Windows

1. Get hold of the font file. You may get it from your friend, from the Internet, or may create it yourself using font creator software.
2. Go to the Control Panel of the Microsoft Windows operating system.
3. Open Fonts folder in the Control Panel.
4. Select File → Install New Font from the menu bar, and follow the instructions. You may have to locate the font file on your computer or network, and select it. You may select more than one font file in a location.
5. You may (or, may not!) have to restart the application software so that the font is listed by the application software.

The above-mentioned procedure has been described for Microsoft Windows XP. Other versions of Microsoft Windows have similar procedures.

Note: Some fonts are in the form of executable program files. If the executable program is run on a computer, the font gets installed automatically. There is not need to install it by the above-mentioned procedure.

Note: After installing the font, one can type in the font. For typing in the non-standard font, one will generally have to follow the visual sequence (and not logical or phonetic sequence) for letter, vowel signs, vowel modifiers and conjuncts.[6] For example, to type कि, one will have to first type the vowel sign ि followed by the letter क; the sequence ि स्‌ and त्र will produce स्त्रि.

Implementation through overlaying software and font

The approach mentioned in the earlier part of this chapter had the problem that the glyphs for English letters were deformed to those in Indic scripts. The 1990s also witnessed another way of writing in Indian languages. In this approach, the reliance is on the first 128 codes of ASCII; but the upper 128 codes or even higher codes were also used to encode Indic characters and glyphs. An eight-bit number can represent 256 codes (2×2×2×2×2×2×2×2). If the lower half (0 through 127) is used for ASCII code representation, then the upper half (128 through 255) can be used for Indic scripts.[7]

This approach required the use of overlaying software. The overlaying software converted the keystroke into another code. For example, when one hit the key for the letter *A* (code 65), the overlaying software changed it to that of another letter or letters, say, ¥ (code 165), § (code 167), © (code 169) or Æ (code 198). The glyphs for these characters with higher codes than normal English letters were tinkered with to give the look of Indian script. In this approach, the upper end of the character set, generally meant for letters/symbols such as Ç, ±, ß, », μ, ¾, ® were used for the Indic scripts.

The overlaying software did complex processing to determine the correct sequence of glyphs based on the keyboard layout for the appropriate visual presentation.

For example, one implementation may be as illustrated below:

Keys pressed:	**abc** (three keystrokes)
Overlaying software converted it to, say:	§¦®±¦ (five codes 167, 166, 174, 177 & 166)
On screen and in print, it looked, say:	वरुण
Because:	§ → ट, ¦ → ा, ® → रु, ± → ए, ¦ → ा

[6] Logical or phonetic sequence has been explained in later chapters.

[7] In many implementations, even the lower 128 codes (0 through 127) were tinkered with to provide for the large number of glyphs needed to design an Indic script. Some implementations also used codes higher than 255.

Note that three key strokes '*abc*' is converted into a different number of (i.e., five) characters '§¦®±¦'. The number of characters is more than the number of keystrokes, but it could be less also. The five characters with numeric codes 167, 166, 174, 177 and 166 produces the look वरुण.

iLeap, ShriLipi, Bijoya and ITRANS etc were the popular software which used this approach. One may obtain any such application software and install in one's computer to understand how it works. However, this book does not recommend this approach.

Note: For typing in Indic scripts using the overlaying software, one has to follow the keyboard layout and procedures prescribed by the overlaying software. Some software requires one to type in logical sequence (as opposed to visual sequence) in Indic script. More on logical sequence and visual sequence for typing is mentioned in Chapter 4.

Implementation of Arabic script based languages

Arabic script based languages are written in the right-to-left direction. As such, desktop publishing in languages like Urdu is done using specific software and non-standard fonts. Figure 5 illustrates typing done in Urdu in the software InPage (version 2.4). It is worth noting that the on-screen keyboard shows QWERTY keyboard layout even though what gets typed in the document is apparently in Urdu.

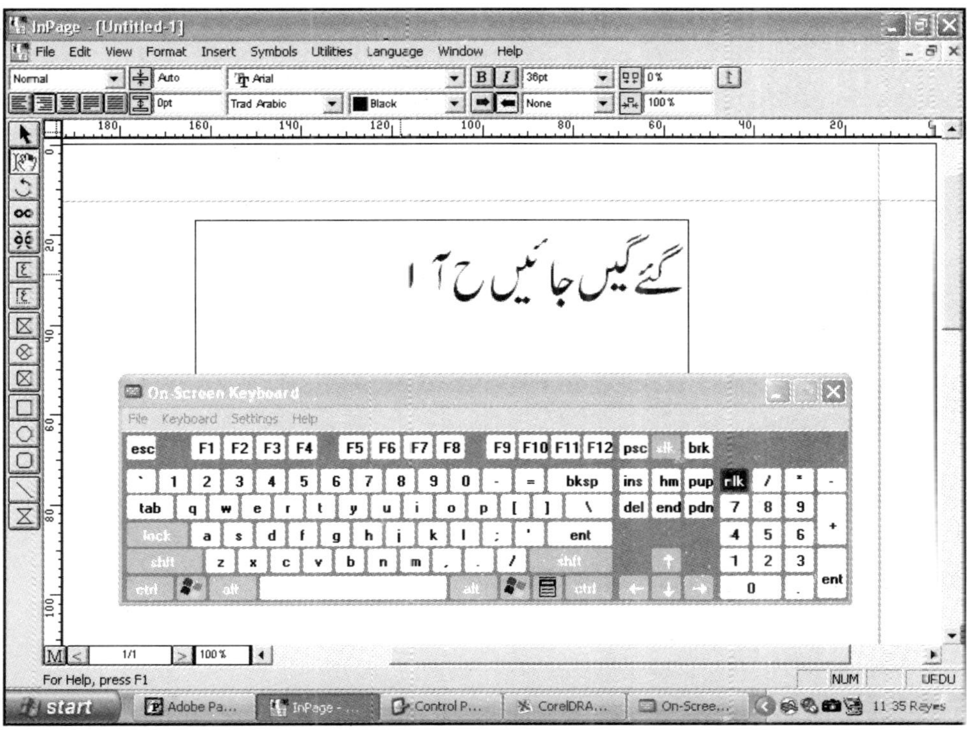

Figure 5: Desktop printing in Urdu in InPage software

Deficiencies of these approaches

Both the above-mentioned non-standard approaches suffer from serious legal and technical limitations. For example,

1. To see the text correctly, one must have the specific fonts installed on one's computer.
2. In another font, the same text may read something very different—even in an altogether different script and language. For example, as explained earlier, हाँ in one font may appear नहीं in another font!
3. This approach cannot be used to search the Internet, or to name the files and folders in Indic scripts.
4. Cut, copy and paste may produce undesirable result.
5. Other software may not recognize the language.
6. Notwithstanding the deceptive Indic language look, the texts are internally in codes reserved for Latin script and possibly in English language. As such, the formatting and auto-correct options, spelling and grammar checking etc of English language are applied by Microsoft Office etc, unless specifically de-selected.
7. The method is difficult to implement in mixed right-to-left and left-to-right languages.

Note: Microsoft Windows 95, 98, ME and NT do not support Indic scripts. Indic languages can be implemented only through the above-mentioned approaches. These versions of Microsoft Windows support European scripts and languages. The popular application software Adobe PageMaker versions 6.5 and 7.0 did not appear to support Indic and Arabic texts; so Indic text could be implemented in PageMaker only through non-standard font methods.

Figure 6 shows the screenshot of a website in "Bengali" language. As the font was not properly installed, what shows up on the screen is a gibberish text.

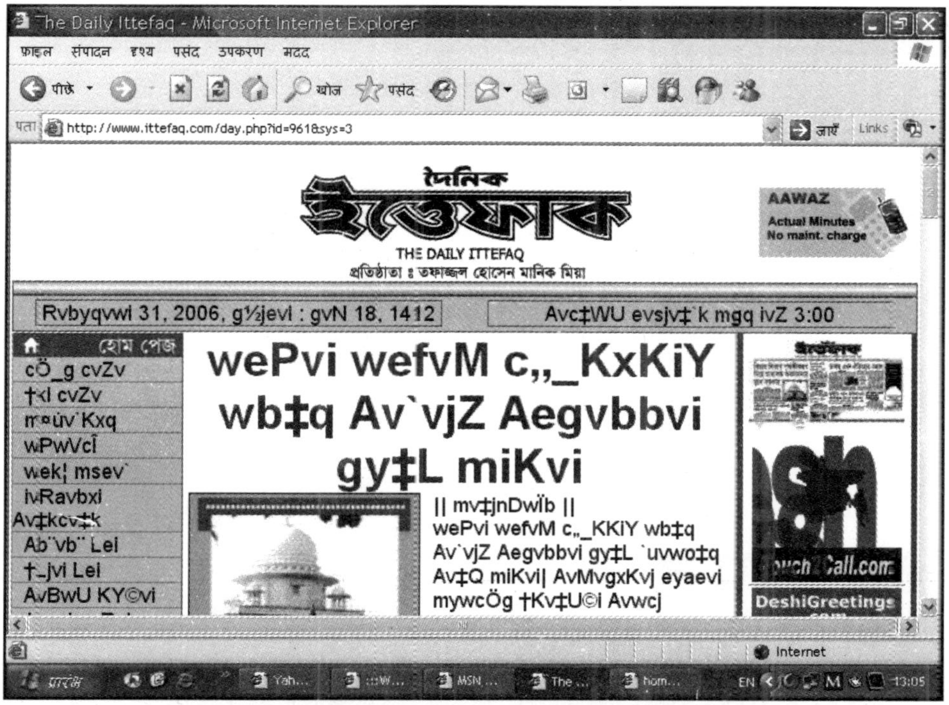

Figure 6: Latin letters show up in absence of font display

In Figure 7, the processing of text by the popular WordArt has been shown, in which attempt has been made to get the text "माइक्रोसॉफ्ट" written in vertical style. If the text is written in "Hindi" using Shusha (or similar fonts), the vertical orientation of the text is what appears on the right-hand side in the figure. The correct orientation of the text appears only when the text is in Unicode (as shown in the left hand side). More on Unicode in later chapters.

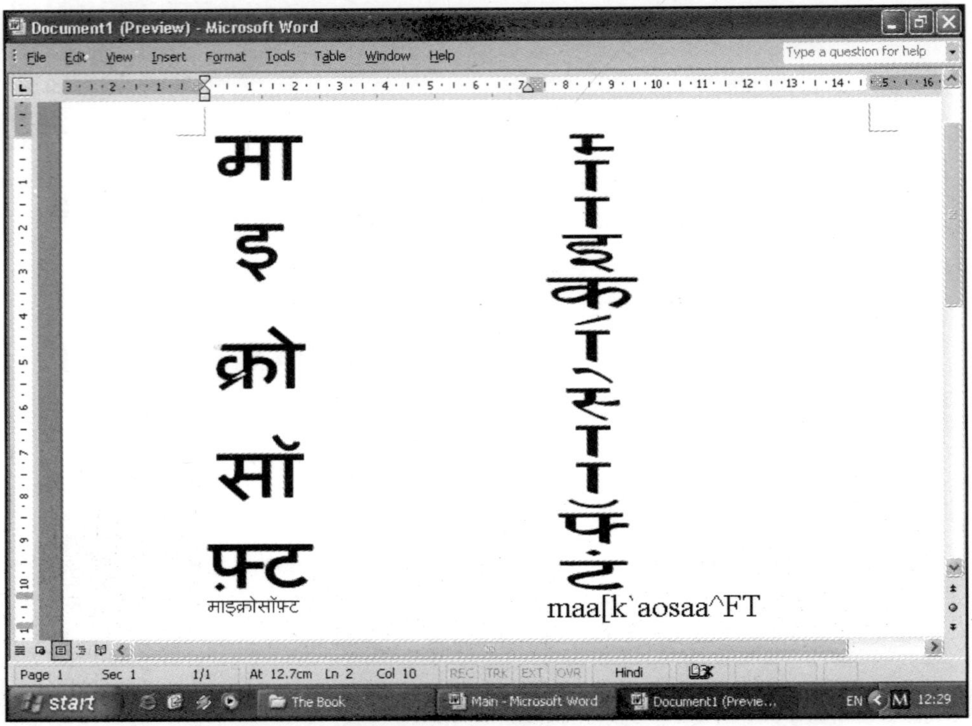

Figure 7: Vertical style for texts in WordArt

What you have learned

1. How to install fonts
2. How to type in Shusha and similar fonts
3. Typing in Indic language using overlaying software
4. Typing in Urdu
5. Deficiencies of the two approaches

2. Indian Script Code for Information Interchange (ISCII)

Note: *To see some of the screenshots given in this chapter, it may be necessary to utilize procedures explained in later chapters. It may be convenient for some readers to skip this chapter, and return to the chapter only after reading Chapters 3 and 4. ISCII is only of historical importance now.*

The BIS ISCII standard

Since the 1970s, different committees of the Department of Electronics and the Department of Official Language have been evolving different codes and keyboard layouts that could cater to all the Indic scripts due to their common phonetic structure. Earlier efforts could not keep the ASCII code intact. The Bureau of Indian Standards (BIS) standards IS 13194:1991 is intended for use in all computer and communication media which allow use of 7 or 8 bit characters. In an 8-bit environment, the lower 128 characters are the same as ASCII character set. The top 128 characters cater to all the ten Indian scripts based on the ancient Brahmi script. In a 7-bit environment the control code SI can be used for invocation of ISCII code set, the control code SO can be used for reselection of the ASCII code set.

Indian Script Code for Information Interchange (ISCII) is a standard code for ten Brahmi-based Indic scripts: Assamese[8], Bengali, Devanagari, Gujarati, Kannada, Malayalam, Oriya, Punjabi, Tamil and Telugu. Bureau of Indian Standards (BIS) granted recognition to ISCII. The BIS standard is IS 13194:1991. It conforms to earlier standard IS 10402:1982 8-bit coded character set for information interchange.

The common Inscript keyboard[9] overlay allows typing of all the ten Indian scripts. This overlay fits on any existing English keyboard. Alternating between the English and Inscript overlay is achieved through the CapsLock key. The Inscript keyboard provides a logical and intuitive arrangement of vowels and consonants. It is based both on the phonetic properties and the relative frequencies of utilization of the letters. Not only does this make the keyboard much easier to learn, but also enables a person to type subsequently in all the Indian scripts.

The ISCII code table is a super-set of all the characters required in the ten Indic scripts. An optimal keyboard overlay for these scripts is made possible by the phonetic nature of the

[8] Assamese script is Bengali script with an extra letter ৱ, and replacing the letter র by ৰ.

[9] Inscript keyboard layout has been explained in Chapter 4 and in Annexure (F).

alphabet. The differences between scripts are primarily in their written forms, where different combination rules get used. The table of ISCII codes is given in *Annexure (B)*.

There are manifold advantages in having a common code and keyboard for all the Indic scripts. Any software which allows ISCII codes to be used, can be used in any of the ten Indic script, enhancing its commercial viability. Furthermore, immediate transliteration between different Indian scripts becomes possible, just by changing the display modes without changing the codes.

The 8-bit ISCII code retains the standard ASCII code while the Indic script keyboard overlay is designed for the Standard English being able to co-exist with Indic scripts. This approach also makes it feasible to use Indic scripts along with existing English computers and software, so long as 8-bit character codes are allowed.

The ISCII code set co-exists with the standard English code. It contains only the basic Indic letters and vowel signs arranged in an order conforming to dictionaries of Indic languages.

As the display rendering of Indic text depends entirely on the composition methodology, it is possible to view the same text in different styles prevalent in the script. It is possible to transliterate the text to Roman script, using diacritical marks on English letters, for removing ambiguities. It is even possible to have the initial letters capitalized in the Roman text.

ISCII is usually based on 8-bit code. With eight bits, one can encode 256 characters (that is, 2^8 or 2×2×2×2×2×2×2×2 characters). The lower seven bits—00000000 through 01111111 binary, or numeric codes 0 through 127—are used to represent 128 characters (that is, 2^7 or 2×2×2×2×2×2×2 characters) of ASCII, which is used for writing in usual English. The higher seven bits are used to represent 128 characters (that is, 2^7 or 2×2×2×2×2×2×2 characters) of Indic scripts.

The same codes are used for different scripts. The languages encoded in ISCII have same or mostly the same alphabets. There is one-to-one—well almost—relation between the letters in different scripts, as may be seen in the table at *Annexure (B)*.

Note: The codes 128 to 255 are used in Unicode to represent certain Latin ligatures and accent marks etc. This has been shown in *Annexure (B)*.

Example: जय श्री राम is encoded in ISCII as follows: (please refer to *Annexure (B)* for codes)

ज य space श ् र ी space र ा म
i.e., 186, 205, 32, 213, 232, 207, 220, 32, 207, 218, 204
i.e., ºÍ ÕèÏÜ ÏÚÌ

Note: The ISCII codes for हिन्दी and हिंदी are different notwithstanding their being same in Hindi grammar in both meaning and pronunciation. This is because न् comprises two ISCII characters with codes 198 and 232 (i.e., for न and ् respectively) in that sequence whereas *anusvara* (ं) comprises a single character with code 162.

हिन्दी is encoded as ह ि न ् द ी, i.e., 216, 219, 198, 232, 196 and 220; and हिंदी is encoded as ह ि ं द ी, i.e., 216, 219, 162, 196 and 220. Similarly, पांच and पाँच are encoded differently in ISCII, so are साई, साईं and साईँ. More on encoding of texts in Indic scripts and sequence of characters are given in later chapters, especially in Chapter 4 and *Annexure (E)*.

Note: To be able to see the ISCII Indic language characters correctly in Microsoft Windows, the conversion table must have been installed. Whether the conversion tables have been installed may be seen in Microsoft Windows XP by opening the Regional and Language Option under the Control Panel. (It has been explained in Chapter 3 as to how to open the Regional and Language Option.) In the "Regional and Language Option" window, the Advanced tab may be clicked, and ensured that the conversion table is installed for the desired languages. If the conversion table for the language is checked, then it is already installed. (See Figure 8)

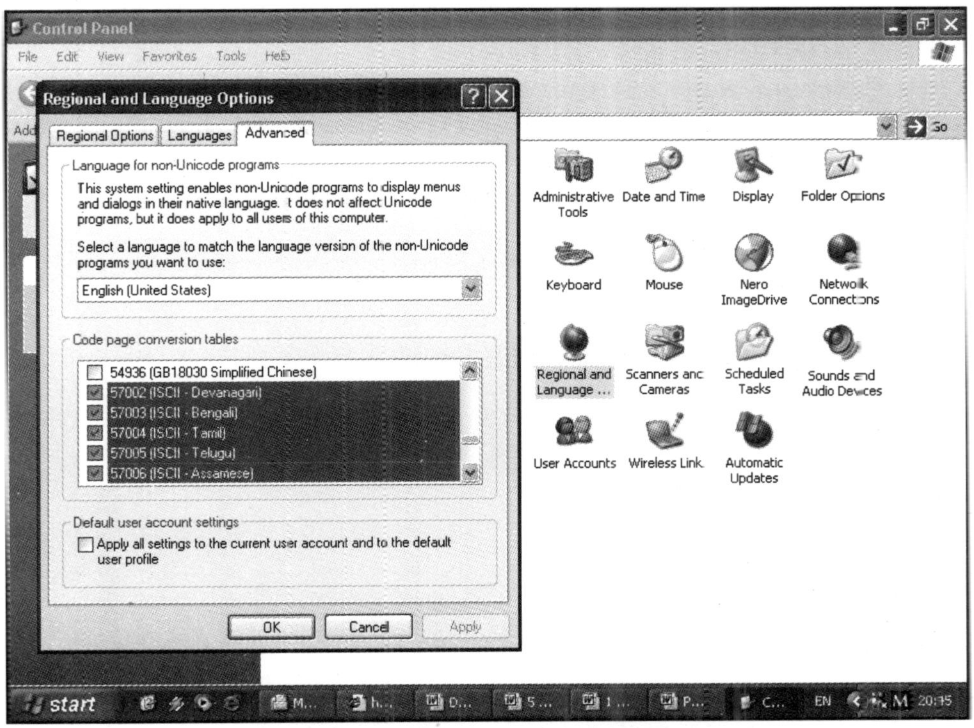

Figure 8: Selecting ISCII conversion tables in Microsoft Windows

ISCII to Unicode conversion and vice versa

ISCII to Unicode conversion

It is possible to convert a text written in ISCII code to Microsoft Word document in Unicode. For this conversion, one will have to follow the following steps:

1. Ensure that Microsoft Word is set to confirm conversions when it opens an encoded file.
   a. On the **Tools** menu, click **Options**, and then click the **General** tab.
   b. Select the **Confirm conversion at Open** check box, and then click **OK**.
2. On the **File** menu, click **Open**.
3. Click the arrow next to the **Files of type** box, and then click **Text Files**.
4. Locate the Indian Script Code for Information Interchange (ISCII) text file[10], and click **Open**.
5. In the **Convert file from** box, click **Encoded Text**, and then click **OK**.
6. Click **Other encoding**, and then click the original ISCII encoder, specifying the script/language. In the correct encoding, Preview frame will show meaningful text in the desired script (see Figure 9). Click **OK** button.
7. Save the file as a Microsoft Word document.

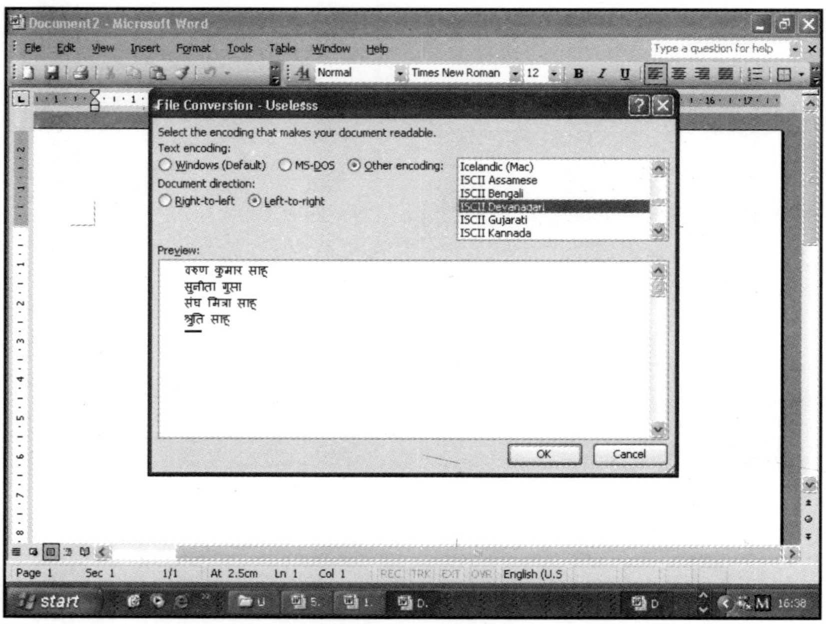

Figure 9: Selecting ISCII Devanagari encoding

[10] This is the file where text has already been written in an Indic script in ISCII. It is assumed that someone has already written Indic text in ISCII.

Unicode to ISCII conversion

It is also possible to convert a text written in Unicode in Microsoft Word to an ISCII text file. For this conversion, the following steps are to be taken:

1. Open in Microsoft Word the document containing the Indic text in Unicode that is to be converted to an ISCII text file.
2. On the **File** menu, click **Save As**.
3. In the **Save as type** box, click **Plain Text**.
4. Click **Save**, and then verify you want to save the file to this format.
5. Click **Other encoding**, and then click the ISCII encoder you want, specifying the script/language.

Note: It is recommended that when working with Indic languages in Microsoft Office, the support for the specific languages are enabled through Microsoft Office Language Settings. See Chapter 6.

Warning: If the Indic script text in Unicode is saved in some other format (say, Japanese), then the text may not be saved appropriately, and it may not be possible to recover the text.

Transliterating from one Indic Unicode to another via ISCII

The ten Indian scripts supported by ISCII have similar alphabets, though not exactly the same. The same numeric codes are used in all the scripts for a particular letter. One can take advantage of this to transliterate from Unicode in one Indic script to another Indic script via ISCII. To do this, the following steps are to be taken:

1. Type the text in the source Indic script in Unicode in Microsoft Word. (Typing in Unicode has been explained in later chapters.)
2. Save the Microsoft Word document as ISCII text file using the method explained earlier ("Unicode to ISCII conversion"), and thereafter close the file.
3. Re-open the text file from Microsoft Word as explained earlier ("ISCII to Unicode conversion"). However, while opening the text file, choose the ISCII encoding for the target script. The text will now appear in the target Indic script, i.e., transliterated in the target script.
4. Save the file as a Microsoft Word document by **Save As...**. The new Microsoft Word document will be in Unicode in the target script.

Warning: Unicode encodes many more characters for Indic scripts than are encoded in ISCII. So, the above-mentioned procedure may fail for the Unicode characters not included in the ISCII code set. Moreover, the formatting may be lost.

Warning: Some letters in Indic alphabets do not follow one-to-one relation. This means that it may not always be possible to convert back a letter to itself by reconverting the text to the original script. For example, Bengali script does not have the letter व (va). If Devanagari letter व (va) is converted to Bengali script, it will transformed to ব (ba). If this ব (ba) is reconverted to Devanagari script, what will be obtained is ब (ba), and not व (va). Thus, व (va) will become ब (ba) on re-conversion.

Typing in ISCII

Usually, Inscript keyboard layout is used for typing in ISCII. Ligatures and vowel signs are typed in the unique spelling. The keyboard layout and typing of ligatures and vowel signs in Inscript have been explained in Chapter 4.

Note: ISCII standard recommends that CapsLock key be used to switch between typing in ASCII and ISCII codes. So, uppercase English alphabets can be typed with Shift key only, and not with CapsLock.

Tips: There is an interesting way of keying in characters with higher codes, i.e., codes from 128 to 255. For this, one has to (i) know the code of the character in decimal number, and (ii) use the numeric keypad of the keyboard to enter the code in decimal number (that is, one may not use the number keys which are part of the main keyboard and are in a row just below the function keys and just above the English-letter keys). Suppose, one wants to key in ISCII Indic script codes in Notepad utility. For this, one will have to open Notepad, and place the cursor at an appropriate location. To key in a character, one has to press the Alt key, and while keeping the Alt key pressed, type the code of the character in four decimal digits in decimal number system; and then release the Alt key. It should be ensured that the numeric keypad is used to enter numbers, and that the NumLock is in ON position. For example, the following table illustrates a few combinations:

Table 2: Inputting character through code

Key combinations	Character that is entered
Alt 0032	*blank space*
Alt 0050	2
Alt 0193	Á
Alt 0200	È
Alt 0222	Þ
Alt 2309	अ
Alt 2310	आ

Note: In Table 2, the codes used in the last two entries are above 255, and are in the Unicode. Unicode has been discussed in later parts of the book.

Webpage design in ISCII

There is hardly any website in ISCII. Anyway, one will have to use the correct encoding in the Internet Explorer to browse a website designed in ISCII encoding. Appropriate encoding may be selected by following the options in the menu bar of the Internet Explorer window as follows: View → Encoding → *the appropriate encoding*, i.e., ISCII-*Language*. This has been illustrated in Figure 10, where ISCII-Gujarati encoding has been selected.

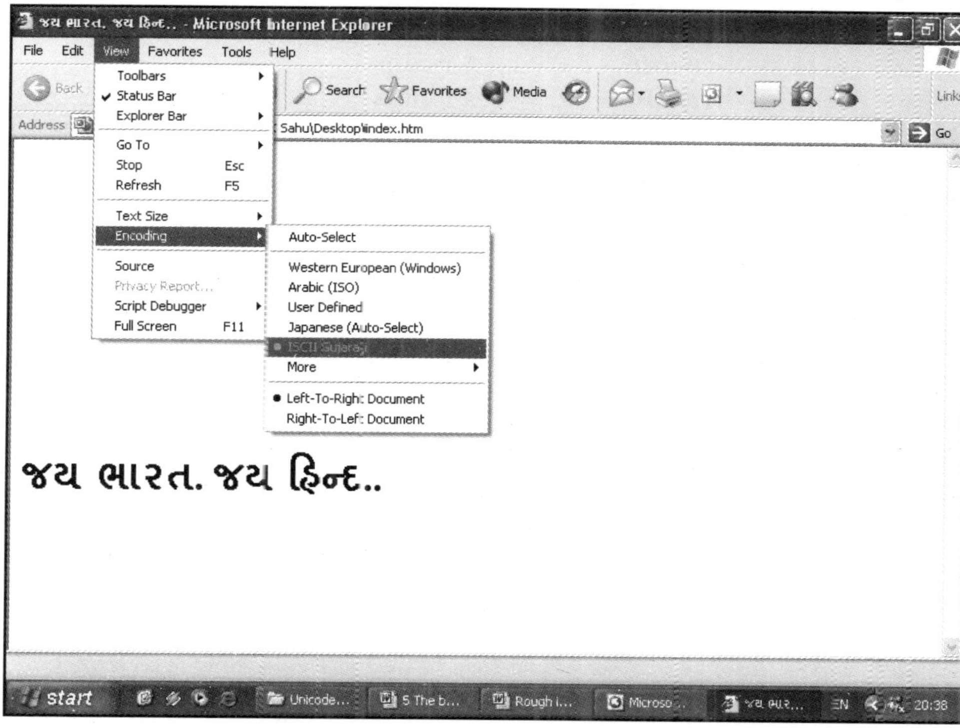

Figure 10: Website in ISCII code

Note: To create an HTML document in ISCII, it is necessary to use the meta tag given below. With this meta tag, the contents of the ISCII string can be viewed without explicit conversion of the ISCII code to Unicode. The web browser does the conversion from ISCII to Unicode internally using the system installed Indic font.

```
<meta http-equiv="Content-Type" content="text/html; charset=x-iscii-de">
```

The meta tag is for showing the text in Devanagari. For other scripts, one will have to use the appropriate charset as per the following table:

Table 3: Charset codes in ISCII

Script	*Charset*
Assamese	x-iscii-as
Bengali	x-iscii-be
Devanagari	x-iscii-de
Gujarati	x-iscii-gu
Kannada	x-iscii-ka
Malayalam	x-iscii-ma
Oriya	x-iscii-or
Punjabi	x-iscii-pa
Tamil	x-iscii-ta
Telugu	x-iscii-te

As an illustration, the following HTML code produces "जय भारत। जय हिन्द।।"

```
<html>
<head>
<meta name="GENERATOR" content="Microsoft FrontPage 6.0">
<meta name="ProgId" content="FrontPage.Editor.Document">
<meta http-equiv="Content-Type" content="text/html; charset=x-iscii-de">
<title>New Page 1</title>
</head>
<body>
ºÍ ËÚÏÂê ºÍ ØÛÆèÄêê
</body>
</html>
```

If the charset is changed to **x-iscii-or**, then it produces the same in Oriya: "ଜୟ ଭାରତ. ଜୟ ହିନ୍ଦ..". If it is changed to **x-iscii-gu**, the same text appears in Gujarati script as shown in Figure 10.

Note: In the above method, Internet Explorer converts the text in ISCII code to Unicode for displaying in the browser screen. If one does "cut" or "copy" from the browser screen, then the text that is copied in the clipboard is in Unicode, and not in ISCII.

Note: The Internet can be searched in ISCII, even though not much resource is available in the cyberspace in ISCII. For example, to search the Internet with search key हिन्दी, one will have to search with "ØÛÆèÄÜ" (codes D8, DB, C6, E8, C4 and DC in hex), which is the ISCII code for हिन्दी (spelled ह, ि, न, ्, द and ी).

Note: ISCII is for Brahmi-based Indic languages. On the lines of ISCII, C-DAC developed PASCII (Perso-Arabic Script Code for Information Interchange) codes for encoding Arabic-script based languages of the subcontinent. More can be seen at C-DAC website http://parc.cdac.in. However, in view of Unicode, PASCII has little use.

Deficiencies of ISCII

One disadvantage of ISCII is that it is difficult to work with more than one Indic script in the same document. This is because the same codes are used to denote all the ten scripts supported by ISCII. This restriction has been removed in Unicode system, described later in the book.

Many glyphs, signs and symbols used in Indic scripts were not encoded in ISCII. ISCII contains bare minimum letters and vowel signs, and is very rudimentary. Even Unicode character sets for Indic languages need improvements.

There are not many application software and websites in ISCII. The popularity of Unicode has overshadowed ISCII. The Hindi website of even the Bureau of Indian Standards, which recognized ISCII, is in Unicode, and not in ISCII!

Nonetheless, it was an important step. Unicode for Indic scripts was influenced by ISCII. Moreover, non-Unicode encodings similar to ISCII were used for different languages in other parts of the world.

What you have learned

1. ISCII standard for Indic scripts
2. ISCII conversion tables in Microsoft Windows
3. Conversion from ISCII to Unicode and vice versa
4. Transliterating Unicode text in one Indic script to another
5. Designing webpage in ISCII
6. Deficiencies of ISCII

3. Installing Languages in Microsoft Windows

Installing Indic/Arabic/East Asian etc languages

Microsoft Windows 95, 98, ME and NT contain no support for Indic scripts. So, ***Indic languages cannot be implemented*** in these operating system environments. However, certain European languages can be added under these environments.

Microsoft Windows 2000 supports Devanagari and Tamil scripts. Microsoft Windows XP supports Bengali (XP SP2[11]), Devanagari, Gujarati, Gurmukhi, Kannada, Malayalam (XP SP2), Tamil and Telugu Indic scripts. Complex text support needs to be manually enabled in Microsoft Windows 2000 and XP.

In Windows Vista, complex script support is supposedly automatically enabled. It supports Bengali, Devanagari, Gujarati, Gurmukhi, Kannada, Malayalam, Oriya, Tamil and Telugu scripts.

Under Microsoft Windows 98

Installing an additional language under ***Microsoft Windows 98*** has been illustrated in Figure 11. Language can be installed by the following procedure:

1. Go to the Language tab by Control Panel → Keyboard → Language tab.
2. Click the "Add…" button, and select the desired language from the drop-down list.
3. Click "OK" button.
4. Several languages can be added by repeating the above steps.

While installing a language, Microsoft Windows CD may asked, which may be provided or its location may be browsed. An installed language may be removed by clicking Remove button after selecting the language.

[11] Service Pack 2.

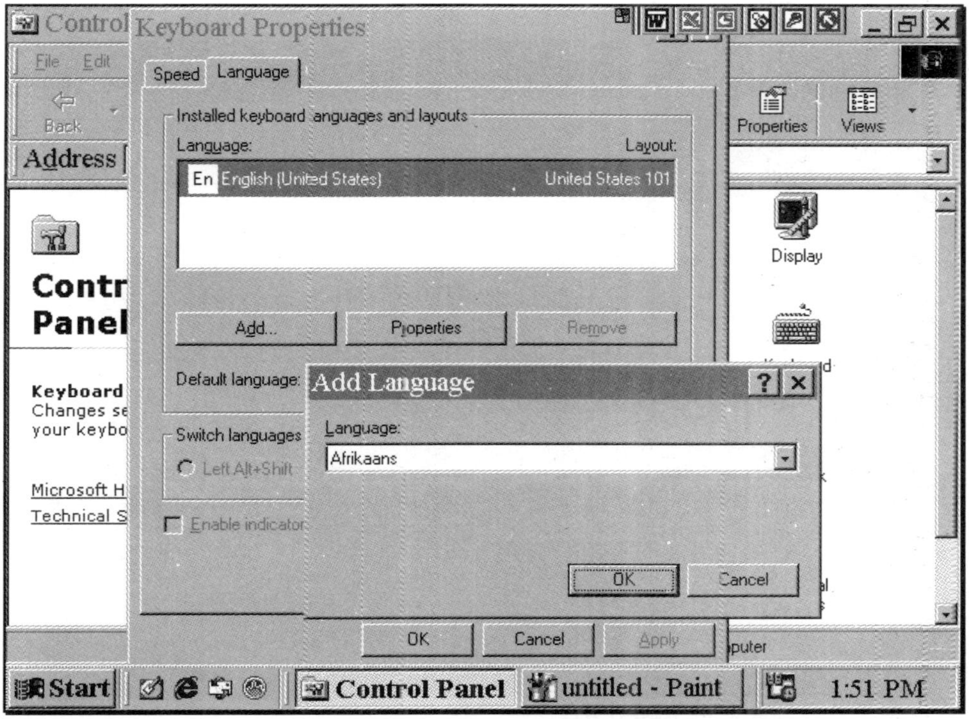

Figure 11: Languages under Microsoft Windows 98

Under Microsoft Windows XP

To install files for Indic languages under ***Microsoft Windows XP*** environment, the following steps should be taken:

1. Open Control Panel of Microsoft Windows operating system.
2. Open the Regional and Language Options by clicking on the icon in the Control Panel. If you have opened the Control Panel in the category view, then you may find the Regional and Language Options under the category "Date, Time, Language and, Regional Options".
3. Click on the Languages tab. See Figure 14.
4. Check the check box "Install files for complex script and right-to-left languages including Thai" as shown in Figure 14.

How to go to Control Panel? Click the Start button of Microsoft Windows (which is usually in the left-bottom corner of the screen). From the list that pops up, choose Control Panel as shown in Figure 12.

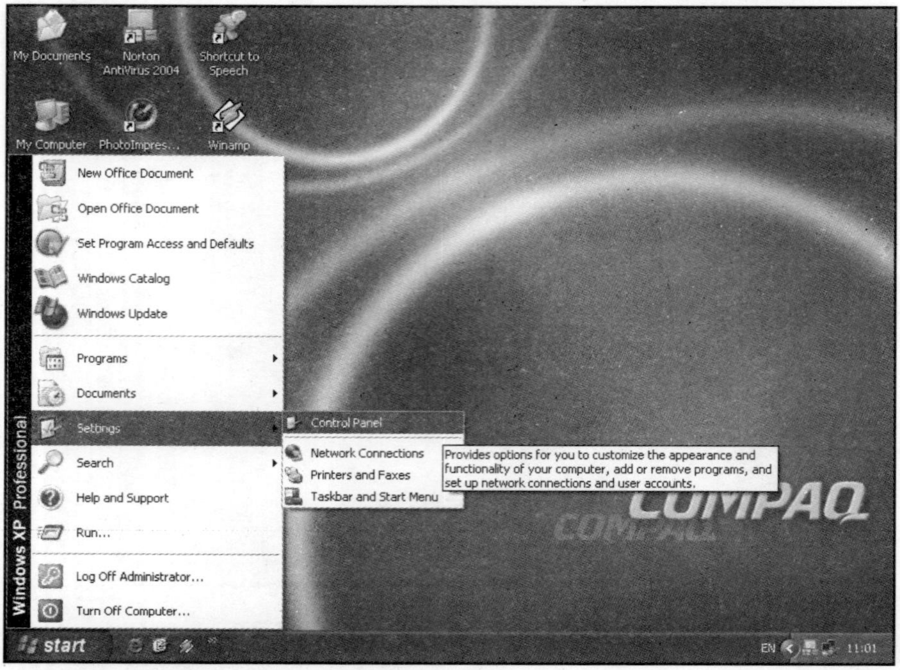

Figure 12: Opening "Control Panel"

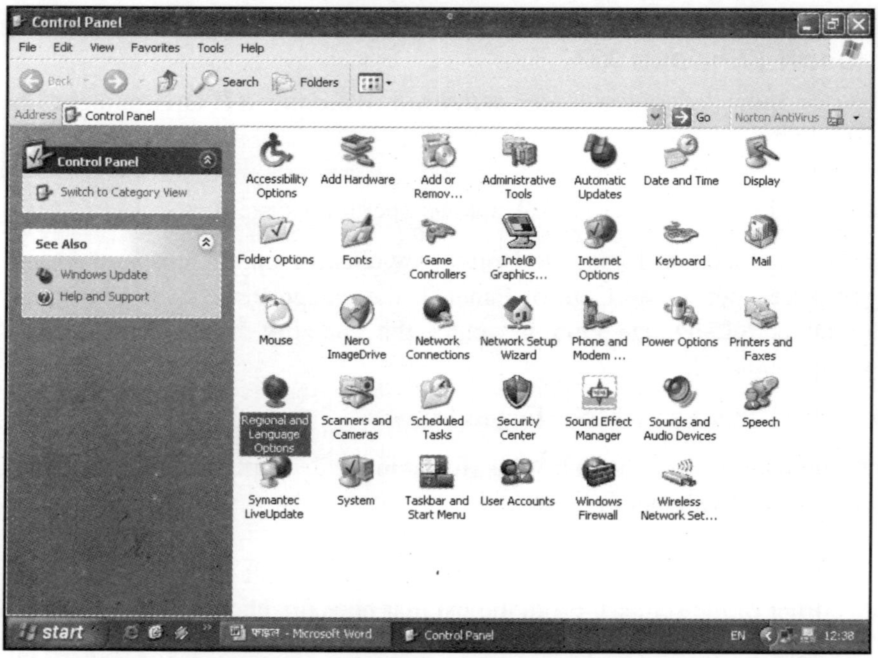

Figure 13: Opening "Regional and Language Options" in classic view

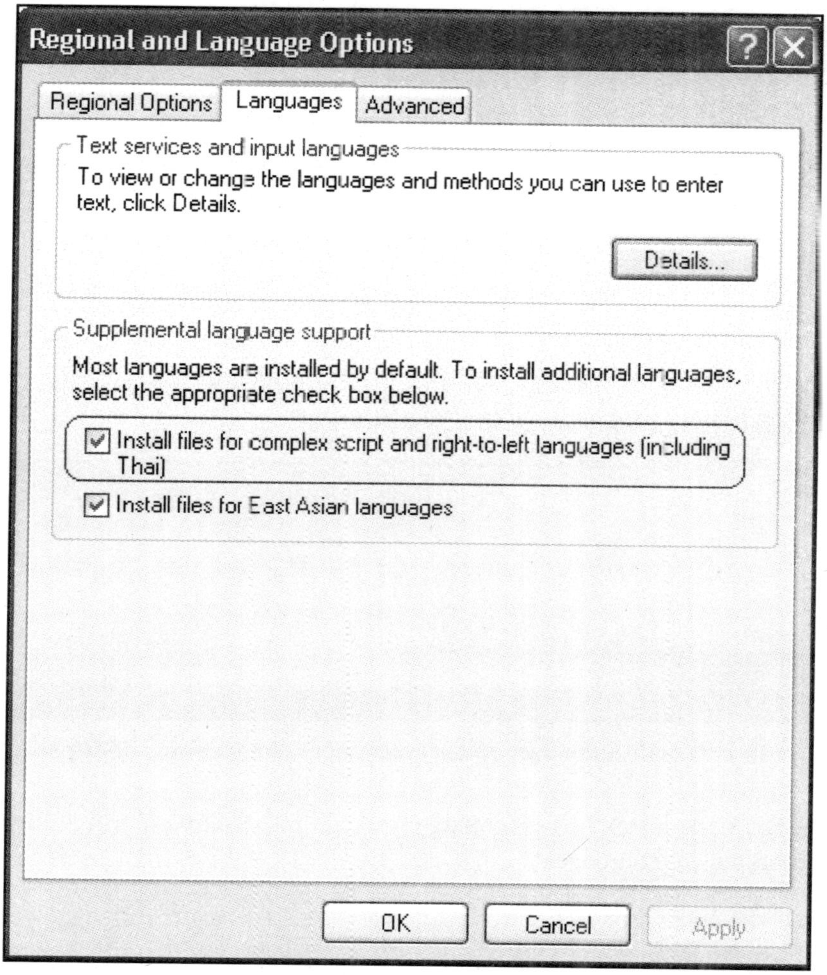

Figure 14: Selecting complex scripts and East Asian languages

Note: If the check box is already checked, then files for Indic, Arabic etc scripts and languages are already installed on the computer. The check box must not be cleared if one wants to use Indic and Arabic etc languages.

Note: In Indian language version of the Microsoft Windows, the check box for complex scripts and right-to-left languages will be checked by default. The option will be dimmed, so it cannot be unchecked (Figure 15).

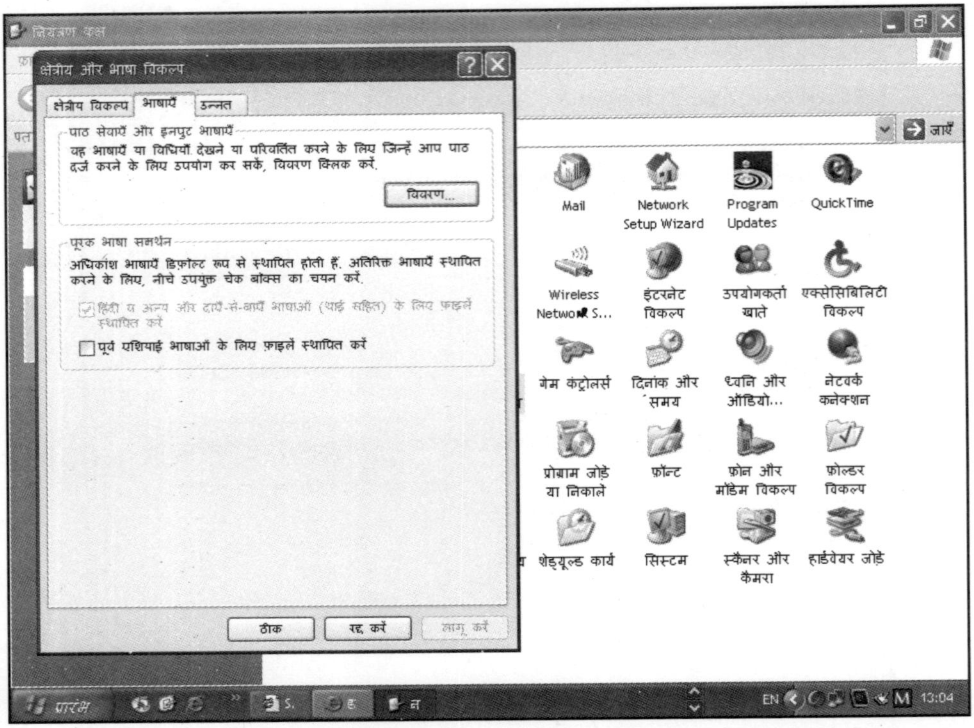

Figure 15: Indic/Arabic languages already selected in Hindi version of Microsoft Windows XP

Warning: If the check box is already checked, un-checking it will uninstall the files for Indic, Arabic etc languages!

Tips: If the check box entitled "Install files for East Asian Language" is also checked, then East Asian languages such as Chinese, Japanese and Korean will also be installed in the computer (see Figure 14). If one does not want to work with Indic languages but only with East Asian languages, then one need to check only the box meant for East Asian languages.

5. Thereafter, click "Apply" or "OK" button.
6. As the installation of files for the languages/scripts selected by you starts, Microsoft Windows may ask for the Windows CD. You may either provide the CD, or locate where the Windows CD files are stored.

Note: Windows will not ask for the CD during the un-installation of language files by de-selection of the check box(es).

7. After the above steps are completed successfully, the files for Indic, Arabic, Thai, etc languages has been installed in your computer. If you had selected East Asian Languages, then files for these languages have been installed in your computer.

Note: Support for Latin, Greek, Cyrillic etc scripts is automatically enabled in Microsoft Windows XP and later versions.

Note: It has been assumed that one is logged on the computer as an administrator or a member of the Administrators group, and that the network policy settings do not prevent one from completing the procedure.

Note: After the completion of the above procedure, one will be able to read the documents in the relevant languages. However, to be able to also write (that is, to input data and text) in the language, the keyboard layout/IME for inputting data will have to be selected as described later in the chapter.

Under Microsoft Windows 2000

Note: Slightly different steps are to be followed for installing Indic languages In ***Microsoft Windows 2000***. The steps are as follows.

1. Go to Control Panel → Regional Options → General tab (see Figure 16).
2. In the "Language settings for this system" frame, check the box next to "Indic."
3. Copy the appropriate files from the Windows 2000 CD when prompted.
4. If prompted, reboot the computer once the files have been installed. Microsoft Windows 2000 supports Devanagari and Tamil scripts.

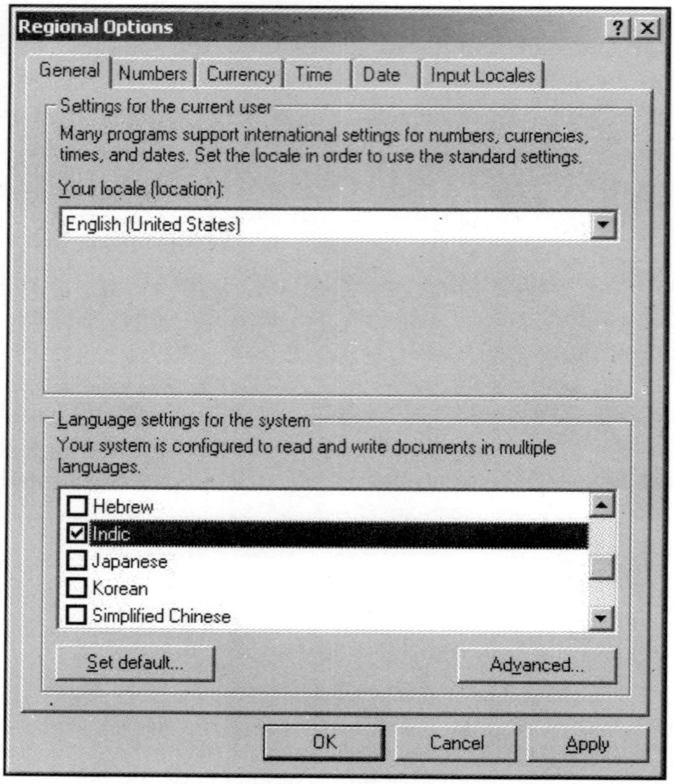

Figure 16: Selecting Indic script in Microsoft Windows 2000

Note: Microsoft Windows is supporting more and more languages. One may need to update the operating system to be able to work in language that has been supported later by the operating system.

Warning: Implementation of languages in computers is an evolving process. Even the Unicode standard undergoes change. As such, features of the languages may undergo change.

Tips: One reason why Indic and East Asian languages were not selected by default (that is, these are to be specifically selected) is that installing the language files slows down the computer's performance slightly!

Under Linux

Secondary languages can be selected under Linux operating system environment. This can be done through "Control Center." One having privilege of the Administrator (root) may open the "Language" under the group "System" as shown in Figure 17.

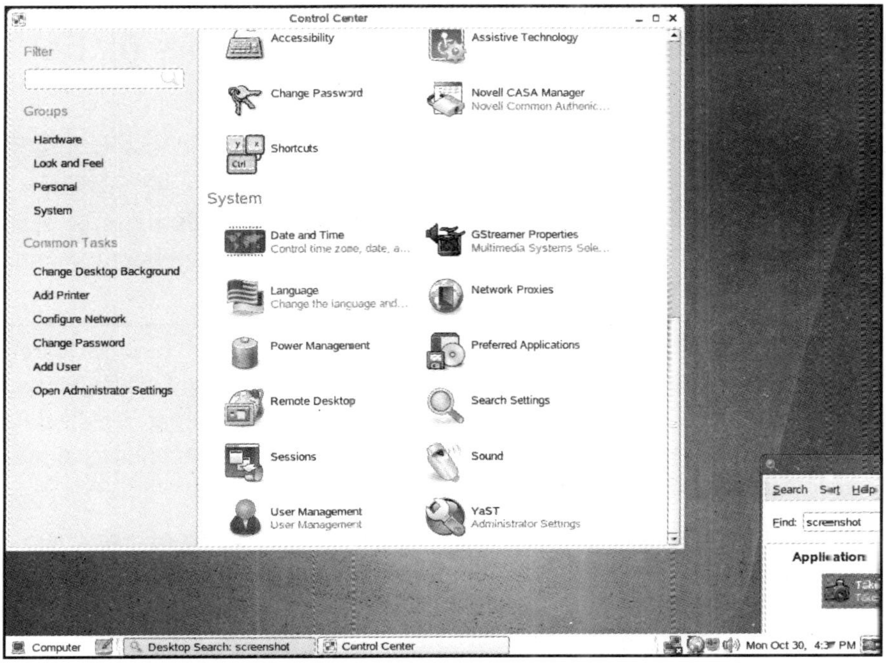

Figure 17: Control Center in SUSE Linux

The secondary languages may be selected from among the available languages, as shown in Figure 18.

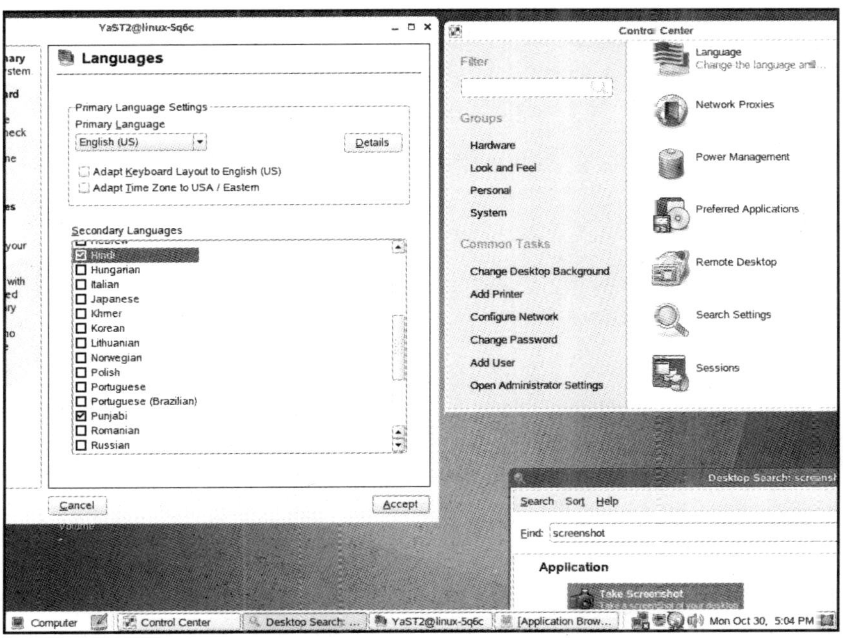

Figure 18: Selecting secondary languages under Linux

Installing keyboard layouts/Input Method Editors (IMEs)

One has to install appropriate keyboard layout(s)/input method editor(s)to be able to type texts in the desired languages and scripts. Without such installation, it may not be possible or convenient to type in those languages.

Note: The files for the Indic/Arabic/East Asian languages must be installed in the computer as described in the previous section, before the keyboard layout/IME can be installed for these languages.

Input Method Editor (IME): An input method editor (IME) is a program or operating system component that allows computer users to enter complex characters and symbols (such as Indic, Tibetan, Arabic, Japanese, Chinese, and Korean characters), using a standard Western keyboard. The term IME originated from the Microsoft Windows operating system. The use has now gained acceptance in other operating systems.

One keystroke on the keyboard does not necessarily mean inputting of one character, or one glyph. In normal English writing, one keystroke (other than that of Alt, Control, CapsLock etc) corresponds to one character and one glyph. However, it is not so in case of complex scripts such as Indic, Arabic and East Asian languages. Keystroke and encoding are distinct, and depends on the Input Method Editor (IME).

With the procedure mentioned in the previous section, it will be possible to read texts written in complex scripts and East Asian scripts in Microsoft Windows with correct formation of ligatures. However, it will not be possible to key in text in these languages using the keyboard, as the keyboard will type text in the default language, which may be English (US). To be able to key in text in the language(s) using the normal keyboard, it will be necessary to select the keyboard layout/IME as described below. Any number of input languages can be installed.

In Microsoft Windows 98 (See Figure 19):-

1. Open the Language tab by Control Panel → Keyboard → Language tab.
2. Add the desired language by clicking Add… button, if it is not already installed, as explained earlier. See Figure 11.
3. Select the desired language by clicking on it.
4, Click Properties button while the language is selected.
5. Select the keyboard layout from the drop-down list, and click OK button. See Figure 19.
6. Default input language may be changed (if so desired) by clicking the button "Set as Default" while the language is selected.
7. Click OK/Apply button.

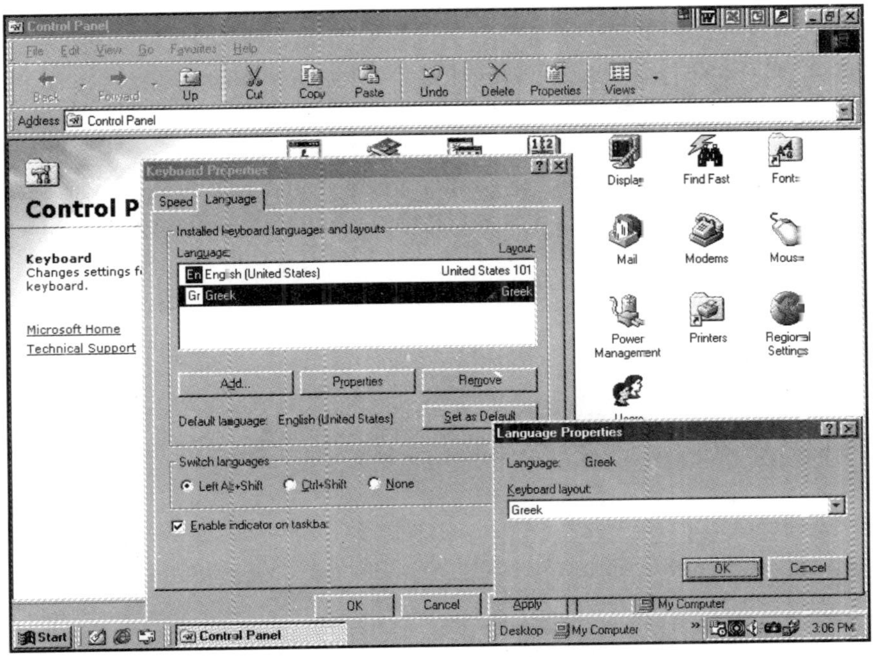

Figure 19: Selecting keyboard layout in Microsoft Windows 98

In Microsoft Windows 2000

1. Select "Input Locale" tab in keyboard icon in Control Panel.
2. Click the "Add" button in the "Installed input locales" frame.
3. Select the desired language in the "Input Locale" drop-down box on the "Add Input Locale" dialog box.
4. Select the appropriate keyboard layout.

In Microsoft Windows XP

1. In the screen as shown in Figure 14, click the button "Details...." The window entitled "Text Services and Input Languages" will appear as shown in Figure 20. Select Settings tab.
2. Click the button "Add...." A window entitled "Add Input Language" pops up as shown in Figure 21.
3. Select the desired language and the keyboard layout/IME from the combo list, and click "OK" button. In the illustration at Figure 21, Marathi language is being added in Marathi keyboard layout.

Tips: When a language is selected, the default keyboard layout/IME for the language appears in the keyboard layout/IME drop-down list, unless it has already been selected previously.

4. Repeat the previous two steps for adding all the languages and keyboard layouts/IMEs you want to use in the near future for typing from keyboard. The selected language(s) and keyboard layout(s)/IME(s) will appear in the "Installed Services" frame as shown in Figure 21.

Tips: The input language(s) and the keyboard layout(s)/IME(s) can be added and/or removed later. As such, it is recommended to select only the languages and keyboard layouts/IMEs that will be needed in the near future. That is, one need not select all probable the languages and keyboard layouts/IMEs that one is ever going to use. Selecting unnecessary keyboard layouts/IMEs will make typing cumbersome.

5. Click "OK" or "Apply" button in "Text Services and Input Languages" window.

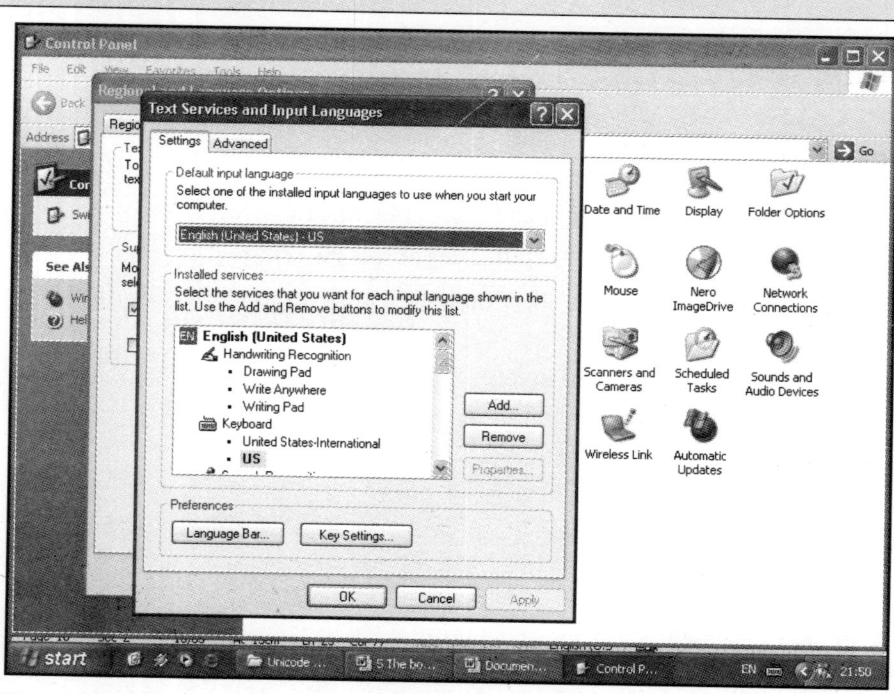

Figure 20: "Text Services and Input Languages" window

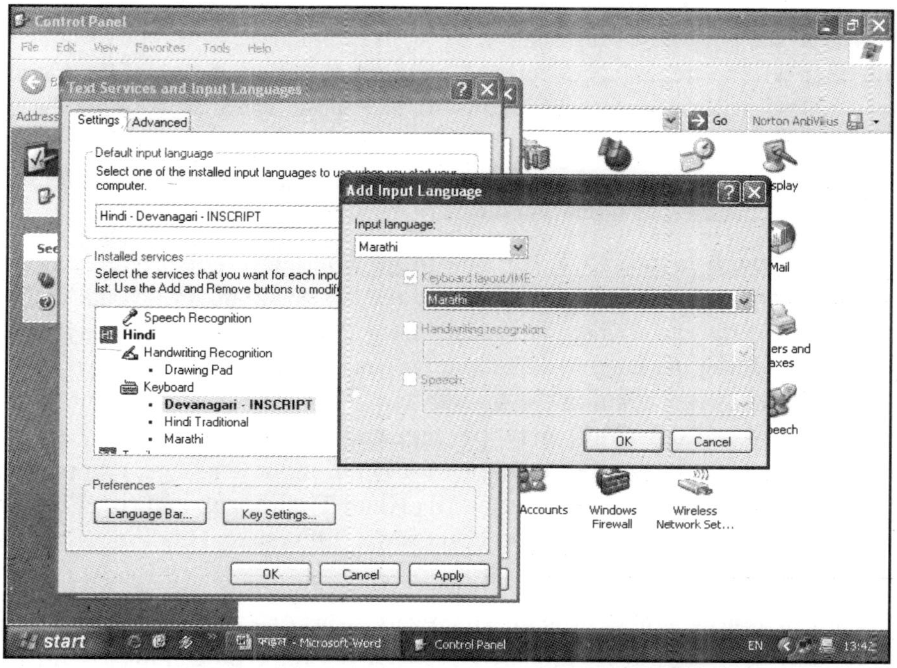

Figure 21: Selecting keyboard layout/IME

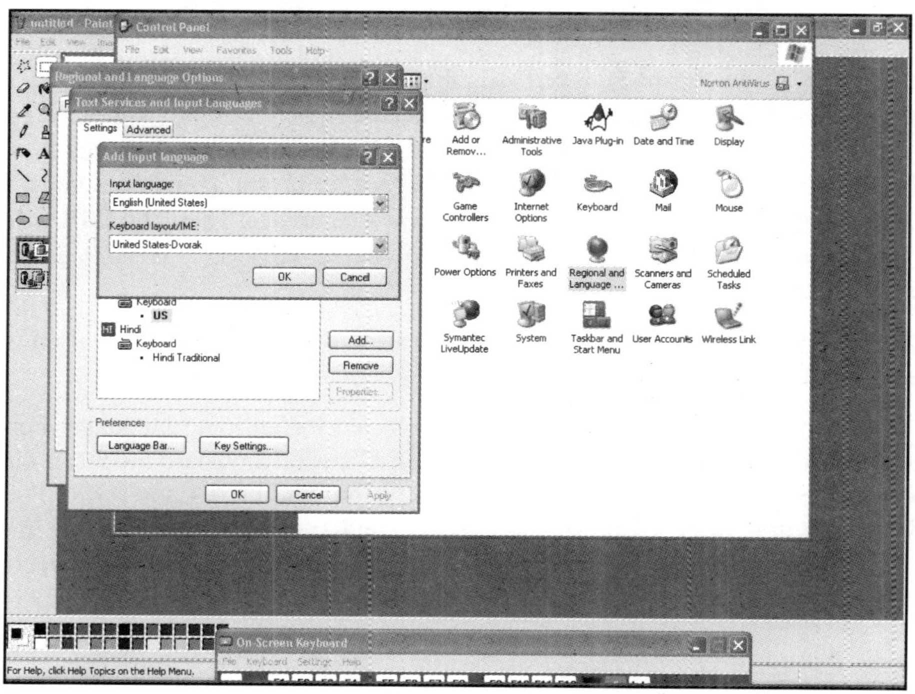

Figure 22: Selecting keyboard layout/IME (another example)

Note: For the purpose of installation of Input Languages, different variants of the same language will be treated as different languages. All the variants of the language should be installed separately, if one wants to use these variants as input languages. For example, English (US) and English (UK) will be treated as two different languages. If one wants to work in both American English and British English, then both English (US) and English (UK) must be installed as input languages.

More than one keyboard layout/IME for one input language: It is possible to have one or more than one keyboard layouts/IMEs for one language.[12] The keyboard layouts/IMEs may be in the same script or in different scripts. To install more than more keyboard layout/IME for an input language, after adding the language as input language with a keyboard layout/IME, one has to add the same input language again in the similar way (as described above), but this time with a different keyboard layout/IME. This may be repeated to install any number of keyboard layouts/IMEs for a single language. For example, for Hindi input language, one may install three keyboard layouts/IMEs: (i) Devanagari Inscript, (ii) Hindi Traditional, and (iii) English (US), the last one being not in Devanagari script, but in Latin script. Of course, Hindi input language can be installed with even more keyboard layouts/IMEs.

Note: A keyboard layout/IME may contain characters from one or more scripts. For example, most Indic language keyboard layouts/IMEs permit typing numerals in Latin script. Indic full stop sign (।) has been encoded in Devanagari script only. Devanagari full stop sign is to be used in typing the punctuation mark in Bengali, Punjabi, Gujarati etc scripts.

Note: In addition to the keyboard layouts/IMEs that come with Microsoft Windows, additional software for keyboard layouts/IMEs are also available. For example, software for various keyboard layouts/IMEs in Devanagari script is available. For instance, Remington, Typewriter and Phonetic etc keyboard layouts/IMEs for Devanagari script are available. One will have to obtain the third party IME software, and install it in one's computer. Then, the IME will appear in the list of "keyboard layout/IME" (see Figure 21). Moreover, one may design customized keyboard layout as explained in *Annexure (G)*.

Note: The keyboard layout/IME determines the script(s) that will be used to type the selected language.

Note: Any keyboard layout/IME can be selected for an input language. For example, one can select Hindi as the input language with English-US as its keyboard layout. If one does so, the text typed will be marked as being in Hindi language, but will be in Latin script. For example, even though the text is in Latin script, it is marked as Hindi, as is apparent from the status bar of Microsoft Word. However, it is recommended that a language be typed in the recommended script only. Features on the language may be available only in the recommended script.

---

[12] Of course, one can use only one keyboard layout/IME at one time. However, one can switch among the keyboard layouts/IMEs as one goes on typing.

How does one select a specific input language and a specific keyboard layout/IME for the input language? This question has been answered later in the chapter.

<u>Removing an installed input language or keyboard layout/IME</u>: An input language or the keyboard layout/IME for the input language can be removed. For this, one has to take the following steps:

1. In the settings tab of "Text Services and Input Languages" window (see Figure 20), select the language or keyboard layout/IME by clicking on it in the Installed services frame.
2. Click the "Remove" button.
3. Repeat the earlier steps to remove all the unwanted languages or keyboard layouts/IMEs.
4. Click "Apply" or "OK" button. The input language(s) or the keyboard layout(s)/IME(s) will be removed.

Note: It will be possible to read the text already typed in the language even after the input language has been removed.

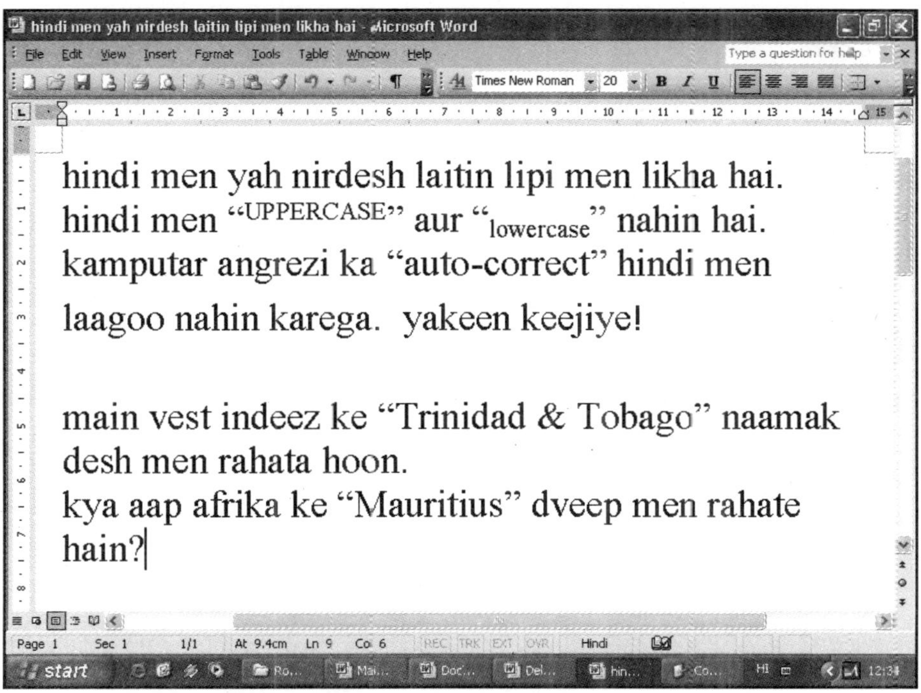

Figure 23: Hindi language written in Latin script

Selecting default input language

Default input language is the specific language (or variant of the language) along with the keyboard layout/IME that is used as input language and keyboard layout/IME by default. The default input language and keyboard layout/IME can be changed, and changed again and again. Usually, the default input language is English (US) with keyboard layout as English-US. However, a different default input language and keyboard layout/IME can be selected. Any of one of the languages with keyboard layout/IME listed in the "Installed Services" frame (see Figure 20 and Figure 24) can be selected as default input language.

To select the default input language and keyboard layout/IME, one has to select the default language under "Default input language" drop-down list as shown in Figure 24, where Tamil language in Tamil keyboard layout is being selected as the default input language in place of Hindi in Devanagari-INSCRIPT keyboard layout. Thereafter, one should click "Apply" or "OK" button. If the language/keyboard layout/IME is not listed under "Installed Services," then first it will have to be added as explained earlier (see Figure 21).

Tips: Many Indian users write in British English, and not in American English. English (UK) can be chosen as the default input language instead of English (US) by the above-mentioned procedure. However, one may have to select "English US" keyboard layout. This is because "United Kingdom" keyboard is slightly different (for example, it has keys for £ and ¬) and most Indian keyboards have keys printed as per "English US" keyboard layout.

Warning: Most computers in India have American English as the default language, and not the British English popular in India. Naturally, words like *aeroplane*, *colour*, *practise* and *programme* etc are marked as wrongly spelled in Microsoft Word. Some users of such computers add the British English words to the "custom dictionary" (described in Chapter 9) so that the British English words are not marked as spelling errors. However, this approach is defective for the following reasons: (i) The text remains marked as being in American English, (ii) All the word forms of the British English words are to be added to the custom dictionary that could be a bit too many (for example, *practise*, *practises*, *practised*, *practising*, *practising's* for the word *practise*), (iii) American English words are still recognized as correct spelling (for example, *practiced* is recognized as a correct spelling along with *practised*!).

Note: Default input language and keyboard layout/IME will appear in bold letters in the "Installed Services" frame (see Figure 20, Figure 21 or Figure 24).

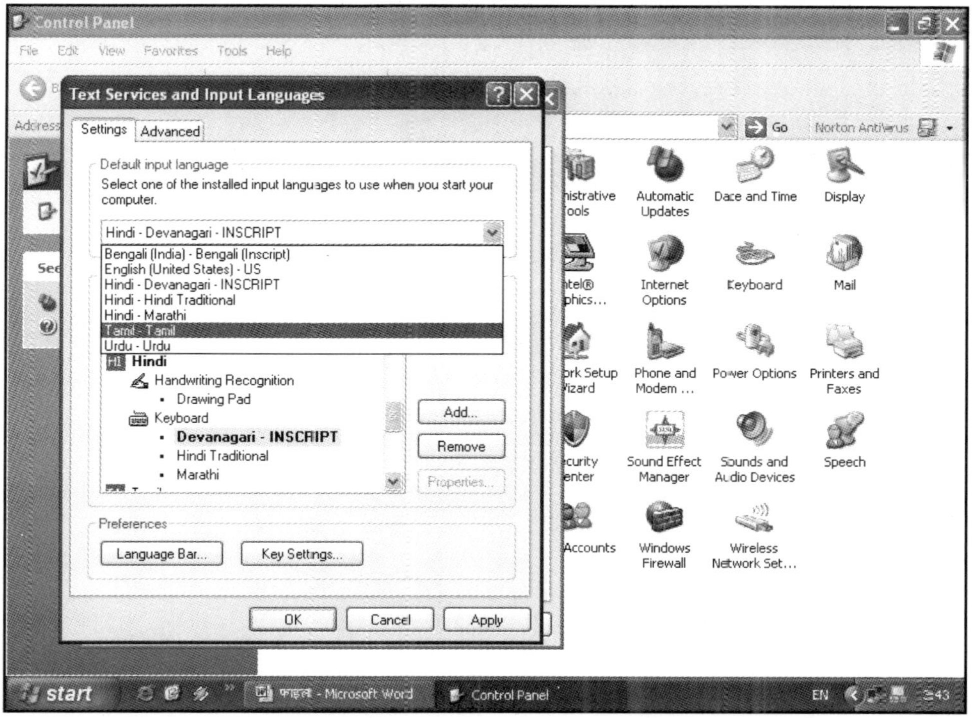

Figure 24: Selecting default input language

Language bar settings

If more than one input language, and/or more than one keyboard layout/IME have been installed, then it is worthwhile to have Language Bar on the desktop and the additional Language Bar icons in the taskbar. This will show the currently selected language and keyboard layout/IME. This also allows one to select the language and keyboard layout/IME speedily by the click of mouse.

Language bar settings can be set or changed by clicking the “Language Bar...” button under Preferences section (see Figure 24). The Language Bar Settings window will pop up as shown in Figure 25. Appropriate options may be selected.

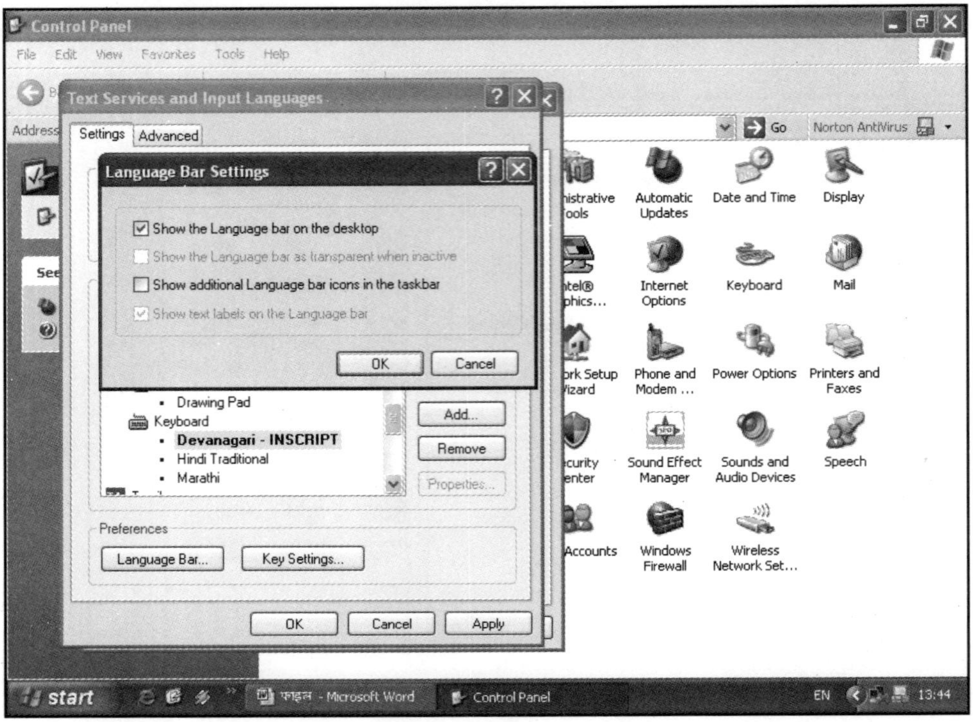

Figure 25: Language bar settings

Changing input language

If more than one input language has been installed, then initially, the default input language will be the input language.

One may switch to the next input language (or, variant of the language) in a cyclical manner by ***pressing Left-Alt and Shift keys simultaneously***. Left-Alt key may be pressed, and while the Left-Alt key is pressed, the Shift key should be pressed; and then both the keys should be released. Each time the key combination is pressed, the current input language advances to the next language in a cyclical manner in the list of the installed input languages. Either Left-Shift or Right-Shift key may be used. Left-Shift and Right-Shift advances the languages in the opposite cyclical direction.

Of course, above-mentioned key sequence is as per the default settings. One may change the default settings by clicking the "Key Settings…" button in the Preferences section under Settings tab of "Text Services and Input Languages" window (see Figure 25 and Figure 26), and selecting the desired options.

Another way of changing the input languages is to click on the language icon (showing the code of the current input language) in the taskbar or the notification area (also called system tray), as the case may be. One will have to select the desired input language from the list of languages that pops up as shown in Figure 27. Also see Figure 28.

Note: This method will have to be used even to switch among variants of the same language, such as from English (US) to English (UK), from English (UK) to English (Australia) etc.

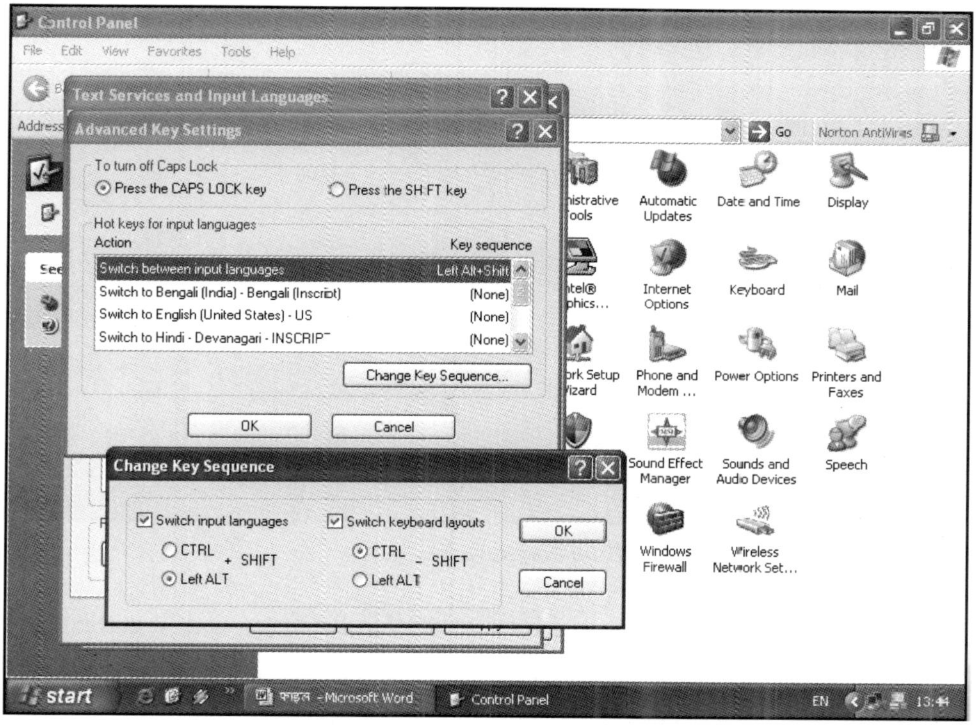

Figure 26: Setting of keys for switching between languages and keyboard layouts/IMEs

Note: If only one input language has been installed, then the procedure will have no impact, as there is no other language to switch over to.

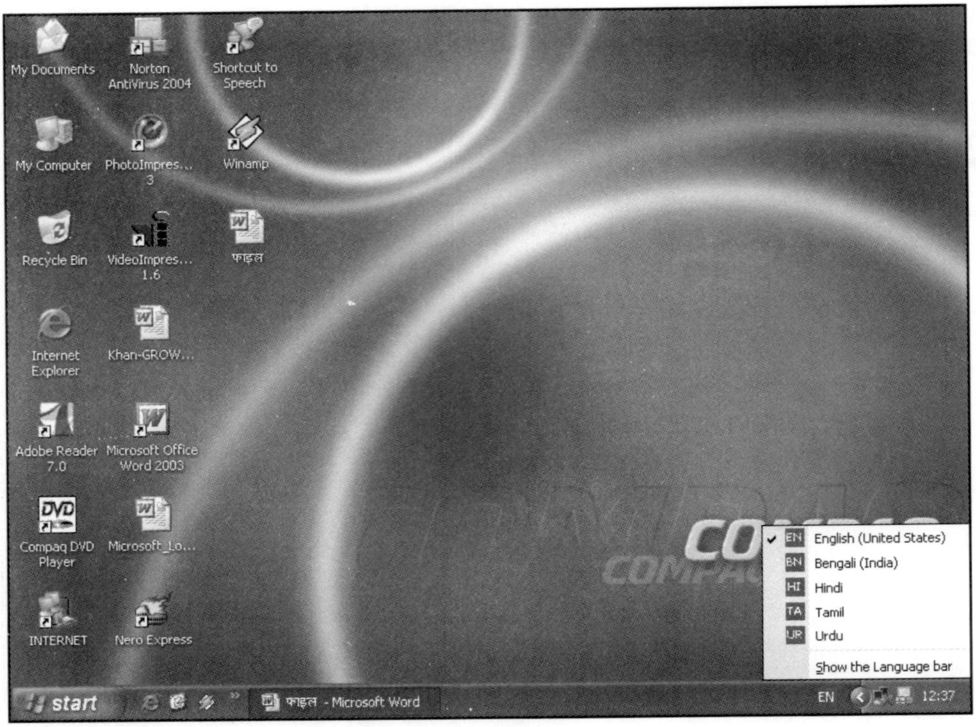

Figure 27: Selecting language from language bar

Note: One can switch directly to a particular language and a particular keyboard layout/IME by pressing customized hot keys. The hot keys can be set by selecting the input language and keyboard layout/IME in Figure 26, pressing the button "Change Key Sequence…", and then selecting the desired key combination.

Note: In Figure 26, one can also select whether Caps Lock will be turned off by pressing the key Caps Lock again or by pressing Shift key.

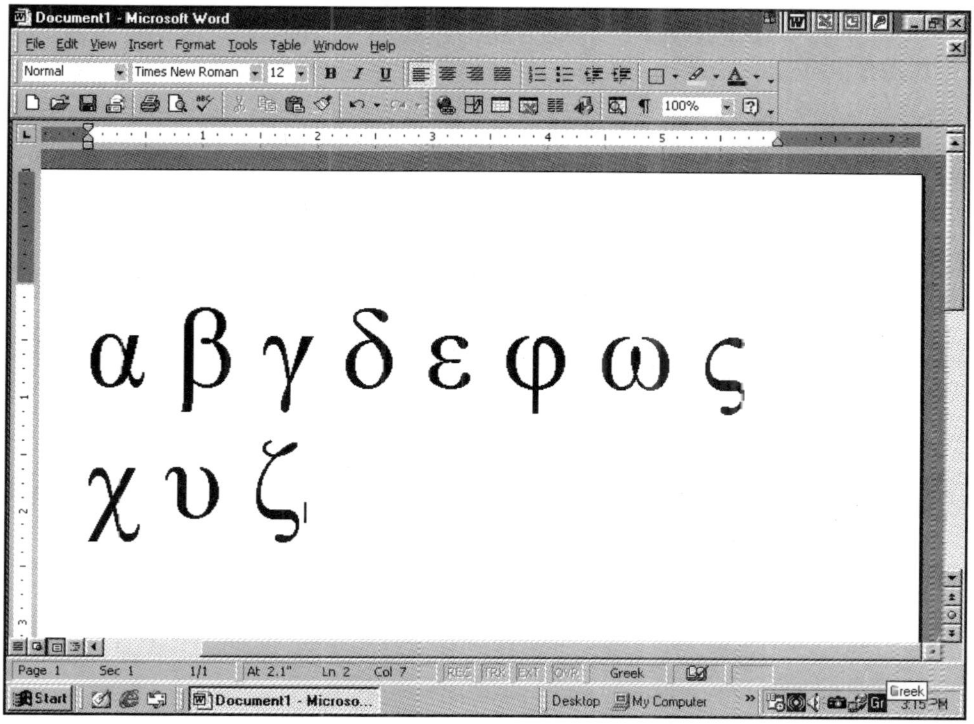

Figure 28: Typing in Greek keyboard layout in Microsoft Windows 98

Changing keyboard layout/IME

If more than one keyboard layout/IME has been installed for the language currently selected as the input language, then one can switch to the next keyboard layout/IME in a cyclic manner by ***pressing Control and Shift keys simultaneously***. Control key may be pressed, and while the Control key is pressed, the Shift key should be pressed; and then both the keys should be released. Each time the key combination is pressed, the current keyboard layout/IME advances in a cyclical manner in the keyboard layout/IME for the language. Either Left-Shift or Right-Shift key may be used. Left-Shift and Right-Shift advances the keyboard layout/IME in the opposite cyclical direction.

Of course, above-mentioned key sequence is as per the default settings. The default settings may be changed by clicking the button “Key Settings…” under Preference in the Settings tab of “Text Services and Input Languages” window (see Figure 26), and selecting the desired options.

Another way of changing the current keyboard layouts/IMEs for the currently selected input language is by selecting the appropriate keyboard layout/IME from the taskbar as shown in Figure 29. The icon for the keyboard layout/IME may be clicked, and appropriate keyboard layout/IME may be selected from the list.

Note: If several keyboard layouts are possible in the selected input method editor (IME), then a specific keyboard layout in the IME may have to be selected. This has been illustrated in Figure 30, where an IME ("Indic IME 1") for Devanagari script has been installed in the computer. In the options that pop up, one has to select a specific keyboard layout for the current input language, unless the default one is to be used.

IMEs in several Indic scripts may be downloaded from the Internet. For example, the website http://www.bhashaindia.com allowed downloads on IMEs in several Indic scripts, including Devanagari, Bengali, Gujarati, Gurmukhi, Telugu, Tamil, Kannada, Malayalam.

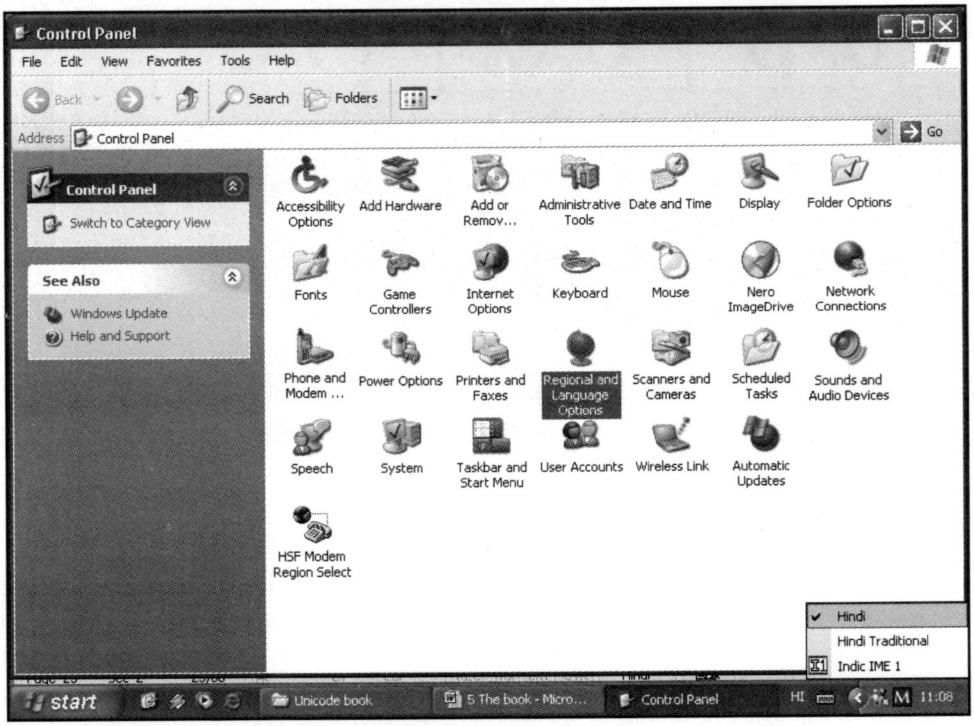

Figure 29: Selecting a keyboard layout/IME

Note: If only one keyboard layout/IME has been installed for the current input language variant, then the Control-Shift key combination will have no impact, as there is no other keyboard layout/IME to switch over to.

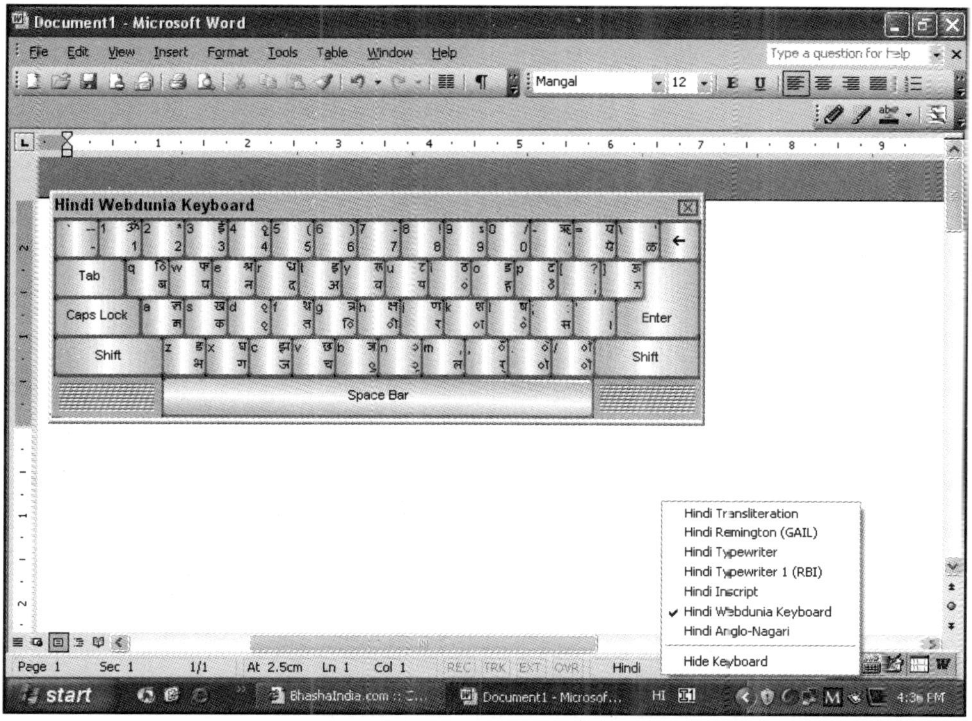

Figure 30: Selecting a keyboard layout in an input method editor (IME)

Note: As one can find from the "Installed Services" frame in the Settings tab of "Text Services and Input Languages" window (see Figure 20 and Figure 21 etc), Microsoft Windows may not (or, by now, may!) support some advanced features for some languages, such as speech recognition and handwriting recognition etc. For example, speech recognition is supported in English (US), but not in Hindi.

Tips: If one is typing in two different windows in two different languages (say, Hindi and Urdu), then Microsoft Windows may remember the language for the two windows separately. That is, one will not have to change language each time one switches between the two windows.

Note: If there is more than one user of a computer, all of them may select different sets of the input languages and keyboard layouts/IMEs.

Selecting keyboard layout under Linux

Keyboard layout can be selected from the "Control Center" item "Keyboard" as illustrated in Figure 31. A Bhutanese (Tibetan) keyboard layout is being selected in the illustration

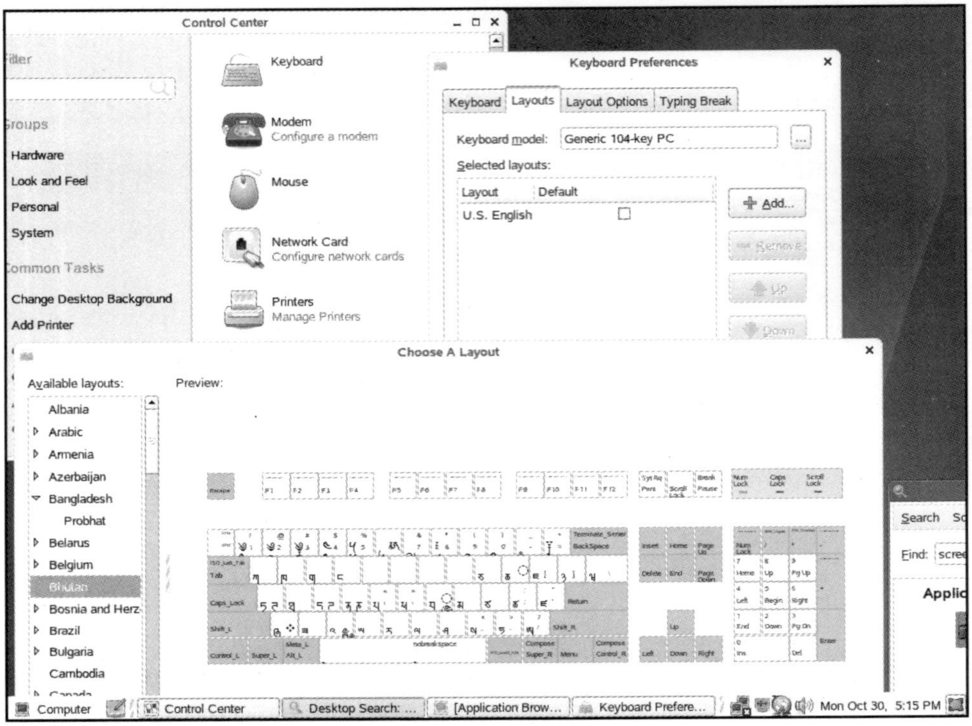

Figure 31: Selecting keyboard layout under Linux

Font insufficient to view text in complex script

For reading a text in a written in a script, one must have the font for that script for visual representation. If the font for that script is not there, what will appear on the screen is a set of hollow rectangular boxes like □ □ □ . An illustration is at Figure 32. The computer has no Unicode compliant font for the character code set for Bengali script. So, what appears on the screen is not text in Bengali language, but hollow rectangular boxes.

Note: Arial Unicode MS (OpenType) is a useful font. It contains glyphs for scripts in Unicode for many languages, and is a biggish font file. However, in the older version of the font, the following languages of the region were not there: Burmese, Sinhala, Silhoti Nagari, Kharoshthi, Old Persian etc. Also, the information on ligature formation of certain scripts were not there.

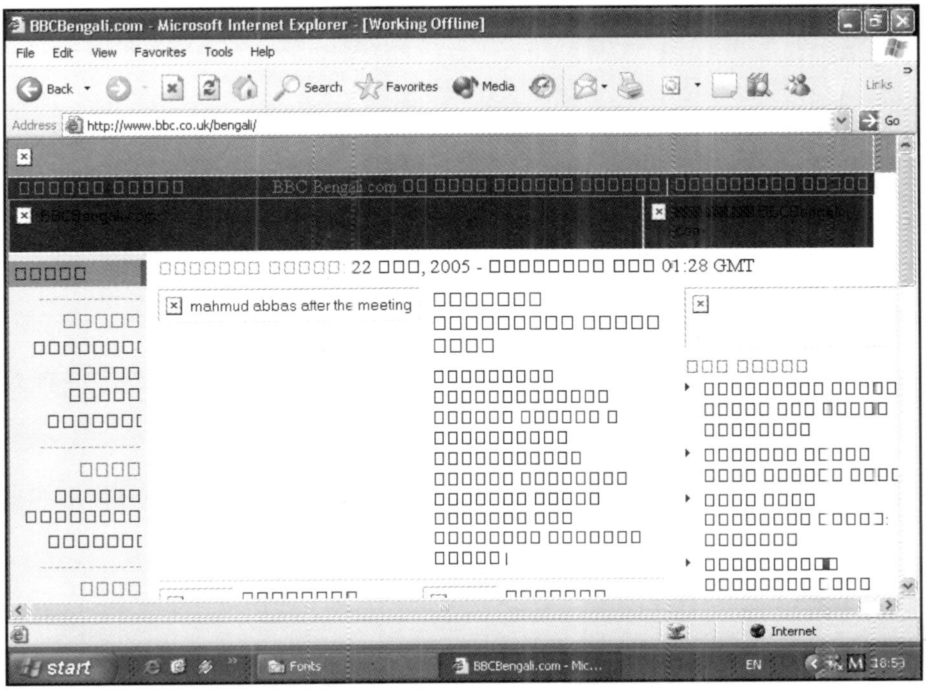

Figure 32: Bengali website seen without Bengali font

While font is necessary to view the text written in Unicode, it is not always sufficient, especially for complex scripts such as Indic and Arabic scripts. The Unicode Standard is strictly concerned with character processing, and presumes that Unicode text strings will be input and stored in a simple sequence defined as 'logical order'. The Unicode Standard also presumes the existence of rendering systems above the Unicode text string that will, as necessary, reorder code-points and affect sophisticated glyph processing to shape the rendering of the text through glyph substitution and positioning features. In contrast, systems and applications that make use of Latin or simple fonts do not need to make a distinction between character processing and glyph processing. In working with such fonts, it is most often convenient to think only in terms of character processing, or simply text-processing: that is, the sequential rendering of glyphs representing character codes as input in logical order.

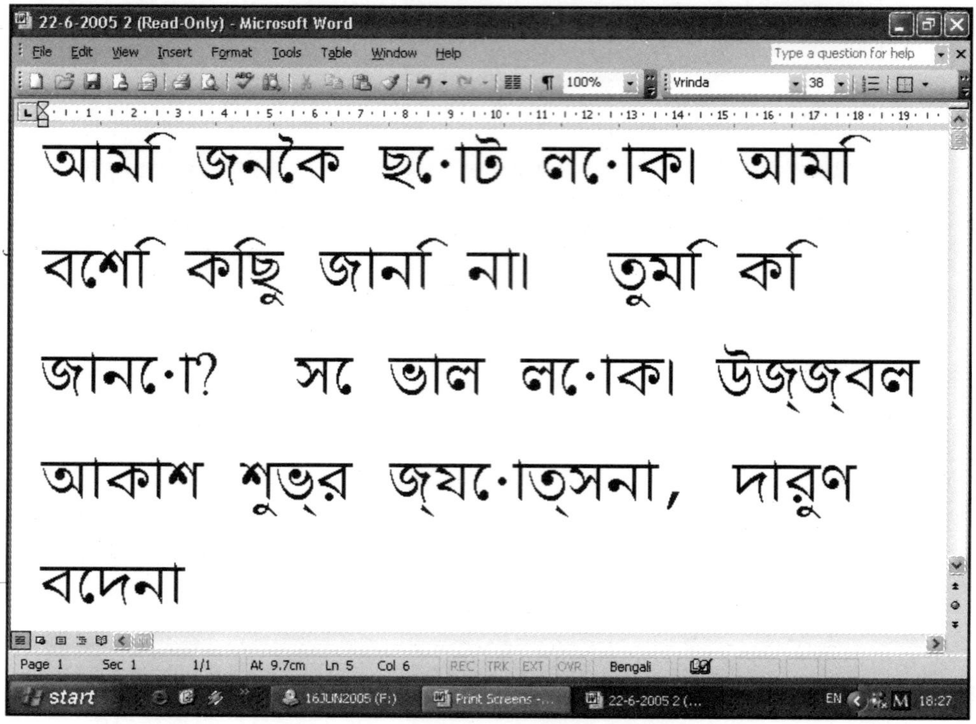

Figure 33: Incorrect glyph rendering of text in Bengali language

The text in Bengali language may be seen in Figure 33 and Figure 34. The text was typed in Vrinda font in Figure 34. However, the same text is viewed in the rudimentary Arial Unicode MS font in Figure 33. Arial Unicode MS did not have information on the glyph rendering and ligature formation of Bengali script. As is evident, the glyph rendering was not correct in Figure 33.

Note: If Microsoft Windows does not support the language/script (or, the language files have not been installed as explained earlier in the chapter), but the name of file/folder or the hint text in a balloon is the script, then instead of the text, hollow rectangular boxes "□□□" may appear.

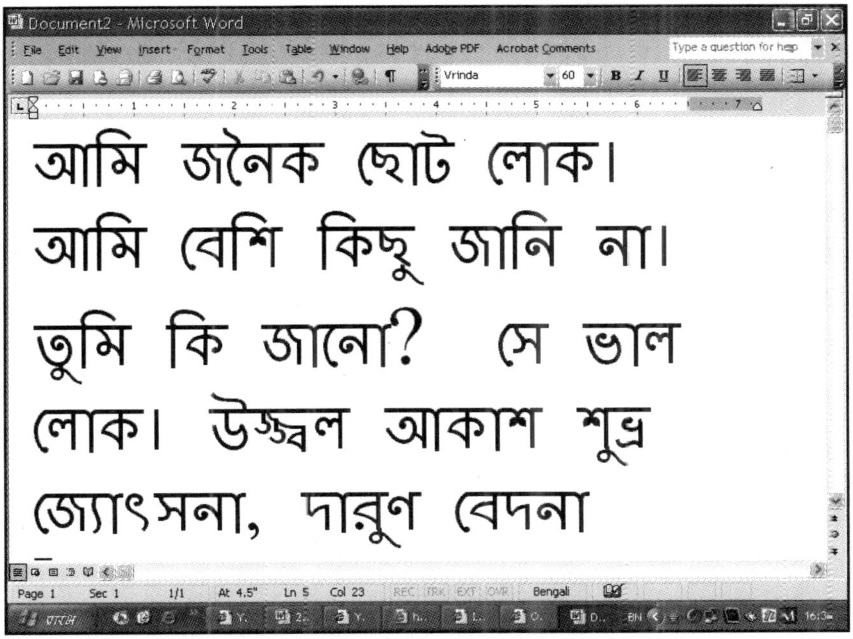

Figure 34: Correct glyph rendering of text in Bengali language

Obtaining Unicode fonts

Many Unicode fonts come with Microsoft Windows and Microsoft Office. Unicode fonts may be obtained from software suppliers. Many Unicode fonts are available on the Internet. The Internet may be searched for Unicode fonts for the script. For example, the website http://www.devanaagarii.net had links to many Unicode-compatible Devanagari fonts.

The Unicode font may be installed in the computer just as any other font is installed (see Chapter 1).

Tips: If the ligatures etc are not being formed correctly in a complex script, the fault may be with the font file. The font file may be defective, or the font file may be an old version.

What you have learned

1. Installing files for complex script and East Asian languages
2. Selecting keyboard layouts/input method editors for input languages
3. Changing default input language
4. Setting English (UK) etc as default input language
5. Changing input languages
6. Changing keyboard layouts/IMEs

4. Typing in Indic and other Languages

A few general ideas

Let us have a look at a few definitions and general ideas. These ideas are important to understand the concepts explained in this book.

Script: Script is a collection of letters and other written signs used to represent textual information in one or more writing systems. One language may be written in one script (for example, Bengali is written only in Bengali script), in more than one script (for example, Sindhi is written in both Arabic and Devanagari scripts separately) or using more than one script (for example, Japanese is written using Han, Hiragana and Katakana scripts).

Character: A character is a unit of text. While most characters have visual forms, some characters do not have any visual form. As explained later, ZWJ and ZWNJ characters are invisible characters, and *halant* character is at times visible and at times invisible. Each character is assigned a numeric code in Unicode.

Warning: There are some confusables characters that look similar, but have distinct use and behavior, and are different characters. Some such characters may have distinct appearance, such as in length or angle. For example, character denoting the minus sign (-), whose code is 002D hex is distinct from that denoting hyphen (-), whose code is 2010 hex. Similarly, the solidus character (/), code 002F hex, is different from "fraction slash" character (⁄), code 2044 hex.

Glyph: A glyph is a graphical unit. A glyph is a particular representation of a grapheme, or graphemes in combination, or only a part of a grapheme. For example, प्रश्न comprises two glyphs प्र and श्न, but as many as six characters प, ◌्[13], र, श, ◌्, and न. In this word, प्र and श्न are consonant conjuncts. In this example, one glyph comprises more than one character. On the other hand, some typewriters require the use of multiple glyphs to depict a single character; for example, two hyphens in place of a dash.

Font: A font refers to a typeface manifesting as an indexed collection of glyphs or glyphs-rendering instructions and associated information that facilitates rendering mapping characters to glyphs and for rendering glyphs in different sizes. In normal English fonts, each character corresponds to a single glyph. However, this is not the case in a font used for a language with a large alphabet or complex writing system where one character may correspond to several glyphs, or several characters to one glyph. Fonts are of OpenType and TrueType.

[13] *Halant* (also called *virama* and *hasant*) is not only a character, but is perhaps the most important and the most used character in Indic scripts.

Ligature: Complex scripts and even Latin script have ligatures. Two or more characters join to form ligature. Examples of ligatures are æ, क्ष and त्र . Ligature is different from digraph. In a digraph, the glyphs remain separate but are placed close together. In a ligature, the glyphs are fused into a single glyph.

Zero-Width Joiner (ZWJ): The zero-width joiner (ZWJ) is a non-printing character used in the computerized typesetting of some cursive or complex scripts. When placed between two characters that would otherwise not be connected, a ZWJ causes them to be printed in their connected forms. The code for ZWJ character in Unicode is 200D hex. For example, श + ् + न produces श्न, but श + ् + ZWJ + न produces श्‍न. ZWJ character has no visual appearance of its own. Nonetheless, it is a character, and an important character in Indic scripts. ZWJ character is called "No-Width Non-Break" in Microsoft Word.

Tips: Zero-Width Joiner character is used in Unicode to write vowel signs in Indic scripts on an invisible consonant—i.e., without the dotted circles. For example, the key sequence ZWJ + ि produces ‍ि; ZWJ + ु produces ‍ु; ZWJ + ौ produces ‍ौ; ZWJ + ॅ produces ‍ॅ etc.

Tips: ZWJ character can be used in writing Chashma र in Devanagari script, which is used in Marathi and Nepali languages. The key combination र, ् and ZWJ produces *chashma* र (i.e., र्‍). For example, the keystrokes व + ा + र + ् + ZWJ + य + ा produce वार्‍या; without ZWJ, it would produce वार्या.

Tips: ZWJ may be used in Arabic script-based languages to control the way the letters are joined. A few examples are given in the table below:

Table 4: ZWJ in Arabic script

Key combination (read right-to-left)	Output (read right-to-left)
ک	ک
ZWJ ک	ک‍
ک ZWJ	‍ک

Zero-Width Non-Joiner (ZWNJ): The zero-width non-joiner (ZWNJ) is a non-printing character used in the computerized typesetting of some cursive or complex scripts. When placed between two characters that would otherwise be connected, a ZWNJ causes them to be printed in their final and initial forms, respectively. This is also an effect of a space character, but a ZWNJ is used when it is desirable to keep the words closer together. The Unicode code for ZWNJ is 200C hex. For example, श + ् + न produces श्न, but श + ् + ZWNJ + न produces श्‌न; also note that as explained earlier श + ् + ZWJ + न produces श्‍न. A blank space character between two letters separates them in two words; however, ZWNJ does not mean the separation of the letters into two words. ZWNJ character has no visual appearance of its own. Nonetheless, it is a character, and an important character in Indic scripts. ZWNJ character is called "No-Width Optional Break" in Microsoft Word.

Tips: ZWNJ may be used in Arabic script-based languages to control the way the letters are joined. A few examples are given in the table below:

Table 5: ZWNJ in Arabic script.

Key combination (read right-to-left)	Output (read right-to-left)
ک ذ	کذ
ک ZWNJ ذ	ک‌ذ

Zero-Width Space (ZWSP): This character is intended for line break control. It has no width, but its presence between two characters does not prevent increased letter spacing in justification. The code of ZWSP is 200B hex.

Note: *Annexure (E)* may be seen for more on use of ZWJ, ZWNJ and ZWSP characters.

Combining Grapheme Joiner (CGJ): The code for Combining Grapheme Joiner character is 034F hex. CGJ does not have any visible display of its own. Despite its name, the CGJ neither joins graphemes together, nor does it create new graphemes. The insertion of a CGJ character into a sequence of combining marks blocks canonical reordering of those combining marks.

Writing direction: Three writing directions are common in modern writing systems: left-to-right, right-to-left and top-to-bottom. However, this book concentrates only on left-to-right and right-to-left languages.

Typing in European languages

This section deals with Latin-script based European languages such as French, Spanish, Portuguese, Italian, German, Catalan, Norwegian etc. Even Cyrillic script based languages such as Russian etc follow the same pattern. Each of the Latin script based European language (including their variants) has its specific standard keyboard layout. The keyboard layouts for French (France) and Spanish (International) languages have been shown at Figure 35 and Figure 36 respectively. (Selecting the input language and the keyboard layout/IME was discussed in the previous chapter.)

Warning: Some languages have variants. Each variant form may have distinct standard keyboard layout. For example, French and Spanish have several variant forms. French (France) keyboard layout is different from French (Canada) keyboard layout, which in turn is different from French (Belgium) keyboard layout etc. Similar is the case with Spanish and other European languages.

Note: Notwithstanding the standard keyboard layout for each language (and variants of the language), it is not necessary to enter text using the standard keyboard layout for that language or variant of the language. For example, English-US keyboard layout may be used to key in text in most Latin-script based West European languages. To type in West European language using English-US keyboard layout in Microsoft Word, one has to choose the input language as explained in Chapter 3 with English-US as the keyboard layout. Alternatively, one may type in English, and then change the language of the text as explained in Chapter 6 (see Figure 69).

Tips: If English-US keyboard is utilized to enter text in Spanish language, the question mark and exclamation point will automatically change to '¿' and '¡' depending on the context. (An interrogative sentence in Spanish language begins with the inverted question mark '¿', and ends with a straight question mark. Also, an exclamatory sentence begins with the inverted exclamation point '¡', and ends with a straight exclamatory point.)

Note: In many European language keyboard layouts, Right-Alt key has special significance. If a key is pressed together with Right-Alt, then a different character gets typed.[14] The keyboard layouts with Right-Alt pressed for French (France) and Spanish (International) keyboard layouts are shown in Figure 37 and Figure 38 respectively.

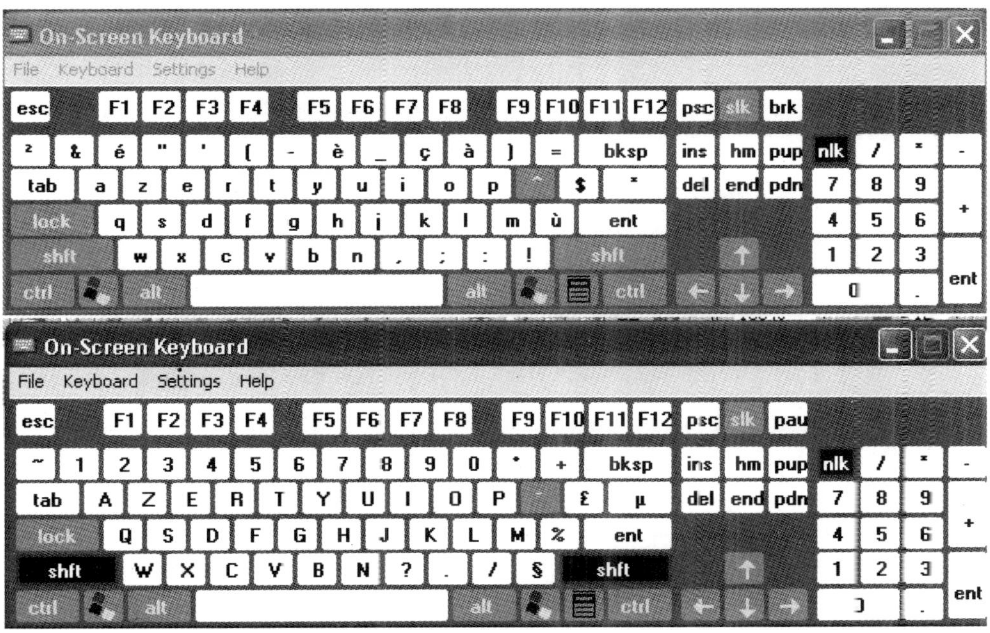

Figure 35: French (France) keyboard layout

[14] The Right-Alt key should be pressed first; and should be released only after the 'another' key has been pressed and released.

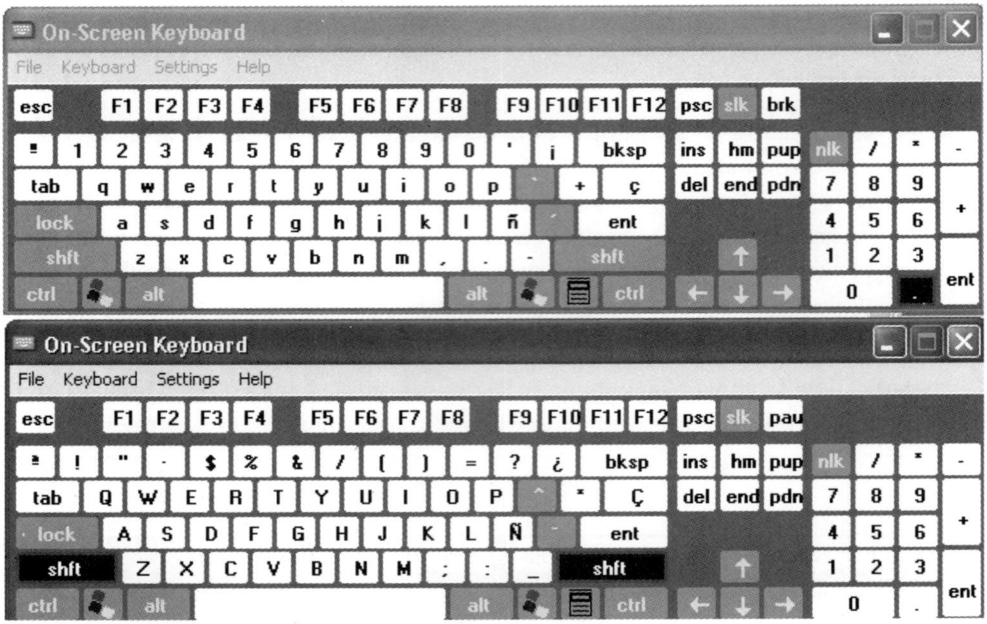

Figure 36: Spanish (International) keyboard layout

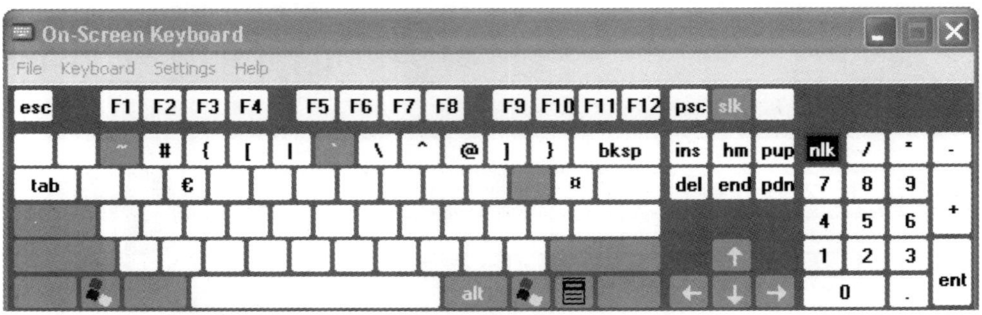

Figure 37: French (France) keyboard with Right-Alt key pressed

Figure 38: Spanish (International) keyboard with Right-Alt key pressed

How to select the input language: It has been discussed in the previous chapter. For example, see Figure 27.

How to choose the keyboard layout: It was also discussed in the previous chapter. For example, see Figure 29.

How to enter diacritical marks: The method of typing letters with diacritical marks is illustrated below with French (France) keyboard layout. The method is similar for other European languages. If there is a separate key for the letter with the diacritical mark, then the letter can be typed by pressing the key. In case of other letters with diacritical marks, a combination of keys in a particular sequence are to be pressed to type it. The diacritical mark is typed using the "dead key." Pressing dead key does not cause inputting of any character; the character(s) that get inputted depends on the subsequent keys pressed. Dead key followed by space character usually produces the dead key character. Dead key followed by a suitable key produces letters with diacritical mark. Dead key followed by other keys produce the diacritical mark followed by the letter denoted by the key.

Here are a few examples (refer to Figure 35 and Figure 37):

Table 6: Typing in French

To type this	Key sequence	Remarks
é	é	Type the letter é directly from the keyboard. The key é is at the key for digit 2 in Figure 35 (without using Shift key).
ô	^ o	In Figure 35, the key ^ appears shaded. Pressing of ^ key will not produce any visual effect, as it is a dead key. The letter ô appears only after the key o is pressed thereafter.
ñ	~ n	The key ~ is selected only in combination with Right-Alt key. In Figure 37, ~ key appears shaded. Pressing ~ key will not produce any visual effect, as it is a dead key. The letter ñ appears only after the key n is pressed thereafter.
^	^ *<space>*	Circumflex key, followed by space bar key.
~	~ *<space>*	Tilde key, followed by space bar key.

Note: United States (International) keyboard layout and other keyboard layouts may be used in a similar manner to key in texts in European languages. United States (International) keyboard layout is being chosen in the illustration at Figure 39. A few examples of key combination in United States (International) keyboard layout are given Table 7.

Table 7: Typing in US (International) keyboard layout

To type this	Required key sequence
'	' <space>[15]
"	" <space>
^	^ <space>
`	` <space>
ç	' c
é	' e
è	` e
í	' i
ì	` i
ñ	~ n
ô	^ o
ö	" o
û	^ u
ü	" u

Double (or, multiple) letters such as *ch*, *ll*, *sh*, *hr*, *rr*, *fl*, *fi* in European languages are treated as a sequence of two (or, more) letters, i.e., characters, and not as independent one character each.

Figure 39: Selecting United States (International) keyboard layout

[15] Apostrophe key, followed by space-bar key.

Keyboard layout for Russian language is shown in Figure 40. Belarusian, Ukrainian etc languages are also written in Cyrillic script, but have different keyboard layouts.

Figure 40: Russian keyboard layout

Note: The German small letter sharp s (ß) is different from the Greek small letter beta (β). Notwithstanding the similar look, the two characters have different numeric codes. Several characters are also different, notwithstanding the deceptively similar (or, even exactly same!) look.

Seeing the keyboard layout on the screen: If one is not well acquainted with a keyboard layout, and the keys have been defined differently than what is printed on the keys in the keyboard, it may be convenient to see the keyboard layout on the screen. To see the keyboard layout on the screen of the computer, one may use On-Screen Keyboard utility under Accessories → Accessibility as shown in Figure 41. Selecting “Always on Top” under Settings in the menu bar in the On-screen Keyboard window ensures that the keyboard layout popup is always visible. The keyboard layout popup can be closed any moment. As Shift, Alt etc keys are pressed, the on-screen keyboard display also changes. (Text can be entered by clicking on the onscreen keys also instead of typing from the keyboard.)

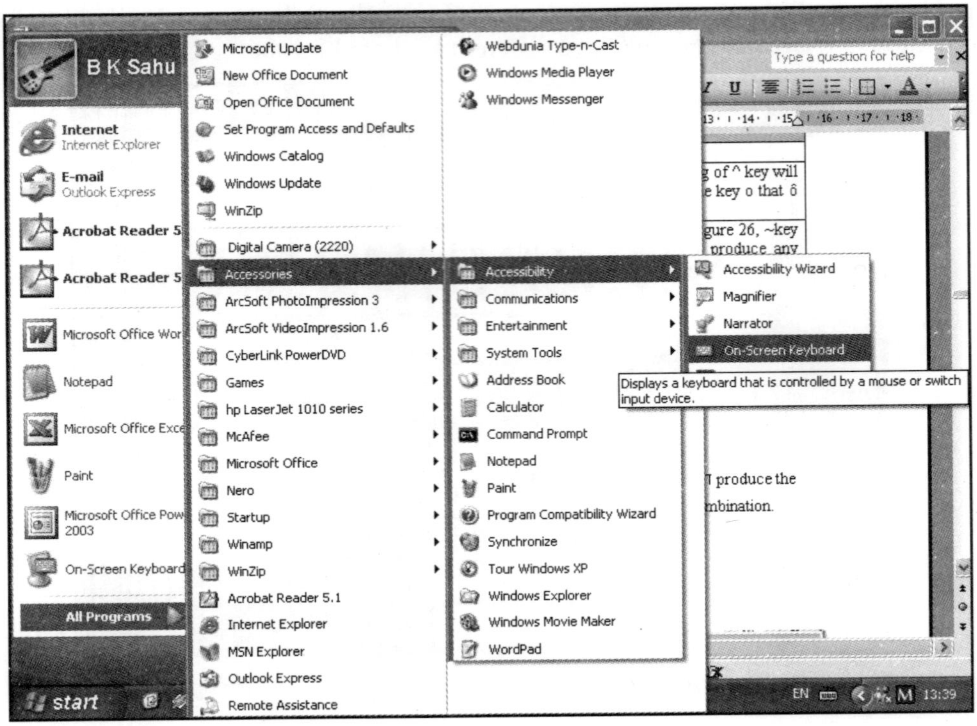

Figure 41: On-Screen Keyboard

Warning: If the input method editor is being used, then the on-screen keyboard layout may not show correctly. Often, as the characters inputted depends on the context (i.e., the keys pressed previously), a key does not correspond to specific characters. Figure 42 illustrates the on-screen keyboard display while typing in East Asian languages using input method editor. While typing in Hindi using phonetic IME (see Figure 52), the on-screen keyboard does not show Devanagari letters/conjuncts in the display.

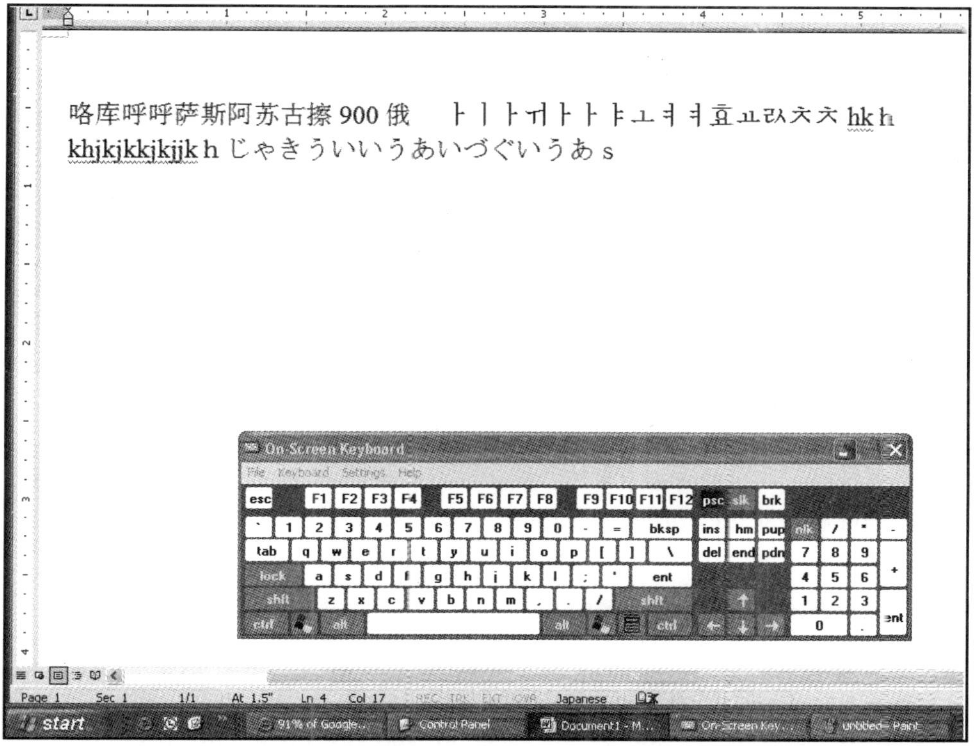

Figure 42: On-screen keyboard while typing in East Asian languages

Note: In the implementation of a language through non-standard font (see Chapter 1), the on-screen keyboard display will show the Latin keys. For example, in Shusha font, the on-screen keys will be displayed as *q*, *w*, *e*, *r*, *t*, *y* etc, and not ट, द्व, ए, र, त, ट etc as per Figure 1.

Combining character sequence

Many Latin letters with diacritical marks have been coded as separate characters. These are under the sets "Latin-1," "Latin Extended-A" and "Latin Extended-B." However, it is also possible to produce the visual effect of Latin letters with diacritical marks using combining characters under the "Combining Diacritical Mark" subset of Unicode. For example, the visual effect of the letter cee with cedilla (ç, code 00E7 hex) can be produced by the two character sequence cee and combining cedilla, i.e., c and ̧ (codes 0063 and 0327 hex). Similarly, the visual effect of à can be produced by typing the two characters in sequence: the letter a and combining grave accent, i.e., a and ̀ (codes 0061 and 0300 hex).

A base character can be followed by any number of combining characters. For example, z̴̫̐ can be typed by typing the base letter zee (z, code 007A hex) followed by three combining diacritical characters ̐, ̫, ̴ (0310, 032B, 0334 hex), not necessarily in that sequence.

The codes of characters Combining Diacritical Marks range from 0300 to 036F hex. In this, 034F hex is the CGJ character. The codes of characters in “Combining Diacritical Marks Supplement” range from 1DC0 to 1DFF hex, that of characters in “Combining Diacritical Marks for Symbols” range from 20D0 to 20FF hex, and that of “Combining Half Marks” range from FE20 to FE2F hex.

Note: Combining diacritical characters need not be used only with Latin letters. For example, combining diacritical marks can be used in combination with letters in Indic scripts also. For example, one can type क̫̃ by typing the character sequence क̫ and ̃ (codes being 0915, 032B and 0303 hex); अ̸̼ can be typed by typing the character sequence अ̼ and ̸ (codes being 0905, 033C and 0338 hex). (Typing in Indic scripts is explained later in the chapter.)

Warning: For typing *anusvara*, *chandrabindu* and *nukta* sign in Indic scripts, these characters of the concerned Indic script are to be use (as explained later in the book). The combining diacritical characters should not be used for typing *anusvara*, *chandrabindu* and *nukta* sign in Indic scripts.

Note: It has just been shown that the visual effect of typing letters with diacritical marks can be achieved in two ways: one, by inputting the character with the diacritical marks in Unicode, and two, by a sequence of base letter followed by combining diacritical character. The two way of typing the same letter with diacritical marks are canonically equivalent. However, it does not mean that no Unicode-conformant process can treat canonically equivalent sequences differently in any way. The canonically equivalent sequences consists of different character codes and different number of characters and bytes.

Note: Combining characters may be used to type odd texts in various languages in Latin script such as Azerbaijani, Cornish, Croatian, Czech, Dutch, Esperanto, Estonian, Finnish, French, German, Greenlandic, Hungarian, Icelandic, Igbo, Irish, Italian, Latvian, Lithuanian, Maltese, Macedonian, Polish, Portuguese, Romanian, Sami, Serbian, Slovak, Slovenian, Spanish, Turkish, Vietnamese and Welsh etc. It can also be used in Indic transliteration, Pinyin and International Phonetic Alphabet (IPA).

Typing in Indic languages

Halant character

Halant is variously called *hasant*, *virama* etc. *Halant* denotes the absence of the implicit a-vowel ending in the preceding consonant. Certain Bengali vowels can also be succeeded by *halant* character as part of *ya-pahalaa* formation as described later in the chapter.

Even though *halant* does not figure in the letters of alphabets of Indic scripts as taught in primary schools, *halant* is an important character. Indeed, it is the most important character of Indic alphabets. The consonant conjuncts have not been encoded in Unicode. All the consonant conjuncts are to be formed with the use of *halant* character. For example, as there is no separate code for the conjunct क्त, the conjunct has to be represented as the sequence of three consecutive characters: क, ् and त in this order. The operating system or the software takes care of the correct visual rendering of the sequence of characters as क्त.

Different Indic scripts have different *halant* character codes in Unicode. For example, the code for Devanagari *halant* is 094D hex, that for Bengali *halant* is 09CD hex, and that for Tamil *halant* is 0BCD hex as is evident from the table at *Annexure (D)*.

Halant character at times has visual and printable form. But at times, it has no visual or printable form, and only affects formation of ligatures.

Vowel, vowel sign and vowel modifier characters in Indic scripts: In Devanagari script, letters अ, आ, इ etc are vowel characters, ा, ि, ी etc are vowel sign characters, and ँ, ं and ः are vowel modifier characters. Corresponding characters in other Indic scripts are vowel, vowel sign and vowel modifier characters in those scripts.

Indic phonemes: Indic phonemes (*varna*) are of two types: vowel phonemes (*svara varna*) and consonant phonemes (*vyanjana varna*). अ (a), आ (aa), इ (i), ई (ii) are vowel phonemes as well as vowel syllables. क् (k), ख् (kh), ग् (g) etc are consonant phonemes, whereas क (ka), ख (kha), ग (ga) etc are consonant letters (i.e., consonant syllables with implicit अ-ending). Like ISCII, Unicode does not recognize the consonant phonemes as the unit characters. Rather consonant letters (i.e., consonant syllables with implicit अ-ending) are treated as unit characters. Also, vowel signs (ा (aa), ि (i), ी (ii)) etc are treated as unit characters. Thus, for example, in Unicode का is to be viewed as a sequence of two characters क (0915 hex) and ा (093E hex), and not two phonemes क् and आ.

Typing in Inscript keyboard layout

Inscript keyboard layout is a popular[16] keyboard layout for most Indic languages such as Hindi, Bengali, Gujarati, Kannada, Malayalam, Marathi, Oriya, Punjabi, Sanskrit, Tamil, Telugu, Konkani, Nepali etc. The same keyboard layout is also used in ISCII (see Chapter 2) though there are a few minor differences as explained later. An understanding of Devanagari Inscript keyboard layout will provide insights into the Inscript keyboard layout for other Indic scripts also, such as Tamil, Gujarati, Kannada, Bengali etc.

Figure 43 shows the keyboard layout of Inscript keyboard layout for Hindi. A more general Inscript keyboard layout showing special characters of South Indian scripts[17], and Gurmukhi, Bengal and Oriya scripts is shown in *Annexure (F)*.

[16] Or, at least easy to comprehend.

[17] The letters ऒ (ॊ), ऎ (ॆ), ऩ and ऴ are in South Indian scripts, and य़ are in Bengali and Oriya scripts.

As will be obvious from *Annexure (F)*, Right-Alt key is to be used to type the following letters, vowel signs, symbols, and Vedic accent marks[18]: ॠ, ॄ, ऌ, ॡ, ॢ, ॣ, ॐ, ॥, ऽ, ॰, ◌॓, ◌॔, ◌॒, and ◌॑. Also, Right-Alt key is to be used for typing Indic numerals in Inscript except in Marathi, where Right-Alt produces international numerals, and normal number keys produce Devanagari numerals. For example, pressing Right-Alt and '1' keys together produces १. Furthermore, Right-Alt can be used to key in letters with *nukta* sign such as क़, ख़, ग़, ज़, ड़, ढ़ and फ़, which are one character each in Unicode.

Tips: Letters क़, ख़, ग़, ज़, ड़, ढ़ and फ़ can be typed in two ways. One way is by using Right-Alt key as explained above. Alternatively, these letters may be typed as a combination of a consonant followed by *nukta* sign (◌़). क + ◌़ = क़, ख + ◌़ = ख़, ग + ◌़ = ग़, ज + ◌़ = ज़, ड + ◌़ = ड़, ढ + ◌़ = ढ़, फ + ◌़ = फ़.

Warning: Unicode standard specifies that the two ways of writing क़, ख़, ग़, ज़, ड़, ढ़, फ़ as explained above are equivalent and that य़ (095F hex) and य + ◌़ are equivalent. However, they have not been implemented as exact equivalents. For example, क़ is a single character with code 0958 hex; however, even though क + ◌़ produce the same visual look, it consists of two characters with codes 0915 and 093C hex respectively, and not one character with code 0958 hex.

Figure 43: Hindi Inscript keyboard layout

Phonetic sequence and not visual sequence: To type text in Inscript, one will have to follow the spelling or logical sequence[19] of characters (i.e., letters, vowel signs, *halant* character, etc), and not the visual look. For example, to type the word कि (ki), one will have to type the letter क (ka) followed by the vowel sign ि (i), and not the other way, i.e., not ि followed by क. This, even though the sign ि precedes क in the visual look of कि. (In Shusha font, discussed in Chapter 1, on the contrary, one were required to follow visual sequence. Also, as noted in *Annexure (E)*, a Devanagari Unicode font called Gargi allows partial visual sequencing of characters.) As another example, the word राष्ट्रीय comprises the following nine characters in this sequence: र (0930) + ◌ा

[18] The Right-Alt key should be pressed first; and should be released only after the 'another' key has been pressed and released.

[19] This sequence most often corresponds to the pronunciation, or the phonetic sequence.

(093E) + ष (0937) + ् (094D) + ट (091F) + ् (094D) + र (0930) + ी (0940) + य (092F), where the numbers in the parentheses are the hexadecimal codes in Unicode.

Note: Notwithstanding the visual look, र्ष्म is spelled as र + ् + ष + ् – म; र्द्ध is spelled as र + ् + द + ् + ध; र्यों is spelled as र + ् + य + ो + ं, and स्त्रि is spelled as स + ् + त + ् + र + ि. This is because the spelling of these characters is like that. Thus, the Indic texts are to be entered in phonetic or logical sequence, and not based on the mere visual look.

Note: In Tamil, both the key sequence க + ொ (0B95, 0BCB hex) and க + ெ + ா (0B95, 0BC7, 0BBE hex) produce the same visual look of கொ. However, க + ே + ா is an illegal combination, as one consonant cannot have two vowel signs. Similarly, को is not same as का followed by the 'e' vowel sign े. Thus, one has to type Indic texts as per the correct spelling, and not based on visual appearance of the text. Visual appearance is taken care of by the operating system and the software, provided the correct characters are inputted in the right sequence.

Unique spelling: Except for ZWJ, ZWNJ, ZWSP etc characters, there is a unique spelling for each valid word written in Unicode standard.[20] For each grapheme or syllabic ligature, the sequence of characters is as follows:

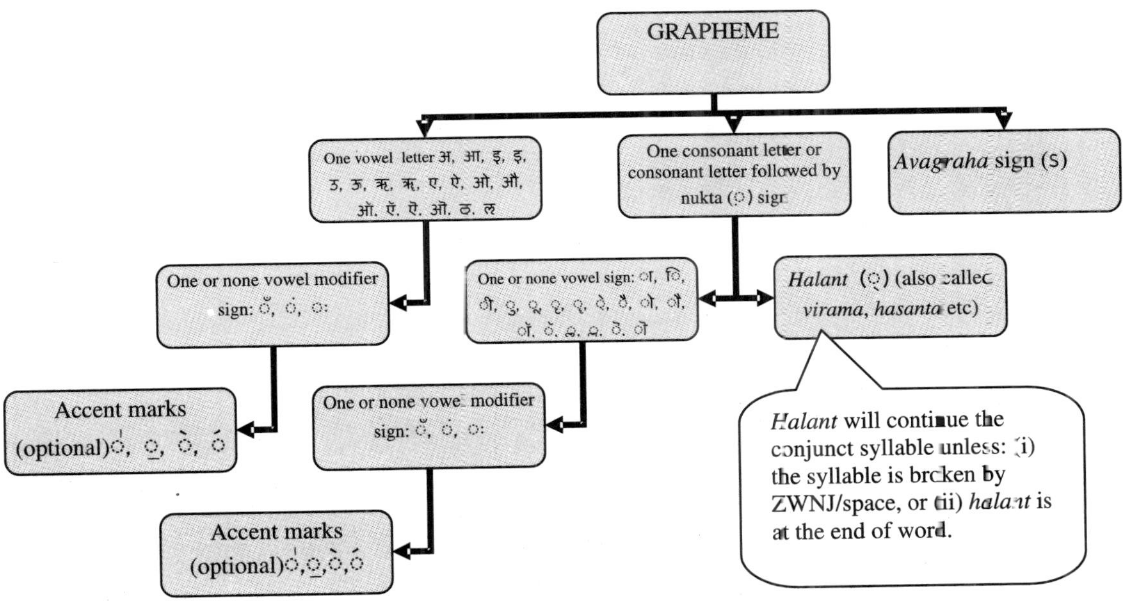

Figure 44: Sequence of characters in Indic script

[20] In current implementations, letters with *nukta* sign can be written in two ways. *Nukta* is usually a sound modifier of a consonant symbolized by a dot sign below the letter. Letters with *nukta* sign are used in writing Urdu or English words in Hindi, such as the 'z' sound, 'f' sound, etc.

Thus, a word consists of one or more conjunct syllables. Each conjunct syllable consists of one or more graphemes. A grapheme may be any one of the following in the given sequence (see Figure 44):

i. An avagraha (ऽ)
ii. A vowel letter,
iii. A consonant,[21] or a consonant followed by *nukta*,
iv. A vowel letter followed by one vowel modifier (◌ँ, ◌ं, ◌ः),
v. A vowel letter followed by accent mark(s) (◌॓, ◌॑, ◌॒, ◌॔ etc),
vi. A vowel letter followed by one vowel modifier, followed by Vedic accent marks,
vii. A consonant (with or without *nukta*) followed by *halant*,
viii. A consonant (with or without *nukta*) followed by a vowel sign
ix. A consonant (with or without *nukta*) followed by a vowel sign, followed by one vowel modifier,
x. A consonant (with or without *nukta*) followed by a vowel sign, followed by one vowel modifier, followed by Vedic accents marks,
xi. A consonant (with or without *nukta*) followed by a vowel sign, followed by Vedic accents marks,
xii. A consonant (with or without *nukta*), followed by accents marks
xiii. A consonant (with or without *nukta*), followed by vowel modifier, or
xiv. A consonant (with or without *nukta*), followed by vowel modifier, followed by Vedic accents marks,

Thus, there is a unique spelling in terms of sequence of characters for a valid word in Devanagari script.

Note: For *ya-phalaa* in Bengali script, Bengali vowel letters অ (a) and এ (e) can also be followed by *hasant* (◌্) and য (*ya*), and the conjunct may be treated as an independent vowel letter. In the current implementation in Microsoft Windows, even other Bengali vowel letters can be followed by *hasant* (◌্) and *ya* (য) characters.

Note: In normal typing, it is necessary to type in the unique sequence as per the spelling without bothering about the formation of ligatures and the placement of the vowel signs and the vowel modifiers. The software will take care of the formation of ligatures, and placement of vowel signs and vowel modifiers. Examples of character sequence for several ligatures and conjunct syllables in major Indian languages are given in *Annexure (E).*

The visual look, formation of conjuncts, and placement of vowel signs and vowel modifiers depend on the font. However, if one wants a specific form of the text, then one has to take resort

[21] Along with the implicit a-vowel ending (i.e., implicit अ-ending in Devanagari).

to ZWJ (200D hex), ZWNJ (200C hex) and ZWSP (200B hex) characters. A few examples of use of ZWJ and ZWNJ are shown below:

Table 8: Typing in Indic script

Character sequence (left-to-right)	*Output (in Mangal font)*
प ◌् र श ◌् न	प्रश्न
प ◌् र श ◌् ZWJ न	प्रश्‍न
प ◌् र श ◌् ZWNJ न	प्रश्‌न
व ◌ा र ◌् य ◌ा	वार्या
व ◌ा र ◌् ZWJ य ◌ा	वार्‍या
च ◌ि ह ◌् न	चिह्न
च ◌ि ह ◌् ZWJ न	चिह्‍न
च ◌ि ह ◌् ZWNJ न	चिह्‌न

ZWJ and ZWNJ characters are used in Arabic and other Indic scripts also.

Note: Letters of Indic scripts join to form ligatures in so many different ways that it is not possible to cover all of them with only ZWJ, ZWNJ and ZWSP characters. Maybe, future versions of the Unicode will take care of these difficulties.

Warning: While one can force formation of half-consonants by the ZWJ character, and that of consonants with *halant* by ZWNJ character, the formation of actual ligature and the visual look depends on the font. A few examples are given below in two different fonts for illustration, where the visual appearance is different in different fonts for the same character sequence. Also see *Annexure (E)* for Gargi font.

Table 9: Actual formation of ligature depends on font

Character sequence	*Appearance in Mangal font*	*Same in DVBOTSurekh font*
अ ङ ◌् क	अङ्‌क	अङ्क
इ क ट ◌् ठ ◌ा	इकट्‌ठा	इकट्ठा
द ◌ृ ष ◌् ट ◌् व ◌ा	दृष्ट्‌वा	दृष्ट्वा
अ ड ◌् ड ◌ा	अड्‌डा	अड्डा

Note: If "Use sequence checking" option is selected in Microsoft Word, then Microsoft Word will not accept incorrect character sequence. For example, it will not be possible to type the character sequence क + ◌ॉ + ◌ि + फ (i.e., कॉ◌िफ), as it is an invalid character sequence[22]—the correct sequence may be क ॉ फ ि, which produces कॉफि. "Use sequence checking" option has been shown in Figure 45. This window can be gotten by the following menu bar option in Microsoft Word: Tools → Options…, and then selecting the "Complex Script" tab.

Now, the implosive Sindhi letters GGA, JJA, DDA and BBA have been encoded in Devanagari as separate characters.

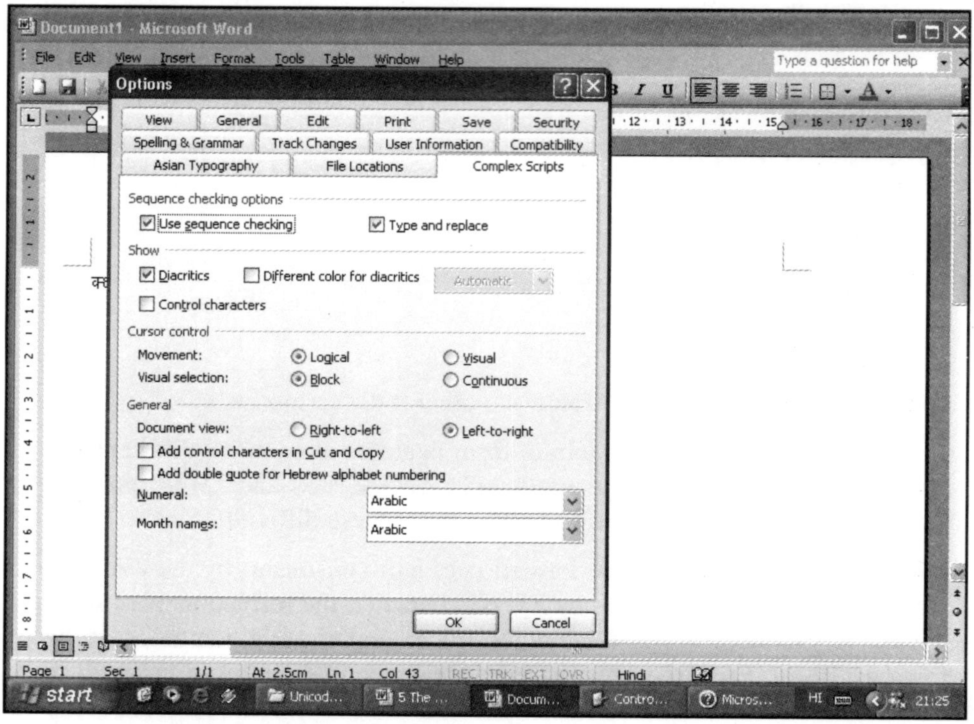

Figure 45: Sequence checking option

Note: हॉं (ह + ॉ + ं), though a valid word, is different from हाँ (ह + ा + ँ), notwithstanding the similar look. Similarly, कॅं (क + ॅ + ं) is not equivalent to कँ (क + ँ), despite the similar visual look.

Note: In normal Hindi typing, the *chandrabindu* mark is often reduced to *anusvara* after certain vowel signs and *reph*-sign (र् above the top line). However, if one types *chandrabindu* in computer, one will get *chandrabindu*, and not *anusvara*. Thus, क्योँ (क + ् + य + ो + ँ) is different from क्यों (क + ् + य + ो + ं), as the codes for *chandrabindu* (ँ, 0901 hex) and *anusvara* (ं, 0902 hex) are different. Similarly, हैँ (ह + ै + ँ) and हैं (ह + ै + ं) are

[22] One consonant letter cannot have more than one vowel signs.

different. Obviously, पाँच, पांच and पाच are also different. In the same vein, दु:ख and दुख are also different.

Note: In Hindi and many other languages, *anusvara* (ं in Devanagari) replaces the nasal consonants[23] belonging to the same class as that of the following consonant in the word. Thus in Hindi, अंग and अङ्ग, पंच and पञ्च, डंडा and डण्डा, पंत and पन्त, and पंप and पम्प are treated as equivalent both in meaning and pronunciation.[24] However, they are not equivalent spellings in Unicode as their codes are different. For example, अंग = अ (0905) + ं (0902) + ग (0917) comprising three characters, whereas अङ्ग = अ (0905) + ङ (0919) + ् (094D) + ग (0917) comprising four characters, where the Unicode character codes are given in hexadecimal number system.

A few disadvantages of Inscript keyboard layout: The consonants are on the one side and the vowels are on the other side. This leads to uneven distribution of keystrokes, and therefore fatigue while typing. There is no key for ZWJ, ZWNJ and ZWSP characters, even though these are important characters.

Other keyboard layouts

There are several other keyboard layouts for Devanagari script—that is, there are several keyboard layouts other than Inscript. Figure 46 shows the Hindi Typewriter keyboard layout. In this keyboard layout, 'LK' key is equivalent to one character *halant* (्, 094D hex), and 'HF' is equivalent to two characters in the following sequence: *halant* followed by ZWJ (i.e., 094D followed by 200D hex).

Figure 46: Hindi Typewriter keyboard layout

Figure 47 shows the Hindi Remington keyboard layout. Note that in this keyboard layout, the keys corresponding to half-letter forms are equivalent to a sequence of three characters in Unicode: the consonant letter, *halant*, and ZWJ character.

---

[23] ङ्, ञ्, ण्, न् and म्.

[24] But not the nasal consonant belong to a different class than the following consonant. For example, वाङ्मय and वांमय. कन्चन and कंचन and संसार and सन्सार etc are not equivalent in Hindi.

For example:

ध्‍ = ध (0927) + ् (094D) + ZWJ (200D)

ष्‍ = ष (0937) + ् (094D) + ZWJ (200D)

भ्‍ = भ (092D) + ् (094D) + ZWJ (200D)

द्ध = द (0926) + ् (094D) + ध (0927), codes in parentheses are hexadecimal numbers.

Figure 47: Hindi Remington keyboard layout

This means that if त्य is typed in Inscript and Hindi Remington keyboard layouts, they will not consist of the same characters despite the same visual look and the font! For example, in Inscript keyboard layout, त्य comprises three characters:

त्य = त (0924) + ् (094D) + य (092F).

But when typed in Hindi Remington keyboard layout, it comprises four characters:

त्य = त्‍ य = त (0924) + ् (094D) + ZWJ (200D) + य (092F), where Unicode character in hex codes are in the parentheses, because त्‍ comprises त (0924) + ् (094D) + ZWJ (200D).

How to remove the unwanted ZWJ character: As explained above, as one presses the ध्‍ key in Remington keyboard layout, what gets typed is ध, ् and the extra ZWJ character. How does one get rid of the extra ZWJ character? The answer is simple: after pressing the ध्‍ key, one should press the backspace key. With this, what one will get is: ध + ् ~~+ ZWJ~~, or 0927, 094D~~, 200D~~, that is, ध + ्, or 0927, 094D.

Entering ZWJ, ZWNJ and ZWSP characters

In the Inscript keyboard layout, there was no specific key for Zero-Width Joiner (ZWJ, code being 200D hex) and Zero-Width Non-Joiner (ZWNJ, code being 200C hex) characters. ZWJ and ZWNJ characters can be entered in Microsoft Word as shown in Figure 48. Insert → Symbol… from the menu bar in Microsoft Word pops up the window shown in the figure. Click the "Special Characters" tab. In the list of special characters, "No-Width Non Break" character is same as ZWJ, and "No-Width Optional Break" character is same as ZWNJ. However, the input language should remain selected correctly while inserting the ZWJ and ZWNJ characters; otherwise, the desired effect in formation of ligatures may not be there.

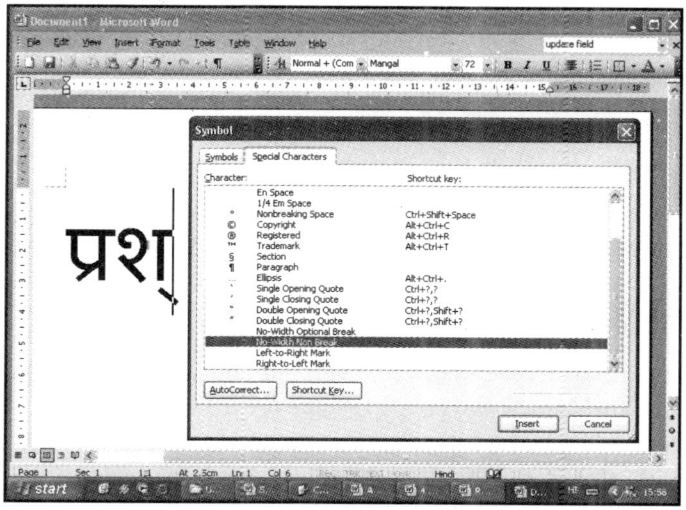

Figure 48: Inserting ZWJ and ZWNJ characters

ZWJ, ZWNJ and ZWSP characters can also be entered in Microsoft Word through Insert → Symbol → Symbols tab, and then selecting the appropriate font and character, and then clicking Insert button. ZWNJ character in Mangal font is being entered in the illustration at Figure 49.

ZWJ, ZWNJ and ZWSP characters can also be entered through Character Map (see Figure 51, where ZWJ character is being inserted).

ZWJ, ZWNJ and ZWSP characters can also be entered by typing their hexadecimal codes followed by Alt-x in Microsoft Word and WordPad. For example, typing Alt-x when the cursor is next to the hexadecimal number 200B produces the invisible ZWSP character.

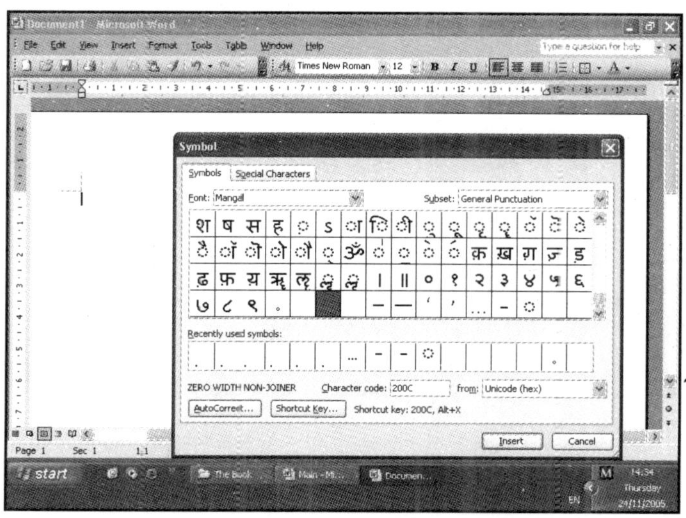

Figure 49: Inserting characters in Microsoft Word

Note: ZWJ character at the end of a word creates a "hanging" half letter. For example, the key sequence अ, ब, ् and ZWJ produces अब्‍.

Marathi and Hindi Traditional keyboard layout

Marathi and Hindi Traditional keyboard layouts are very similar to Devanagari Inscript keyboard layout. However, in Marathi and Hindi Traditional keyboard layouts, pressing [, <, {, & etc keys together with Right-Alt key produces these characters, and not Devanagari letters (ड़, ढ़ etc) as in Devanagari Inscript keyboard layout.

Note: The main difference between Marathi and Hindi Traditional keyboard layouts is in numerals. In Marathi keyboard layout, pressing the number keys produce the same in Devanagari script (i.e., १, २, ३ etc), and pressing number keys with Right-Alt produce the same in default numerals (which is usually 1, 2, 3 etc). In Hindi Traditional keyboard layout, it is just the other way round.

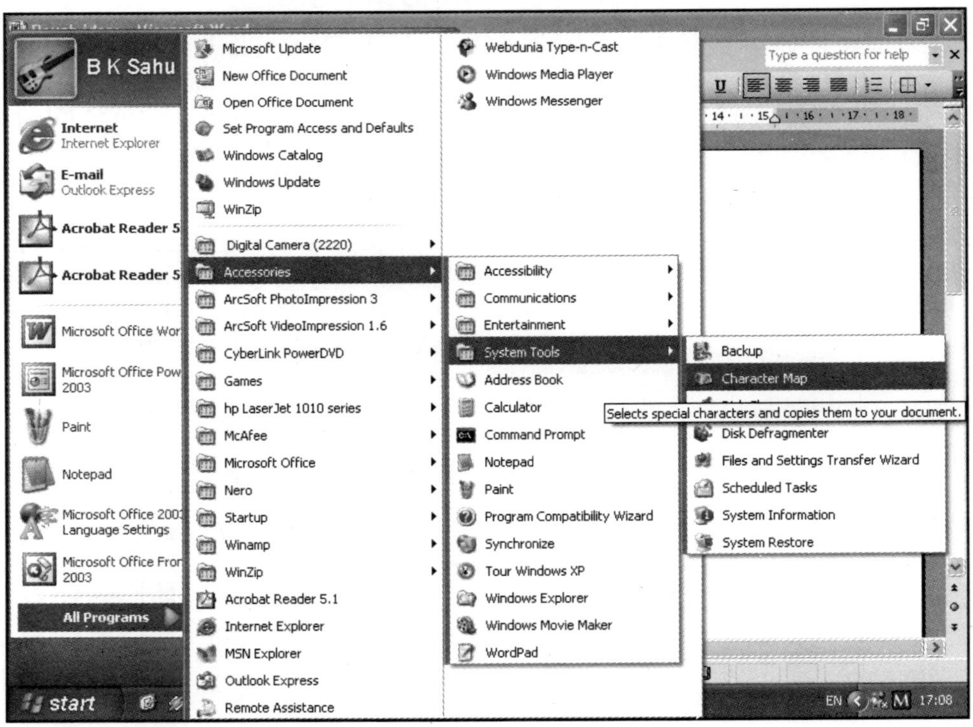

Figure 50: Character Map

Character Map: One can enter an unusual character through Character Map. Character Map is available under Accessories → System Tools as shown in Figure 50. In the Character Map window, one will have to select the appropriate font(s), and the character(s) in the font(s).

The selected character(s) will be copied to the clipboard, which can be pasted. Note that the characters will be in the selected font(s), and Microsoft Office may assign default language to the character(s). For example, for Devanagari character, the default language may be Hindi (but not Sanskrit, Marathi, Nepali etc), for Bengali character, the default language may be Bengali (but not Assamese, Sylhetti etc). Of course, the marked language may be changed as explained in Chapter 6 and Figure 69.

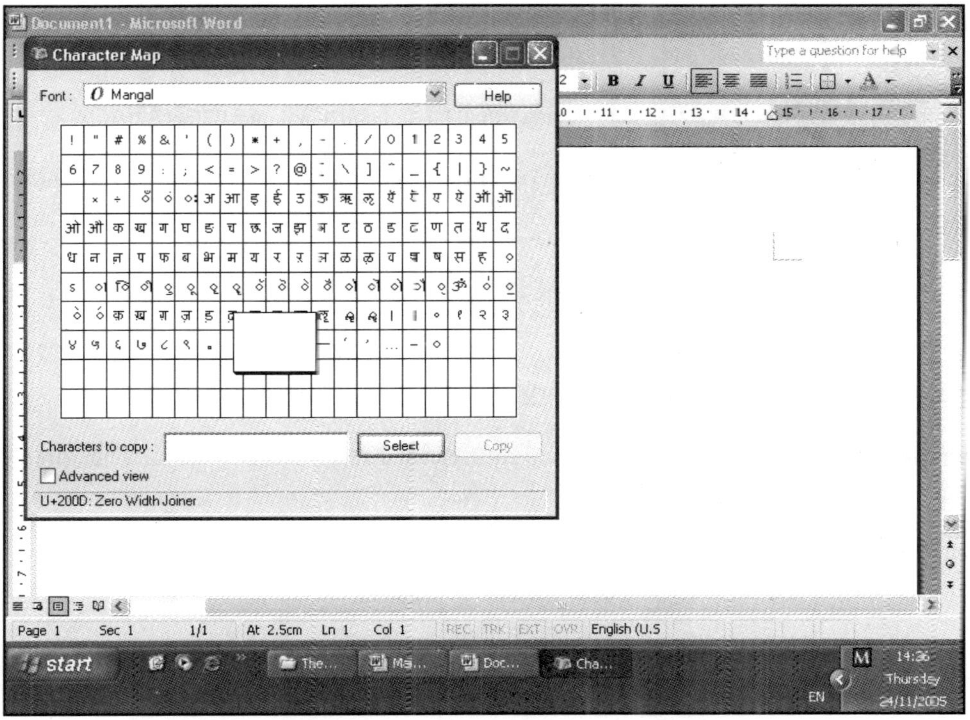

Figure 51: Entering characters by Character Map

Note: An unusual character can also be inserted by Insert → Symbol… in menu bar in Microsoft Word. See Figure 48 and Figure 49.

Some special features of Bengali script

Bengali uses the symbol অ্যা and এ্যা to represent this sound when it begins a word. These symbols graphically appear to be made up of the letters অ (0958) or এ (098F) plus a squiggle ্য known as *ya-phalaa*, and a final া (09BE).

Ya-phalaa is the form the letter য (ya) often takes when it is the last component of a consonant conjunct. For example, ত + ্ + য (ta + *hasant* + ya) may be displayed as ত + ্য (ta + *ya-phalaa*). In many cases a sequence, '… + *hasant* + ya' produces a *ya-phalaa*.

In view of the graphical appearance plus the common '+*hasant*+ya' behavior, the recommendation is to encode these characters as follows:

অ্যা = <0985, 09CD, 09AF, 09BE> (*a- hasant ya -aa*)

এ্যা = <098F, 09CD, 09AF, 09BE> (*e- hasant ya -aa*)

If a *chandrabindu* or other combining mark needs to be added in the sequence it comes at the end of the sequence. For example:

অ্যাঁ = <0985, 09CD, 09AF, 09BE, 0981> (*a- hasant ya -aa candrabindu*)

Ya-phala with Bengali letter র or ৰ (ra) can potentially be in two different forms as shown below:

র + ◌্ + য → র্য
(U+09B0 + U+09CD + U+09AF)

র + ZWNJ + ◌্ + য → র‌্য
(U+09B0 + U+200C + U+09CD + U+09AF)

Also, two Bengali letters 'ta' join to form ligatures in three different ways. The three different forms are:

ত ্ ত → ত্ত
09A4 09CD 09A4 Ligature

ত ্ ত → ৎত
09A4 09CD ZWJ 09A4 Khanda_Ta Ta

ত ্ ত → ত্‌ত
09A4 09CD ZWNJ 09A4 Ta Halant Ta

Note: Earlier, *khanda ta* was not treated as a separate character. But recently, *khand ta* has been recognized as a separate character, and a separate code (09CE hex) has been assigned to it.

Note: Even though *ya-phalaa* is treated as a combination of two characters ্ (*hasant*, 09CD hex) and য (09AF hex), in future it may be treated as a single character. There is a proposal to this effect under consideration by Unicode Consortium.

Note: Oriya script also has *ya-phalaa*. Indeed, Oriya has several *phalaas*: *ka-phalaa*, *kha-phalaa*, *pa-phalaa* etc.

Note: To type Assamese letters ৰ (ra) and ৱ (va/wa) and *Isshar* sign in Bengali Inscript keyboard layout, the following keys are to be pressed as shown in Table 10:

Table 10: Special Bengali/Assamese letters/symbols

Key sequence	Bengali/Assamese letter/symbol
Right-Alt-x	৺ (Isshar)
Right-Alt-j	ৰ (Assamese ra)
Right-Alt-Shift-j	ৱ (Assamese va/wa)

"Delete" versus "backspace" in Indic scripts

Suppose one has typed some text in an Indic script. Let us say the cursor is positioned in the middle of a word. If one presses backspace key, what will be deleted is just one character in the Unicode to the left of the cursor. However, if one presses the Delete key, what will be deleted will be an entire conjunct syllable, i.e., a group of one or more characters which appears as an independent ligature (and which can be traversed by one movement of cursor using left or right arrow keys of the keyboard). For example, say the cursor is in the middle of the word दृष्टि, then backspace will render to दष्टि (i.e., codes 0926 ~~+ 0943~~ + 0937 + 094D + 091F + 093F)—only one character ृ (0943 hex) will be deleted. But delete key will reduce it to दृ (i.e., codes 0926 + 0943 ~~+ 0937 + 094D + 091F + 093F~~)—the entire conjunct syllable ष्टि (i.e., codes 0937, 094D, 091F and 093F hex) will be deleted.

Note: If overwrite option is selected in Microsoft Word, then overwriting of the existing text will be conjunct syllable wise—and not character-wise—as one goes on typing.

Searching in Indic script languages

Very often, it is required to search texts written in Indic script. Say, for example, one is using the search (Edit → Find… or Replace… from menu bar) in Microsoft Word. If the text comprises only one plain vanilla letters without vowel signs etc (for example, कटहल), then the text can be searched with plain vanilla text as search key (for example, कट or टहल etc). However, difficulties arise if the text comprises conjuncts, vowel signs etc. In such cases, Microsoft Word will not search Indic texts character wise or even phonetic element wise. Microsoft Word will only search in terms of complete conjunct syllables, i.e., a ligature that is traversed by one movement of cursor by using left or right arrow keys of the keyboard. For example, let us consider a text contains the words "हिन्दी" (comprising codes 0939 + 093F + 0928 + 094D + 0926 + 0940 hex). It consists of two (and only two) conjunct syllables हि and न्दी. This is because it takes two cursor movements using left (or right) arrow keys of the keyboard to traverse the word हिन्दी. Search operation will not find it using the individual graphemes as search keys ह, न, न्, द or even दी. The search will find it only with the search keys हि, न्दी or the complete word हिन्दी. (However, things are different in Arabic script as explained later.)

It may be noted that the word हिंदी comprises two conjunct syllables हिं and दी.

Note: The vowel signs and vowel modifiers cannot be searched individually. One can search only the complete conjunct syllables. It should be noted that conjunct syllables are broken by the end of the word, ZWNJ, ZWSP, vowel sign[25] together with vowel modifier, if any, etc.

Note: If the text uses ZWNJ, as is "हिन्‌दी" (i.e., 0939 + 093F+ 0928 + 094D + **200C** + 0926 + 0940 hex), then it consists of three conjunct syllables (and not two, as can be verified by traversing the word using left and right arrow keys). Search will find it only using the keys हि, न्‌ (i.e., न + ◌् + ZWNJ, or, codes 0928 + 094D + 200C hex) and दी, or a correct combination of them. Search will not be able to find it using the search key न् (i.e., न + ◌्, or the codes 0928 and 094D hex). Also, it may be noted that number of conjunct syllables is based on spelling, and not the visual look. For example, छ्छ (091B + 094D + 091B hex) consists of only one conjunct syllable. However, छ्‌छ (091B + 094D + **200C** + 091B hex) consists of two conjunct syllables because of the presence of ZWNJ (200C hex) character. It is so notwithstanding the same visual look of the two words. This may be verified by seeing the number of cursor movement it takes to traverse through the words.

Note: Unicode standard requires that Devanagari letters with *nukta* mark be treated as equivalent to the separate code assigned to such letters. However, Microsoft Windows and Microsoft Office do not treat the two as equivalent. For example, if the text contains फ़ (095E hex), then it will not be found if searched with the search key फ़ (i.e., फ + ◌़, or, 092B + 093C hex) and vice versa.

Indic full stop sign (single/double danda/daari etc)

Many Indic languages such as Hindi, Bengali and Punjabi use a vertical bar (।) as full stop sign, whose hexadecimal code is 0964. Also, double vertical bars (॥) are used for the same purpose, whose hexadecimal code is 0956. However, these signs have been encoded only in Devanagari script. The Devanagari code 0964 hex for the *danda* may be used in several scripts, including Bengali, Punjabi, and Oriya etc. Also code 0965 hex may be used as the double *danda* for these scripts. All Unicode characters are equally accessible, and many punctuation marks and symbols are used across several scripts.

Note: Bengali Inscript keyboard layout in Microsoft Windows did not contain keys for *daari* (*danda*) and double *danda*.

Note: Indic language uses many of the punctuation marks of the Latin character set. For example, Devanagari character set does not have separate comma, semicolon, dot etc symbols; these symbols from the character set meant for Latin script are used in Hindi in Devanagari script also. Of course, there is also a separate set of characters for general punctuation marks. One script using punctuation marks of another script is not uncommon. For example, Thaana script uses Arabic comma etc symbols.

[25] Except *halant*, which is not a vowel sign, anyway.

Note: The abbreviation sign used in Assamese resembles that of Devanagari script. At present, there is no abbreviation sign in Bengali script portion of Unicode. So, Devanagari abbreviation sign may be used in Assamese. For example, 'doctor' is written in Assamese in abbreviated form as ড॰, which comprises two characters: Bengali letter ড (Da, 09A1 hex) and Devanagari abbreviation sign ॰ (0970 hex).

Warning: However, vowel signs, vowel sign modifiers, *halant* etc of one script may not be used in another script, even if they may have similar look. For example, *chandrabindus* of Devanagari and Bengali scripts look the same, but one cannot be substituted for another.

Variant characters in Devanagari

Certain Devanagari characters have more than one visual form. For example, letter अ has two forms: अ and ञ्प. Similarly, letters आ, ओ, औ, ऑ, ओ, ऋ, ऌ, श and ण have two forms each. Vowel modifier *anusvara* (◌ं) has twelve variants, and *visarga* (◌ः) has seven variants in Vedic texts. Devanagari digits १, ४, ५ and ८ have two forms each. Letter झ and digit ९ have three forms each. Consonant conjuncts क्ष and ज्ञ have two forms each. Sometimes इ is written as अि, and उ as अु etc. Of course, only the most popular forms have been counted here, and there may be many more obscure forms of the letters, conjuncts and ligatures.

Unicode in its present form does not recognize the variants of the shapes of Devanagari letters and ligatures. This is possibly because of inadequate persuasion from the interest groups. It is possible that in future, Unicode may recognize the variants of Devanagari letters and ligatures. However, until that happens, the variant forms of letters and ligatures can be taken care of only at the font and glyph level.

This holds true for other Indic scripts also.

Typing Vedic hymns

Typing Vedic texts requires several variants of *anusvara* and *visarga*. It also requires several other characters like variants of *jihvamuliya* and *upadhmaniya* etc. Also, Vedic hymns require several forms of accent, stress, *svarochchar chinha* ('pronunciation symbol'), *kampa* ('vibration') and cantillatory marks. Many of them have not yet been encoded in the Unicode standard. Also, encoding of musical texts as written in Indic languages in India requires special underline and over-line notations. It can be expected that in future, Unicode may include characters to encode the entire Vedic texts.

However, even in the current version of Unicode many hymns can be encoded. The Vedic accent marks encoded in the current version of Unicode are: *udatta* (◌॑, 0951 hex), *anudatta* (◌॒, 0952 hex), grave (◌॓, 0953 hex) and acute (◌॔, 0954 hex). Thus, for example, योनि॑र॒प्स्व१‍॒॑न्तः can be typed using the character sequence: य ◌ो न ◌ि ◌॑ र ◌॒ प ◌् स ◌् व १ ZWJ ◌॒ ◌॑ न ◌् त ◌ः (i.e., 092F, 094B, 0928, 093F, 0951, 0930, 0952, 092A, 094D, 0938, 094D, 0935, 0967, 200D, 0952, 0951, 0928, 094D, 0924, 0903 hex).

Nonetheless, it is not possible to encode the following Vedic hymn using the present codes of Unicode standard:

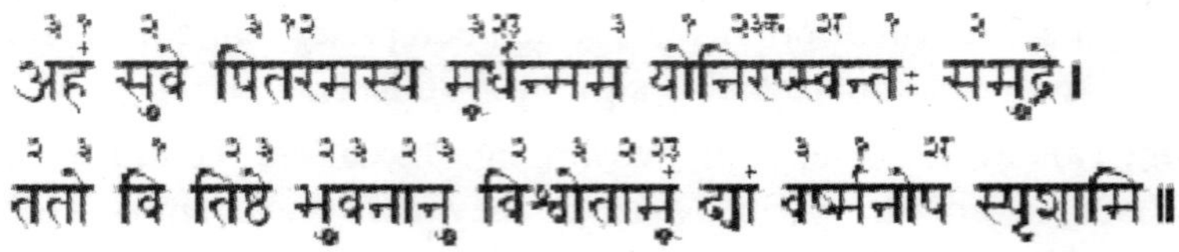

On occasions, Sanskrit text is transliterated in Latin script using diacritical marks. For example, श्रीमद्भगवद्गीता is transliterated as *śrīmad̲bh̲agvadgītā*. Such texts can be typed as explained in the earlier section on typing in European languages. Combining diacritical mark characters (codes 0300 to 036F hex) may be used for unusual diacritical marks on Latin base letters, as explained earlier in the chapter.

ISCII versus Unicode Inscript keyboard layouts

Unicode standard for Brahmi-based Indic scripts draws heavily from ISCII standard. Numeric codes of the consonant and vowel letters in Unicode are based on ISCII. Indeed, except for a few minor differences, the two standards correspond directly. However, unlike ISCII, Unicode is designed to be a multilingual encoding that requires no escape sequences or switching between scripts. ISCII allowed control over character formation by combining letters with the characters *nukta*, INV, and *halant*. Unicode provides similar control with the ZWJ and ZWNJ characters.

The prototypical example is the 'explicit *halant*' (as in श्‌र, as opposed to श्र or श्‍र):

ISCII: *Halant* + *Halant* (for example, श्‌र = श ् ् र)

Unicode: *Halant* + ZWNJ (for example, श्‌र = श ् ZWNJ र)

The 'soft *halant*' of ISCII is expressed (as in श्‍र, as opposed to श्र):

ISCII: *Halant* + *Nukta* (for example, श्‍र = श ् ़ र)

Unicode: *Halant* + ZWJ (for example, श्‍र = श ् ZWJ र)

The ISCII Attribute code (ATR) is not represented in the Unicode Standard, which is a plain text standard. The ISCII Attribute code is intended to explicitly define a font attribute applicable to following characters, and thus represents an embedded control for the kinds of font and style information that is not carried in a plain text encoding.

The ISCII Extension code (EXT) is also not represented directly in the Unicode Standard. The Extension code is an escape mechanism, allowing the 8-bit ISCII standard to define an extended repertoire via an escaped re-encoding of certain byte values. Such a mechanism is not required in the Unicode Standard, which simply uses additional code points to encode any additional character repertoire.

Phonetic/transliteration keyboard layout/IME

Another popular keyboard layout/IME for Indic script is variously called phonetic layout or transliteration layout. In this approach, one apparently presses the English QWERTY keys, and what gets keyed in is text in Indic script. For example, as one presses the keys *m a d a n* or *m a d a n a*, what gets typed is मदन; as one presses the keys *k i s a a n* or *k i s a a n a*, what gets typed is किसान. The following table illustrates it further.

Table 11: Typing in Devanagari in transliteration/phonetic keyboard layout/IME

Apparent key sequence	What gets typed	
	Anywhere in word	**At the end of the word**
k	क्	क
ka	क	क
kaa	का	का
K	क़्	क़
Ka	क़	क़
Kaa	क़ा	क़ा
kh	ख्	ख
kha	ख	ख
khaa	खा	खा
Kh	ख़्	ख़
Kha	ख़	ख़
Khaa	ख़ा	ख़ा

Backspace appears to work 'abnormally' when used in such keyboard layout/IME. For example, if one types 'k', what gets typed is क्; if one types 'h' immediately thereafter, क् gets replaced by ख् (i.e., ख + ◌्). Now, if backspace is typed immediately thereafter, then one will not get back क्, that is, it will not be as if the 'h' has been deleted ("k~~h~~"). Indeed, what one gets is ख, as the *halant* gets deleted (ख ~~+◌्~~). This is because what gets inputted as one types is the Unicode characters, and not English letters. Indeed, backspace works normally, as it deletes the preceding character, which in this was the *halant* sign (◌्). It should be noted that ख् comprises two characters ख and ◌्, having hex codes 0916 and 094D respectively.

Vowels and vowel signs are typed as per the following table:

Table 12: Typing in Devanagari in transliteration/phonetic keyboard layout/IME

Apparent key sequence	Typed text depending on context
a	अ, remove halant
aa	आ, ा
i	इ,ि
ee	ई, ी
u	उ, ु
oo	ऊ, ू
R	ऋ, ◌ृ, ृ
e	ए, े
ai	ऐ, ै
o	ओ, ो
au	औ, ौ
^	◌ं
M	◌ँ
H	◌ः
O	ऑ, ॉ
E	ऎ, ॆ
A	ऍ, ॅ

Apparent key sequence	Typed text
Ka, qa	क़
Ga	ग़
Za	ज़
Fa	फ़
sha	श
Sha	ष
ta	त
Ta	ट
da	द
Da	ड
Na	ण
na	न
Nga	ङ
Nja	ञ
OM	ॐ
cha	च
chha	छ

Note: How does one type अउ in phonetic/transliteration keyboard layout? Typing '*au*' produces औ, and not अउ. To type अउ, one has to type 'a', space, backspace and 'u' in sequence. This is because typing simply 'au' will not produce अउ, but औ. Similarly, 'o', space, backspace and 'o' produce ओओ, whereas 'oo' produce ऊ; 'k', 'a', space, backspace, and 'i' produces कइ, while 'kai' produces कै; 'e', space, backspace and 'e' produce एए, while 'ee' produce ई.

As one types in this keyboard layout/IME, usually a hint appears on the screen as shown in Figure 52.

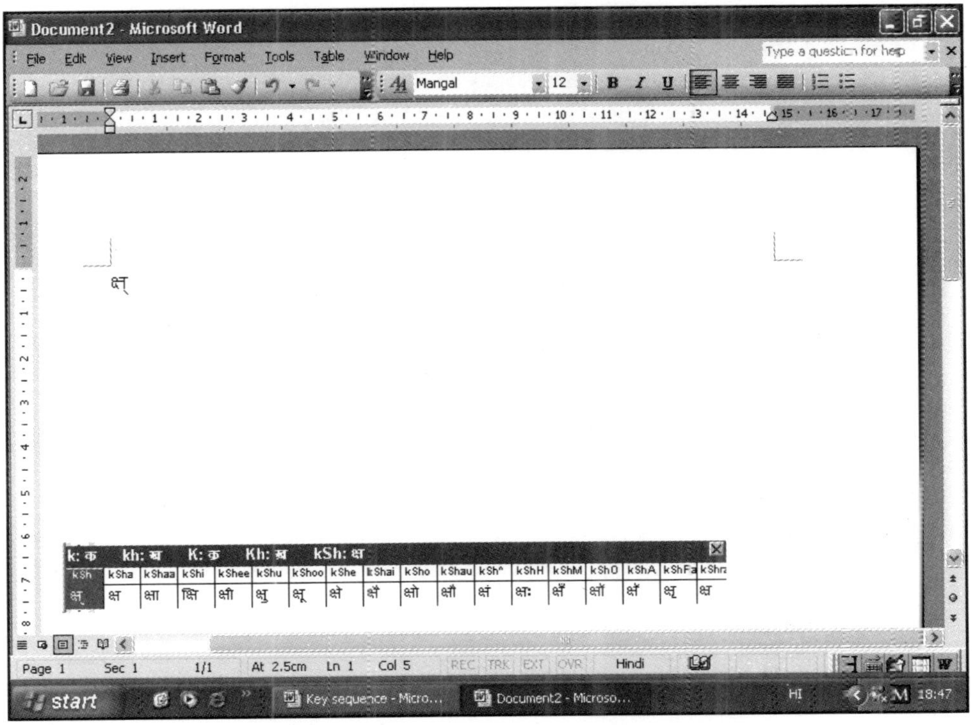

Figure 52: Hints as one types using phonetic keyboard layout/IME

Typing in Arabic script

If a right-to-left language is selected as the input language (see Chapter 3), then the direction of the text is by default right-to-left. The shape of the cursor may change slightly. The backspace and the left and right arrows may move in the opposite direction, i.e., in the logical direction.

Note: The movement of right and left arrows can be changed to the visual direction (as opposed to logical direction) in Microsoft Word by setting Cursor Movement Control to "Visual" as shown in Figure 53. This window may be reached in Microsoft Word by the menu bar option: Tools → Options…, and the selecting the "Complex Scripts" tab.

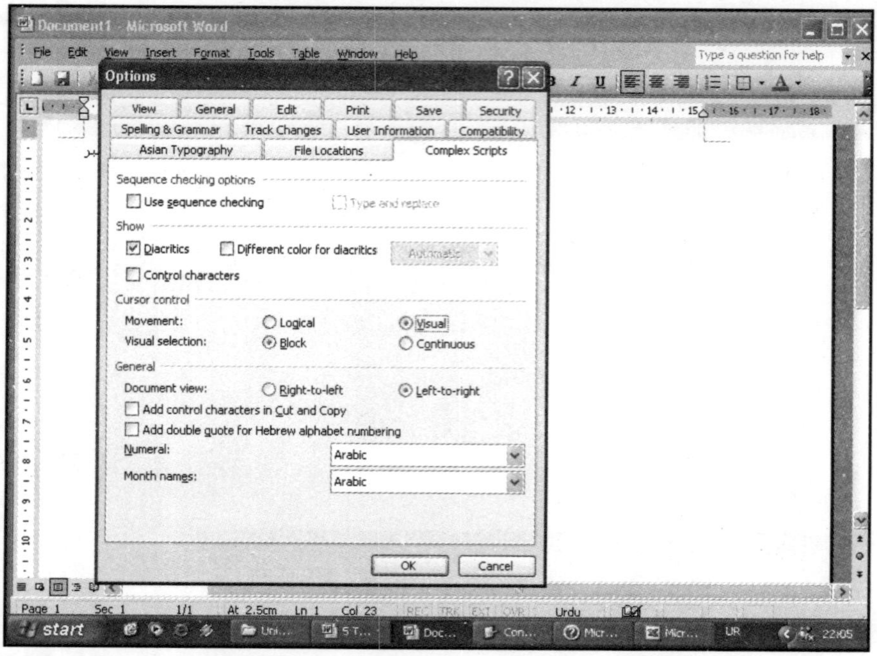

Figure 53: Cursor movement control

The default keyboard layout for Urdu that comes with Microsoft Windows is shown in Figure 54.

Figure 54: Urdu keyboard layout

Different languages based on Arabic script have different default keyboard layouts in Microsoft Windows. For example, the default keyboard layout for Arabic (Saudi Arabia) language that comes with Microsoft Windows is shown in Figure 55.

Note: The Urdu keyboard layout (Figure 54) did not have *zer*, *zabar*, *pesh* etc marks. These marks may be typed by switching to some other keyboard layout for Arabic script, or by inserting these characters as unusual characters as explained earlier in the chapter.

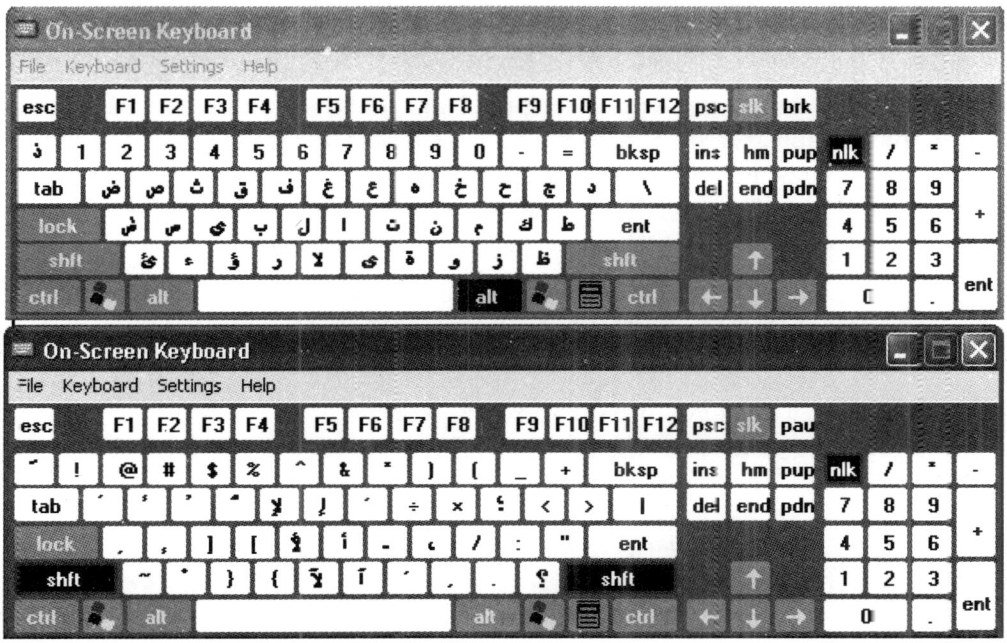

Figure 55: Arabic keyboard layout

To type a text in Arabic script, one is required to key in the letters and signs in the correct sequence without bothering about the formation of ligatures. Ligatures are formed automatically if the consecutive letters can join. Ligatures are broken by ZWNJ, ZWSP and space characters. A space character is added between two consecutive words in Urdu irrespective of the formation or non-formation of ligature. A few examples of typing in Arabic script are given below:

Table 13: Typing in Arabic script

To type this	One should type these characters in right-to-left sequence
اکبر	ا ک ب ر
محمد	م ح م د
برون	ب ر و ن
میرا ہندوستان	م ی ر ا space ہ ن د و س ت ا ن

ZWJ and ZWNJ characters may be used in Arabic-based scripts for controlling the formation of ligatures. ZWNJ ensures that the following character does not join with the preceding character to form ligature within the same word.

Cursor movement in Arabic script: Arabic-script is implemented in computers in considerably flattened and linear form than it is in Urdu calligraphy. Linear and flattened implementation of Arabic script facilitates easy cursor movement and search. Unlike Indic scripts, the cursor movement in languages based on Arabic script is easier. The cursor moves letter-wise[26] within a ligature or conjunct, and not conjunct syllable-wise as in Indic script. Of course, a letter includes the combining marks such as ُ ٌ ً etc. So the word کُ will be traversed in one cursor movement.

Search in languages based on Arabic-script: Unlike Indic scripts, individual characters or letters (or a combination thereof) within a ligature may be searched. What is searched is the logical sequence of characters in the conjunct, rather than the visual look of individual characters. For example, search with the search key containing the letter ک or the word حت will be searched in کحتپ. Even the diacritical marks etc can be searched individually, and can be replaced.

Note: There are two sets of codes for Arabic-Indic digits in Unicode. The Arabic-Indic digit codes 0660 through 0669 hex is meant for Arabic proper, and 06F0 through 06F9 is meant for Persian, Urdu, and Sindhi etc.

Note: The formation of ligatures in Arabic script depends on the font. The following table illustrates how the same texts are rendered visually differently in two different fonts, where the text in Traditional Arabic font is not just right-to-left, but also partly top-to-bottom.

Table 14: Change of directional sense on change of font

Text in "Times New Roman" font	Same text in "Traditional Arabic" font
محمد	محمد
سمج	سمج
نحا	نحا

The directionality of Urdu is not exactly right-to-left. Indeed, within a conjunct, the letters join to form ligatures in roughly top-to-bottom direction also. So, in each conjunct, the directionality is roughly from the right-top corner to left-bottom corner. The peculiar dependence of the directionality on the ligatures is taken care of at the font level.

Numerals are entered in left-to-right direction.

Presentation forms *not* to be used: Unicode includes "Arabic Presentation Forms-A" and "Arabic Presentation Forms-B," the hex codes being FB50 onwards The presentation forms include various forms of different Arabic letters, which are formed as part of ligature. However, it is not necessary to use those presentation forms. Those forms were selected and identified in the

[26] Letters with diacritical marks are traversed in one cursor movement.

early days of developing Unicode when sophisticated rendering engines were not prevalent. A selected subset of the presentation forms was included to provide users with a simple method to generate them. It is strongly discouraged and not recommended to use presentation forms because it does not guarantee data integrity and interoperability. Data files should include only the characters in the Arabic block, 0600 to 06FF hex.

Typing in mixed languages

One can type a sentence with words in as many number of languages and scripts as one wishes, provided the scripts and the languages are supported by Microsoft Windows (and also Microsoft Office, if one is using Microsoft Office). One can switch among languages as explained in Chapter 3. One can even mix left-to-right and right-to-left languages while typing texts in the same sentence—even if it spreads over to more than one line. Figure 66 illustrates multilingual text in several languages.

Note: If one uses a particular keyboard layout frequently, it may be worthwhile to get the characters/ligatures printed on the keys of the keyboard. Alternately, stickers may be used.

Number of keystrokes versus number of characters inputted

This chapter brings home the point that there is no specific relationship between the number of keystrokes and the number of characters that are inputted. The following explanations make it amply clear.

One or more keystroke, no character: Pressing of a key of the keyboard may not result in inputting of any character. For example, in Traditional Hindi keyboard layout, nothing will be inputted on pressing the keys meant for the characters ऐ, ऩ or ऑ. Even in normal English typing, no character is inputted as one presses the keys such as Shift, Control, CapsLock etc.

One keystroke, one character: In normal typing in English, one keystroke usually results in inputting of one character. For example, if one presses the key *a*, what is inputted is code 0061 hex, which shows up on screen and in print as the letter *a*.

One keystroke, many characters: One keystroke may result in inputting of more than one character. For example, as one presses the key for the Devanagari conjunct क्ष, what is inputted is a sequence of three characters: 0915, 094D and 0937 hex, as the conjunct क्ष is a combination three characters क, ् and ष.

Many keystrokes, one character: One may have to press more than one key to input just one character. For example, to input the character ô (code 00F4 hex) in French, one has to press two keys one after the other: ^ (the dead key) followed by o.

More keystrokes, more characters: This does not require much explanation. For example, if one presses the key *a*, one character is inputted; thereafter, if one presses the key *b*, another character is inputted; that is, one key results in inputting of one character, two keys result in inputting of two characters.

More keystrokes, less characters: This is very interesting. As one presses more keys, the number of characters inputted may not only increase or remain the same, but may actually come down! For example, refer to Table 11. In translation/phonetic keyboard layout/IME for Indic script, if one presses the key '*k*' what is typed is क्, which comprises two characters: 0915 and 094D hex (codes for क and ◌् respectively). However, immediately thereafter, if one presses the key '*a*', the inputted text changes to क, which is just one character with code 0915 hex. Thus, with one keystroke '*k*', two characters क + ◌् are inputted, but with one subsequent keystroke (i.e., two keystrokes '*ka*'), it gets reduced to just one character क.

The only exception perhaps is that one cannot type a character with keyboard without any keystroke at all. That is, there cannot possibly be "no keystroke, one or more characters!"

What you have learned

1. How to key in text in European languages
2. How to type text in Indic scripts
3. How to type text containing Vedic accent marks
4. How to type text in Arabic, Urdu etc
5. How to type text in multiple languages in a single document
6. Number of keystrokes versus number of characters entered

5. Settings Specific to Language and Region

Microsoft Windows permits choosing certain settings specific to the region and the language of the user's choice.

Time zone

One can select the time zone on one's computer. One can also change the time zone. For this, one will have to right-click on the clock in the "Notification area" (or, "Date and Time" under Control Panel), and select the option "Adjust Date/Time" in the shortcut menu bar that pops up (Figure 56). One may select the correct time zone from the drop-down list in the Time Zone tab, set the correct time and date in "Date & Time" tab, if necessary, and thereafter click "Apply" or "OK" button.

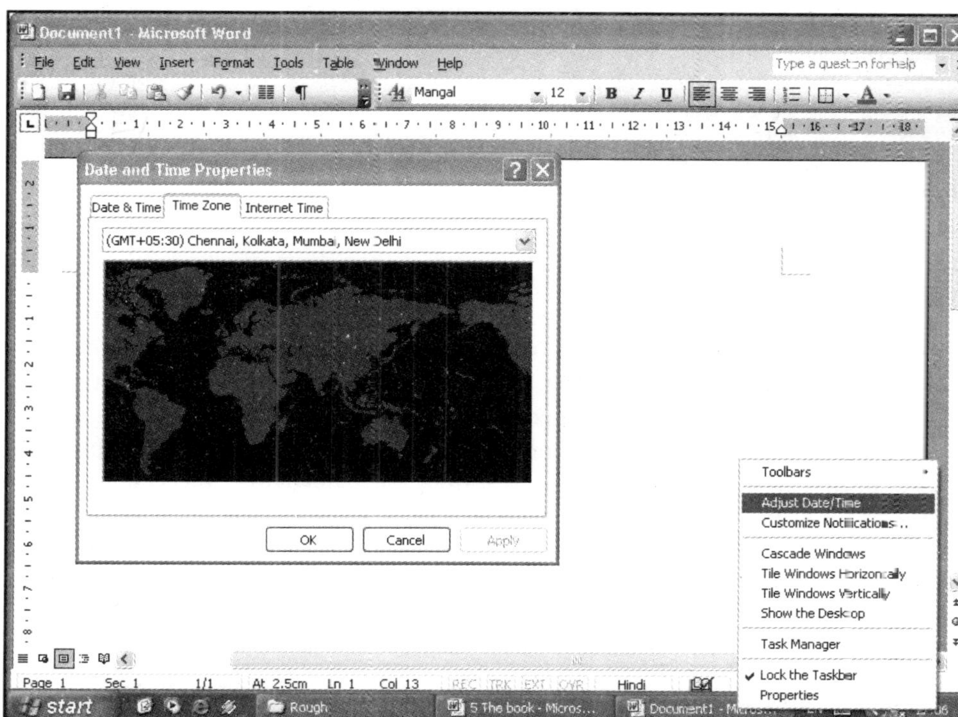

Figure 56: Time zone setting

Time zone can be selected under Linux operating system environment through the "Control Center" item "Date and Time" as illustrated in Figure 57, where a time zone is being selected in the Asian region.

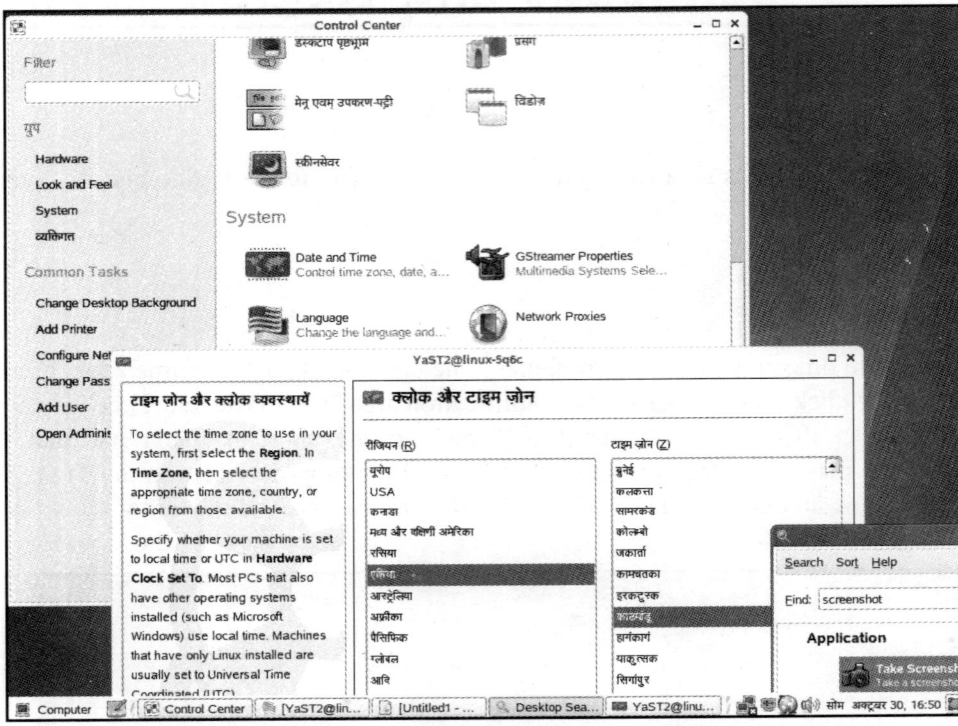

Figure 57: Date and Time under Linux

Default input language

As already discussed in Chapter 3, the desired default input language may be selected, including the keyboard layout/IME. Many computers in India have English (US) as the default language. The default input language can be changed to English (UK), English (India), Hindi, Bengali (India), Tamil, Urdu (India), or any other language of one's choice and supported by the operating system and the application software. Hindi (in Devanagari Inscript keyboard layout) has been set as the default input language in Figure 58 by the procedure mentioned in Chapter 3.

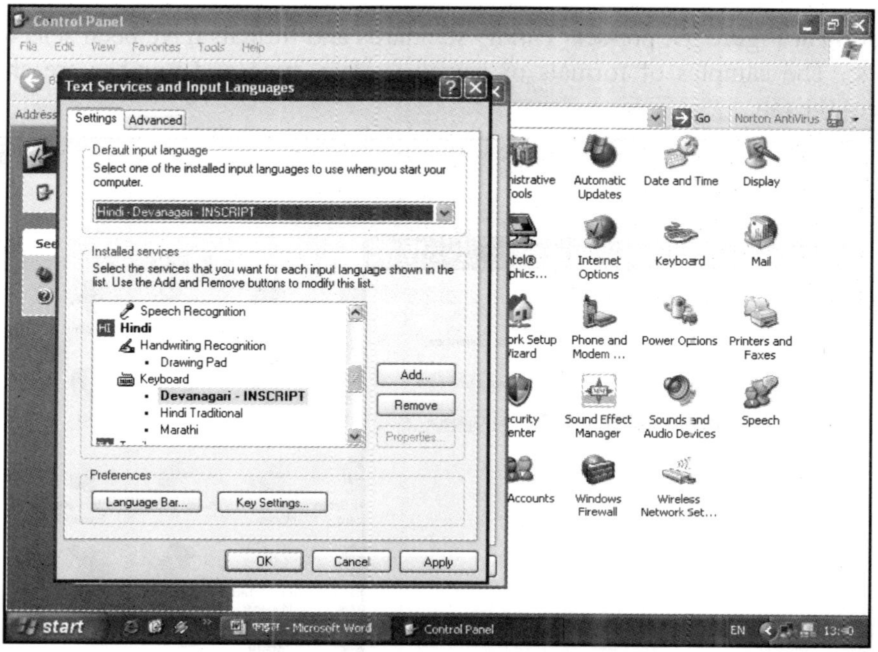

Figure 58: Default input language and keyboard layout/IME

Regional options

Regional Options allow the selection of the formats for date, time, number and currency. The formats in Regional Options are the default formats used by the operating system and many applications. These options affect how some programs format numbers, currencies, dates and time. For example, one may like that the date be formatted as December 03, 2006, as 3 Dec 06, or as Sunday December 3, 2006 etc. Similarly one may format a negative amount of money as (-) Rs 200, Rs (-) 200, or as (Rs 200) etc.

To set the Region Options in Microsoft Windows XP, one will have to do the following:-

1. Open the Control Panel (see Figure 12), then open Regional and Language Options (see Figure 13), and then select the "Regional Options" tab (see Figure 59).
2. In the "Regional Options" tab, the desired location may be selected from the drop-down list. For example, India has been selected as "Location" in Figure 59.
3. One may select any of the pre-set standards and formats of number, date, time and currency, or prepare one's own customized standards and formats (explained later in the chapter). And thereafter, click "Apply" or "OK" button.

In the illustration at Figure 59, pre-set "Hindi" standards and formats have been selected from the drop-down list. The samples of formats of currency, date, time and number are shown in the samples area of the tab.

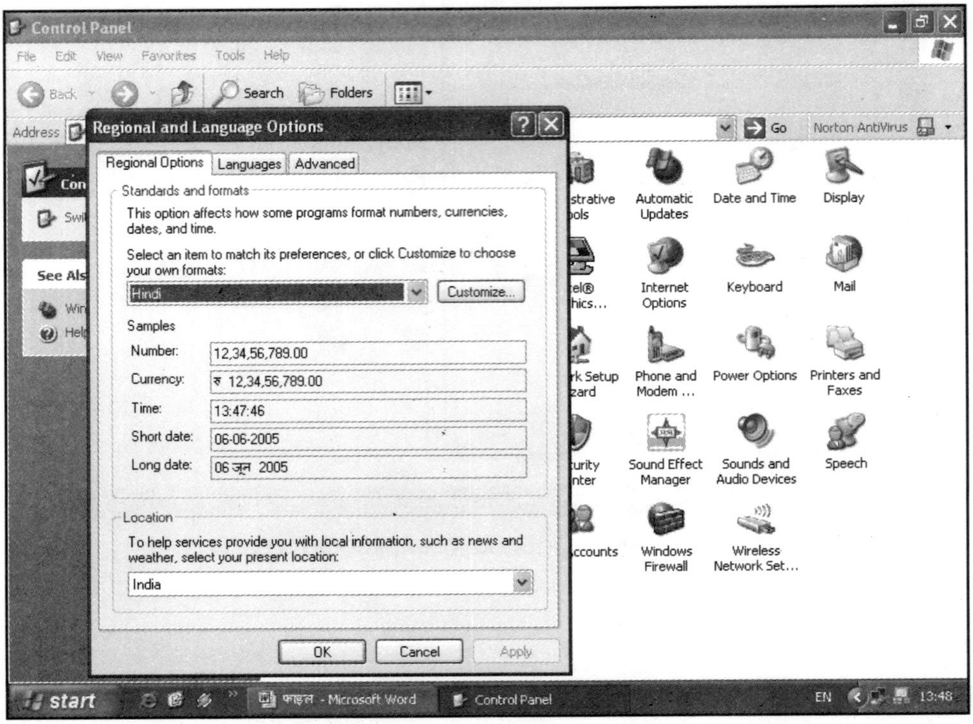

Figure 59: Regional Options tab

Often, instead of selecting pre-set standards and formats, one may like to customize the formats. To customize the formats, one will have to click the "Customize..." button (see Figure 59). Clicking the "Customize..." button will pop up the window with a number of tabs: Number, Currency, Time and Date. See Figure 60.

Number format options

In the number format options, the following may be specified (see Figure 61):

1. *The symbol to be used for decimal sign*: Dot symbol is normally used for decimal sign in English. However, in some languages such as French and Spanish etc, comma is used as decimal symbol and dot is used as digit grouping symbol. A different symbol is used in Arabic script (such as in Urdu language). One may select a different symbol altogether.
2. *Number of digits after decimal*: An option may be selected from the list.

3. *The symbol to be used to indicate digit grouping*: Usually, comma is used to indicate digit grouping. However, as pointed out earlier, in some languages dot is used instead. A different symbol altogether may also be selected.
4. *Digit grouping format*: Any one option may be selected from the drop-down list.
5. *The symbol to be used for negative sign*: Usually, the '–' sign indicates a negative number. However, an altogether different symbol may also be selected.
6. *Negative number format*: A format may be selected from the list.
7. *Whether to display leading zero before decimal*: It is recommended that leading zero be displayed before the decimal sign to make the decimal sign discernible.
8. *The symbol to be used as list separator*: Usually, comma is used as list separator. However, a different symbol may be selected as list separator.
9. *Measurement system*: An option may be selected from the drop-down list.
10. *Standard digits*: An option may be selected from the drop-down list.
11. *Digit substitution option*: An option may be selected from the drop-down list.

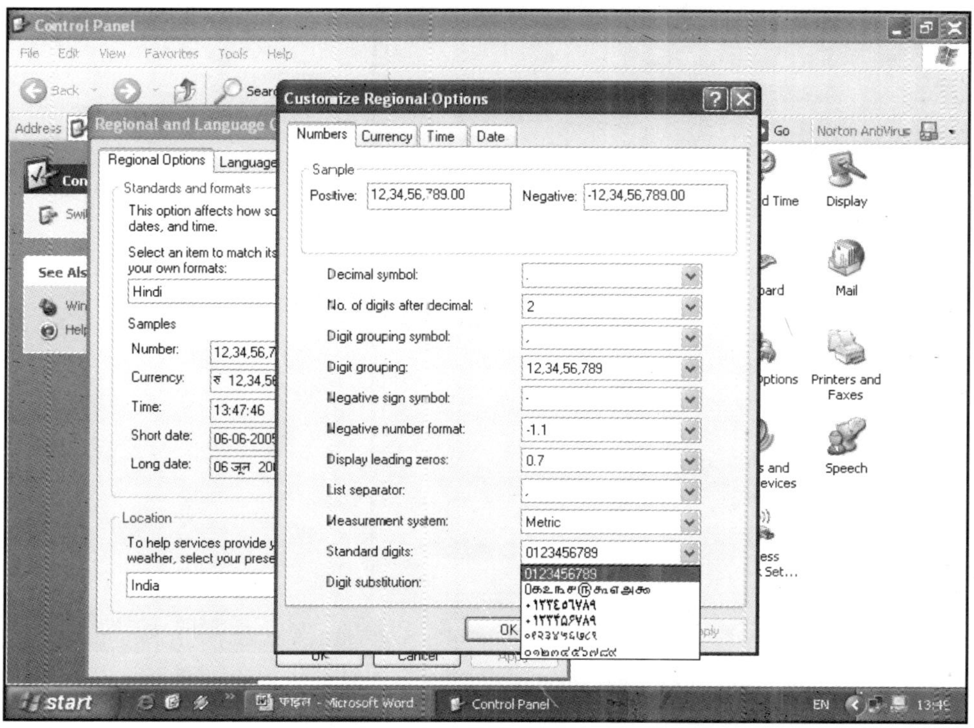

Figure 60: Customization of number formats

Note: If ०१२३४५६७८९ (i.e., Devanagari digits 0123456789) are selected as the "Standard digits," and "Digit substitution" is selected as "National," then at every place where the 0123456789 digits appeared earlier will have digits in ०१२३४५६७८९ format. That is, १ will appear in place of 1 etc. For example, it is worth looking at the English website at Figure 62. In the English webpage, the digits appear in Devanagari script. The original website has not undergone any change. The digit substitution has been done in the local computer, i.e., the front-end Internet Explorer browser. Moreover, the computer clock in Figure 62 displays time in Devanagari numerals, and not in "international" numerals.

Note: In digit substitution, even though the look and the apparent script of the digits change, the hexadecimal codes of the characters do not change. For example, after digit substitution, '1' may appear '१' but the underlying code remains the same; that is, '1' is still coded as 0031 hex, even though it looks like '१' (which is a Devanagari character with code 0967 hex in Unicode). Latin digits '0' through '9' have code 0030 through 0039 hex, and Devanagari digits '०' through '९' have codes 0966 through 096F.

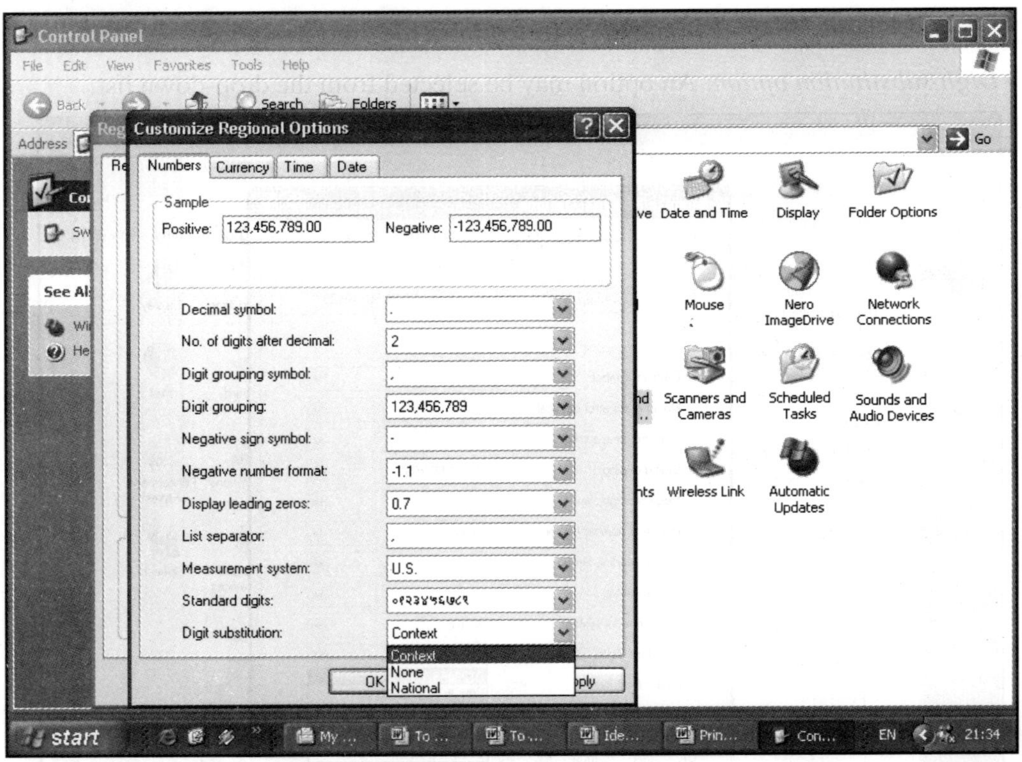

Figure 61: Customization of number formats

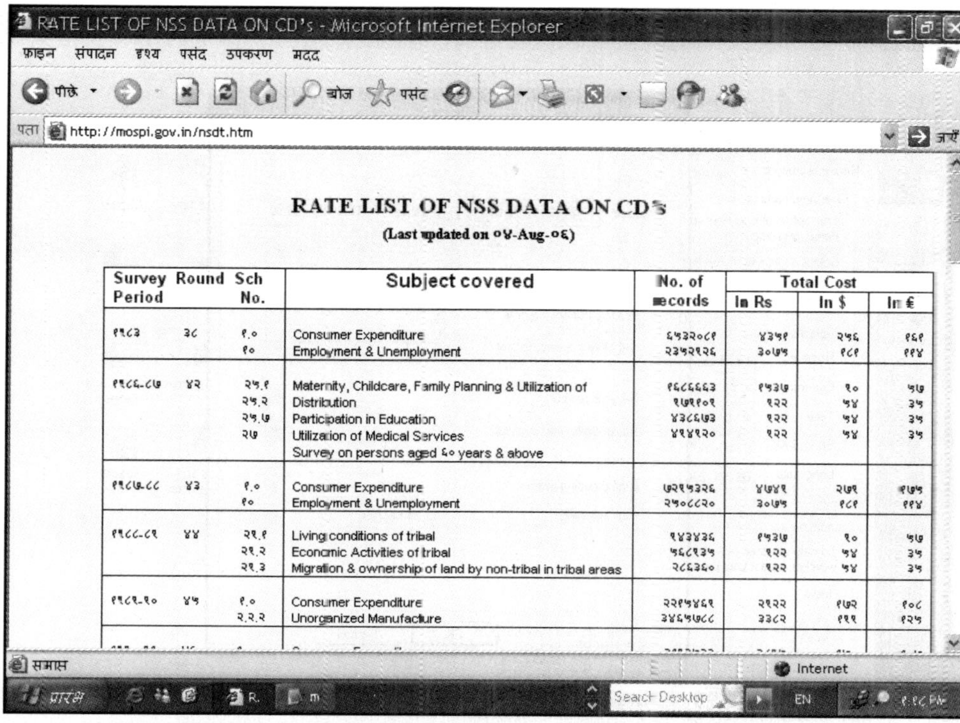

Figure 62: Default number is in Devanagari script, including in the clock

Currency format options

In the currency format options, the following may be specified (see Figure 63):-

1. *The symbol to be used for the currency*: One may either select the symbol from the given list, or type symbol of one's choice to be used for the currency.
2. *Positive currency format*: One may select an option from the drop-down list.
3. *Negative currency format*: One may select an option from the drop-down list.
4. *Symbol to be used for decimal in currency*: One may either select the symbol for decimal in currency from the given list, or type one's own symbol.
5. *Number of digits after currency*: One may select an option from the drop-down list.
6. *Digit grouping symbol*: One may either select the digit grouping symbol from the given list, or type symbol of one's choice.
7. *Digit grouping format*: One may select any one option from the drop-down list.

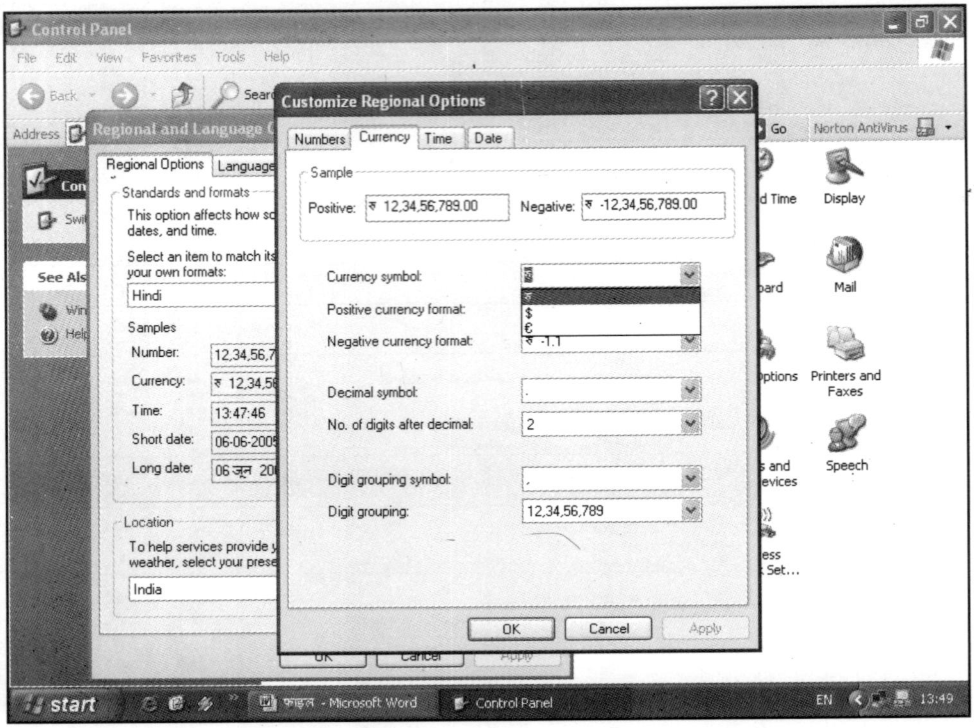

Figure 63: Customization of currency formats

Date format options

In the date format options, the following may be specified (see Figure 64):-

1. *Range of years when two-digit year is entered in a date*: One may select the range of years when two-digit year is entered in a date, such as "07" for "2007" etc.
2. *Short date format*: One may either select an option from the listed formats, or type one's own format.
3. *Date separator*: One may either select a date separator from the drop-down list, or enter symbol of one's choice to be used as date separator.
4. *Long date format*: One may either select an option from the listed formats, or type format of one's choice.

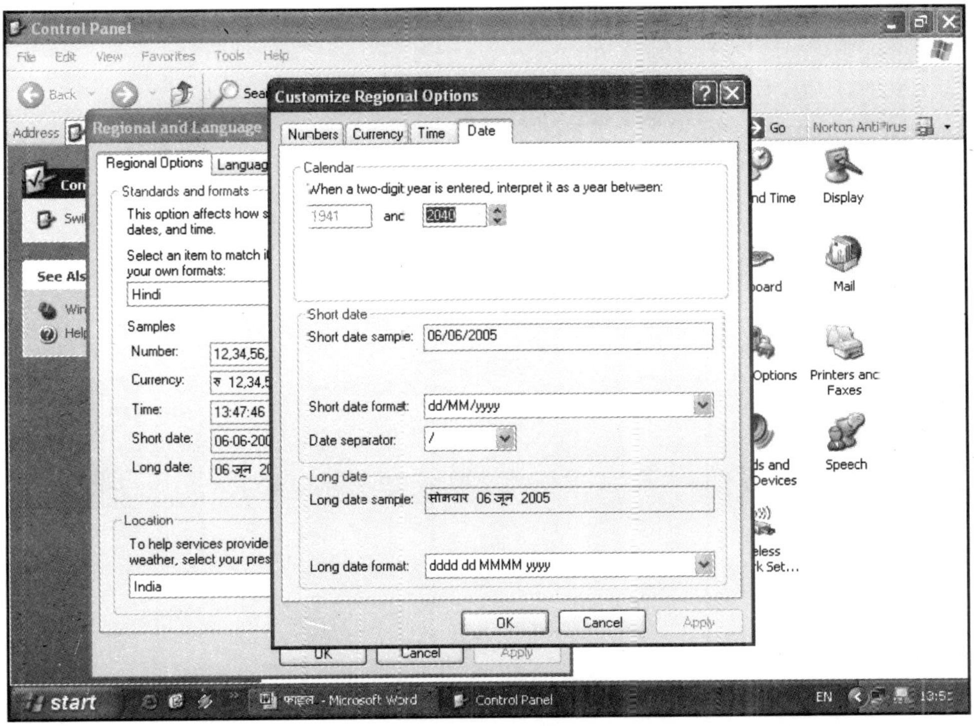

Figure 64: Customization of date formats

Time format options

In the time format options, the following may be specified (see Figure 65):

1. *Time format*: One may either select from the drop-down list, or specify a format of one's choice.
2. *Time separator*: One may either select a time separator from the listed separators, or key in character of one's choice as separator.
3. *AM symbol*: One may either select one of the listed symbols, or key in a symbol of one's choice.
4. *PM symbol*: One may either select one of the listed symbols, or type a symbol of one's choice.

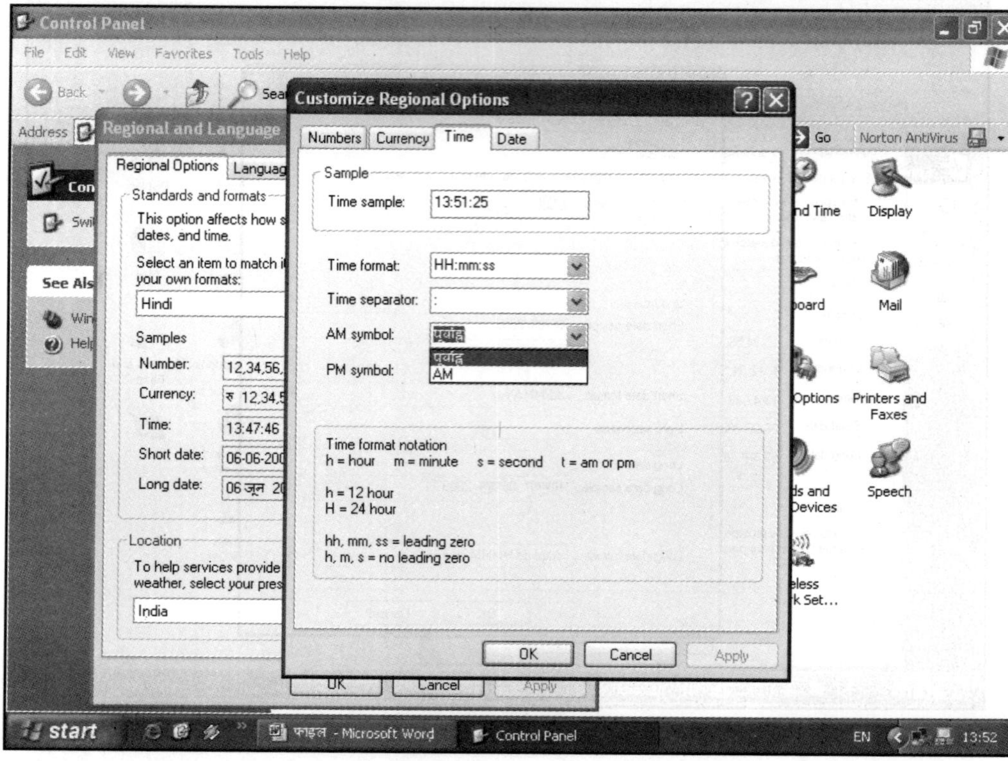

Figure 65: Customization of time formats

Note: The clock of the computer usually appears in the "Notification area" (bottom-right corner). The format in which the time is shown by the clock depends on the settings of date and time format. For example, the time and date are shown in Hindi in Figure 66.

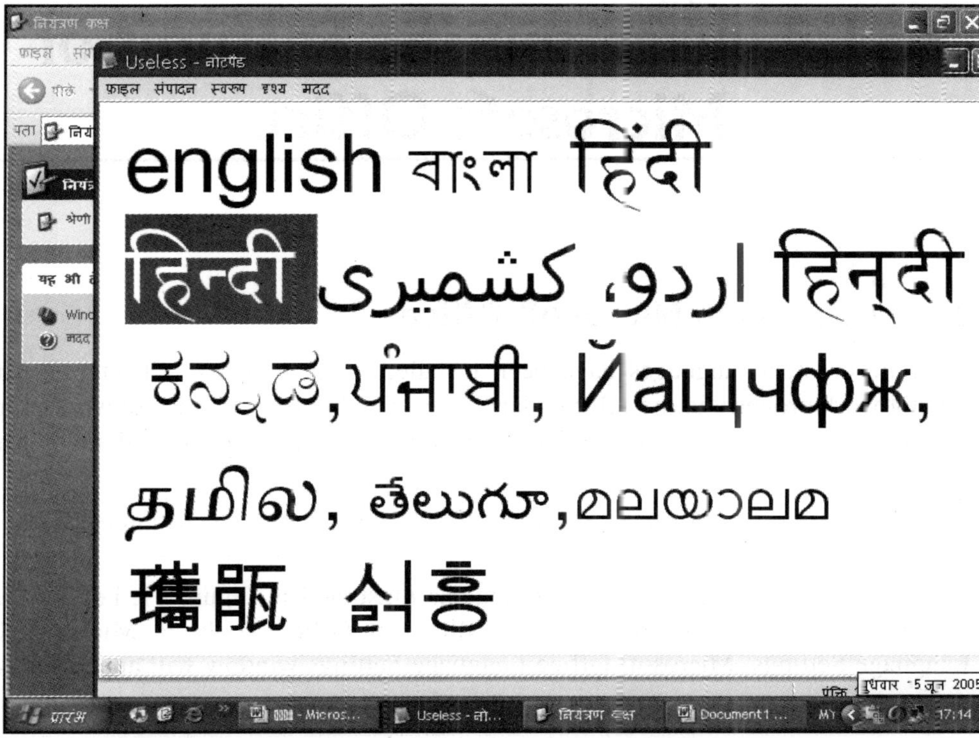

Figure 66: Multilingual text in Notepad, and date and month of the clock in Hindi

What you have learned

1. Time zone settings
2. Number format options
3. Currency format options
4. Date format options
5. Time format options

6. Language-specific Features of Microsoft Office

Language settings in Microsoft Office

Even after Indic or other languages have been installed as explained in Chapter 3, Microsoft Office may not work properly in the selected languages. For Microsoft Office to work properly, it is necessary to specifically select the languages for Microsoft Office. It can be done by Microsoft Office Language Settings.

For the languages settings under Microsoft Office, one will have to do the following:

1. Open Microsoft Office Language Settings as illustrated in Figure 67, i.e., by Start → All Programs → Microsoft Office → Microsoft Office Tools → Microsoft Office Language Settings. Microsoft Office Language Settings window will appears as shown in Figure 68.

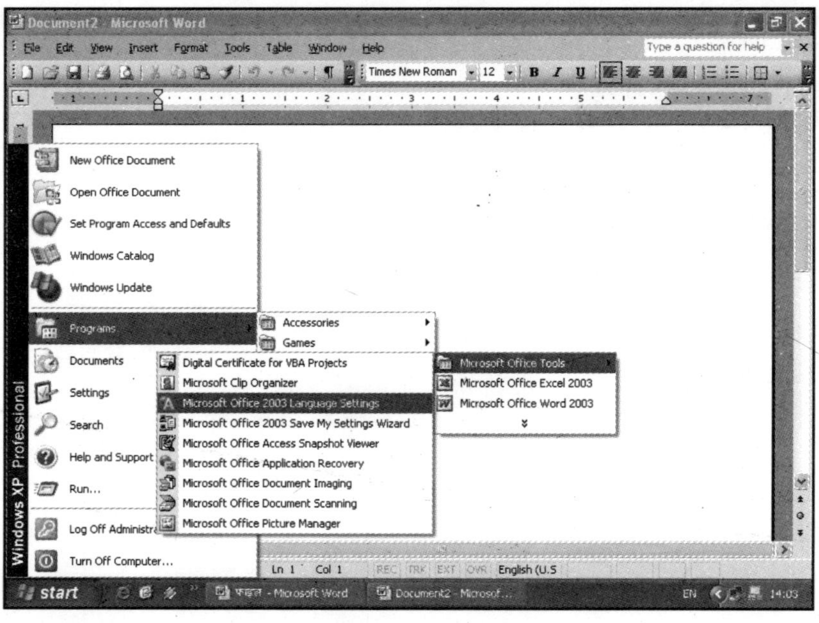

Figure 67: Opening Microsoft Office Language Settings

2. The desired languages are to be selected as enabled languages as illustrated in Figure 68.
3. It will also be required to choose one language that defines the default behavior in Microsoft Office applications. In the illustration, Bengali, English (US), French, Hindi, Spanish, Tamil and Urdu have been selected as the enabled languages, and English (US) has been selected as the default language for behavior in Microsoft Office applications.

Note: If the desired language is not found in the list of languages, or if "limited support" is written next to a language in the "Available languages" frame, it may be necessary to install additional system support for the language. The available support depends on the operating system.

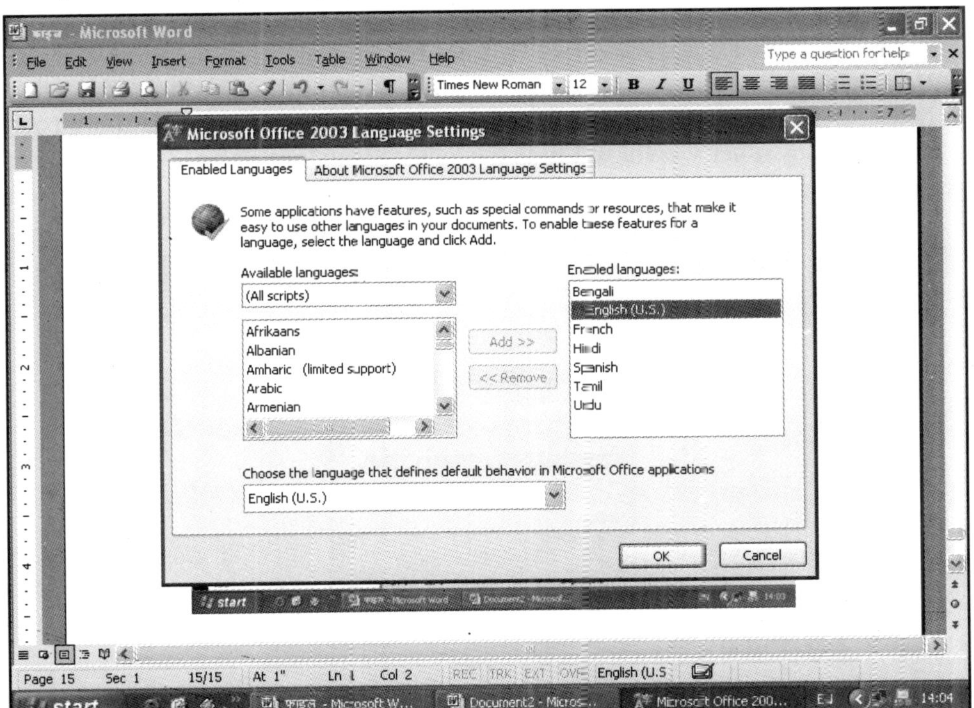

Figure 68: Selecting language(s) under Microsoft Office Language Settings

Language of text

Each portion of the text in Microsoft Office documents is recognized as not only being in one script or the other, but may also be in one language or the other. Language means specific variant of the language; for example, English (UK) and English (US) are treated as two "different" languages. As the cursor is moved in a text in Microsoft Word document or a portion of it is selected, the language of the text is shown in the status bar. In the illustration at Figure 69, the language of the text is Hindi as shown in the status bar, even though it is an apparently English word 'Cow.' (See Chapter 3 and Figure 23 on how to write text in a language in another script; for example, Hindi in Latin script.)

A different language may be set to a portion of a text in Microsoft Word by choosing the appropriate language from the list of languages as shown in Figure 69, which can be reached by the menu bar: Tools → Language → Set Language…. For changing the language of a text, the entire text should remain selected. Moreover, the "Set Language…" option is available under the shortcut menu on right-clicking a word marked as wrongly spelled. However, it may not be possible to set language to a text written in an inappropriate script. If it is desired to write a language in just any script, then one has to take steps as explained in Chapter 3.

Proofing tools and AutoCorrect measures etc in Microsoft Office are specific to the language of the text. That is, English (US) AutoCorrect will not be used for Hindi text and vice versa; only Hindi spelling checker will be used for checking the portion of the text marked in Hindi, unless automatic detection of language has been opted. English (US) AutoCorrect will not be used even for English (UK) or any other variant of English language, and vice versa.

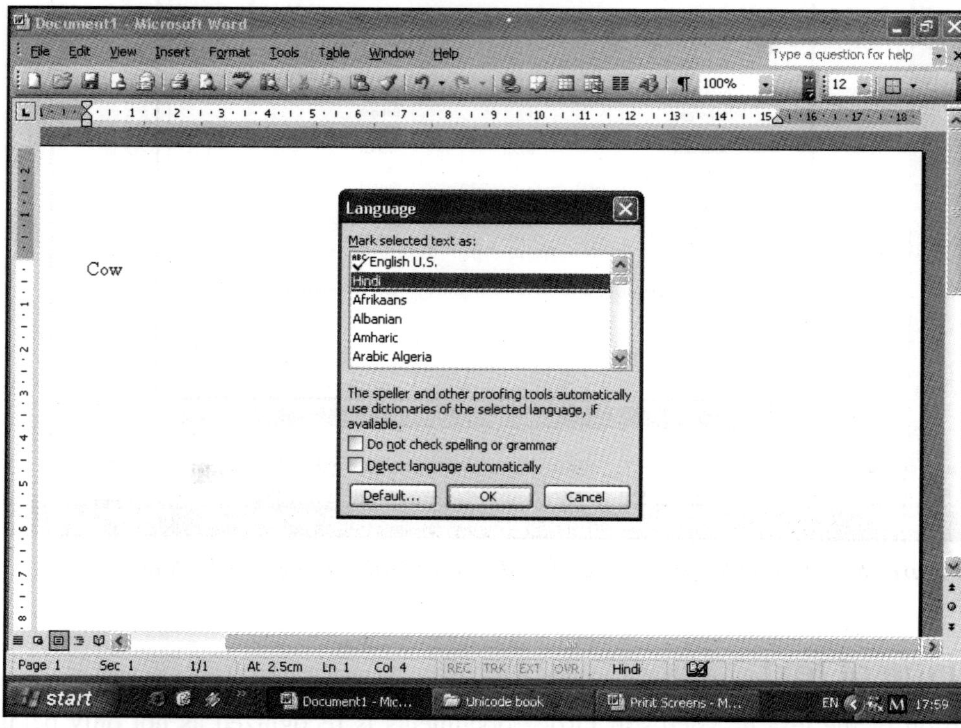

Figure 69: Selecting language of the text

Certain features of Microsoft Word

After the desired language (say, Hindi) has been installed at the Microsoft Windows level through Control Panel as described in Chapter 3, and the language has been selected under Microsoft Office Language Settings, one will find that Microsoft Office supports many features in the language.

As illustrated in Figure 70, the numbered list can be customized to be in Hindi also. The numbers (एक), (दो), (तीन) etc appearing in the list have not been typed by the user, but are generated automatically by Microsoft Word! Of course, the format of the numbered list may be changed to, *inter alia*, any of the following formats by changing the number styles as shown in Figure 70:

(क)	(अ)	(१)	(01)	(First)	(एक)
(ख)	(आ)	(२)	(02)	(Second)	(दो)
(ग)	(इ)	(३)	(03)	(Third)	(तीन)
:	:	:	:	:	:

Warning: In the ordered list with consonants (क), (ख), (ग)…, immediately after (न) comes (ऩ) and only thereafter only comes (प). Also, (ल) is followed by (ळ) and (ऴ), and thereafter only by (व)! The ordered list of vowels (अ), (आ), (इ)… follows even more unnatural pattern: (अ), (आ), (इ), (ई), (उ), (ऊ), (ऋ), (ऌ), (ऍ), (ऎ), (ए), (ऐ), (ऑ), (ऒ), (ओ), (औ), (अं), and (अः)!

Note: In the list (क), (ख), (ग)…, after (ह) comes (कक), (खख), (गग) etc. Similarly, in the (अ), (आ), (इ)… list, (अः) is followed by (अअ), (आआ), (इइ) etc.

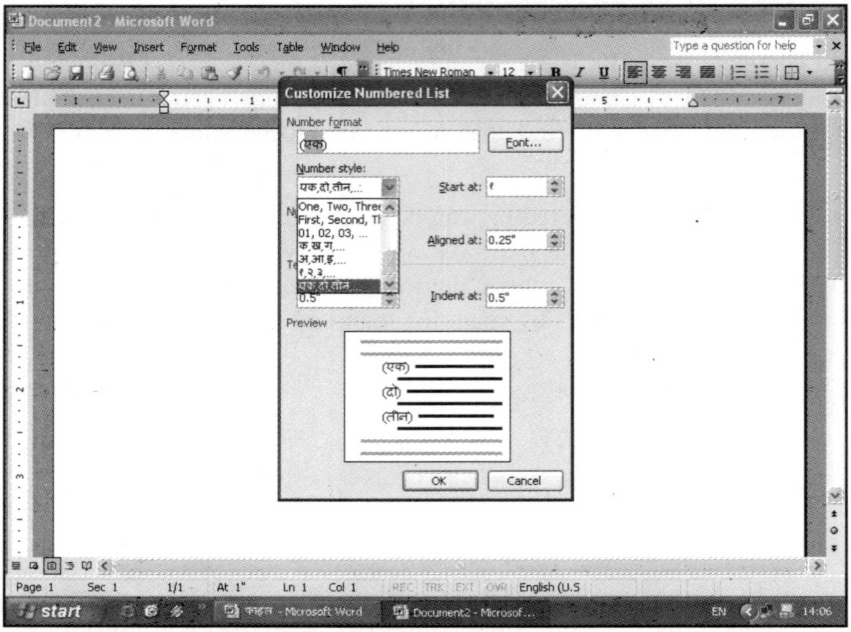

Figure 70: Numbered list in Hindi

The page numbering can also be in Hindi. For this, one will have to choose the appropriate format of the page number. This has been illustrated in Figure 71.

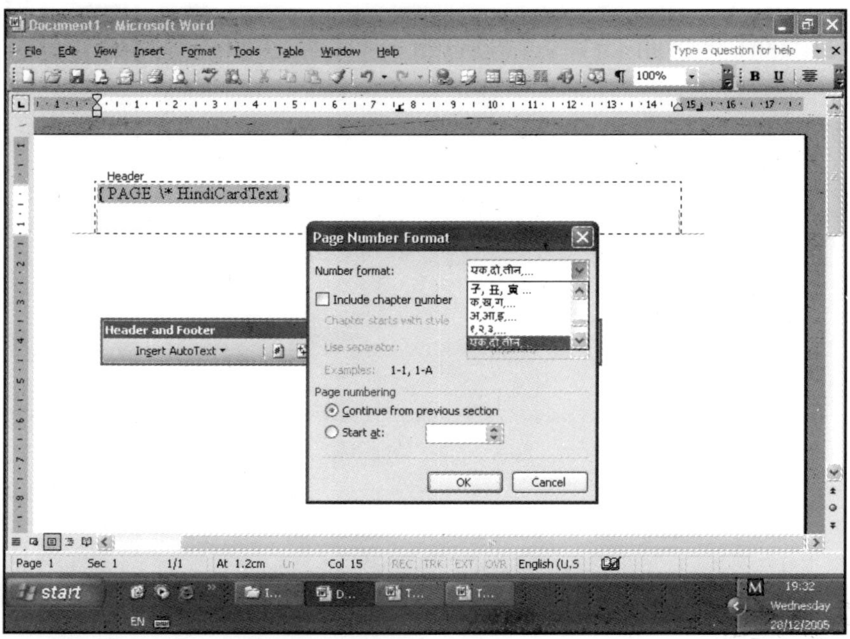

Figure 71: Page numbering in Hindi

One can also use Hindi (or other selected languages) in AutoText and AutoCorrect Options etc in Microsoft Word. As illustrated in Figure 72, AutoText can be in Hindi. The items shown in the illustration are the default ones that come with Microsoft Word.

Note: AutoText and AutoCorrect Options etc are language specific. In the middle of working in English, if one switches to Hindi in the same document, the AutoText and AutoCorrect Options also get switched to the Hindi ones. If one switches to Spanish (International), the AutoCorrect Options also get switched to the Spanish ones.

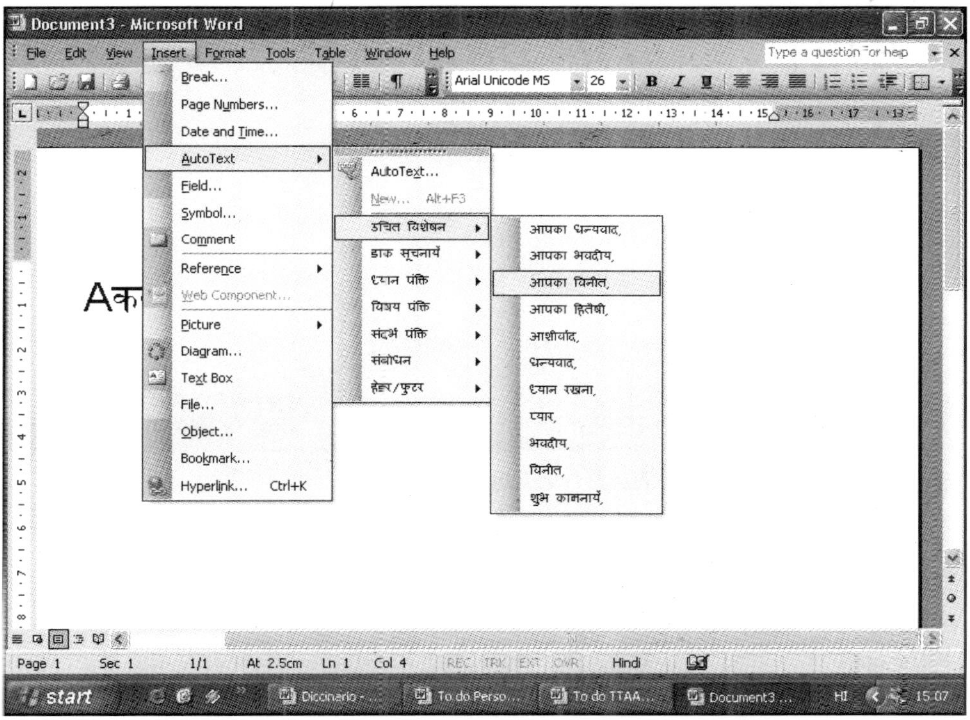

Figure 72: AutoText in Hindi

In Microsoft Word, as one types 'thur,' one gets a hint "Thursday (Press ENTER to Insert)." At this juncture, pressing Enter key causes 'thur' to be replaced by 'Thursday'; pressing Escape key removes the hint. Similar is the case with other days of the week, and several other auto-complete words. This facility is there even in other languages. For example, in Figure 73, as one types मंगल, the hint appears: "मंगलवार (Press ENTER to Insert)." Pressing ENTER key will insert the word मंगलवार; pressing ESC key will remove the auto-complete hint.

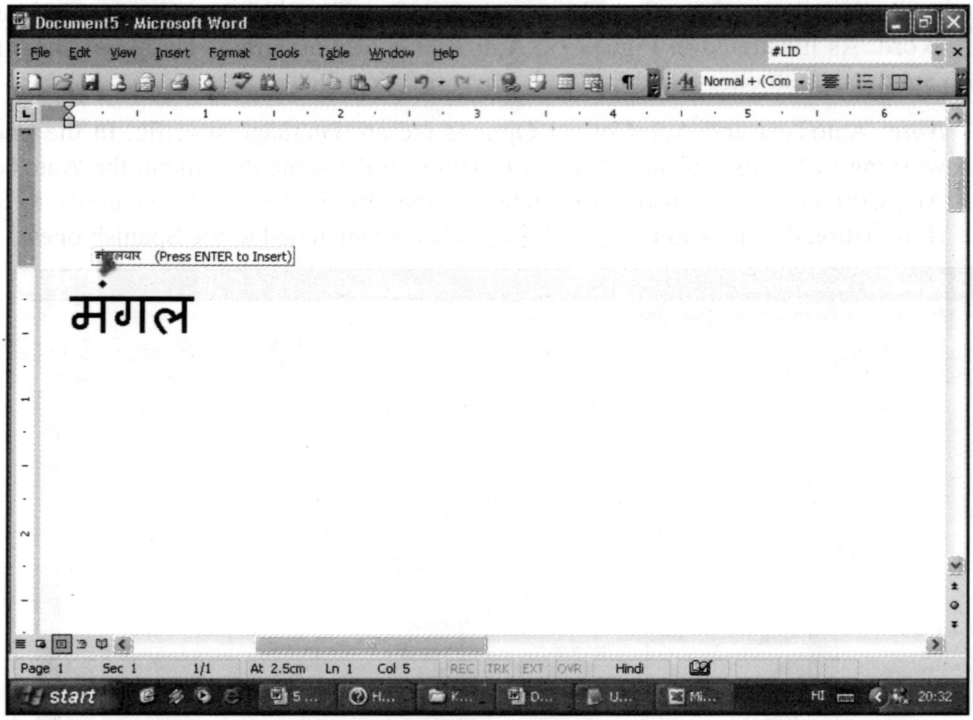

Figure 73: Auto-complete in Hindi (weekdays)

Microsoft Word allows user-defined captions. The captions can be defined in Indic or any other language. Figure 74 shows an example, where popular quadruplets dedicated to Lord Hanuman has been numbered by defining a new caption called चौपाई. Caption may be defined by following Insert → Reference → Caption… from the menu bar in Microsoft Word, and then clicking the button "New Label…," and later by selecting the number format for the label. This may be useful in numbering Vedic hymns and hymns from other scriptures etc.

If one no longer needs to type in the specific user-defined caption, it may be deleted.

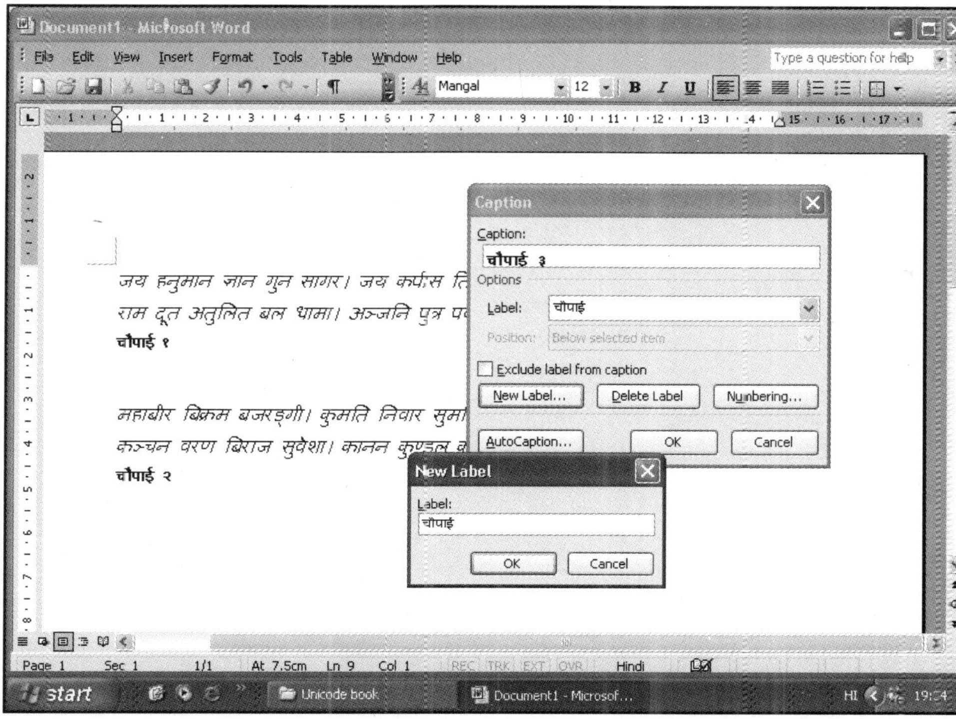

Figure 74: User defined caption in Hindi

The user-defined captions in Indic language can be used in indexing and tabulating. This has been illustrated in Figure 75. The used-defined caption may be selected as shown in the figure, which can be gotten by following Insert → Reference → Index and Tables… in Microsoft Word, and selecting the appropriate tab and options.

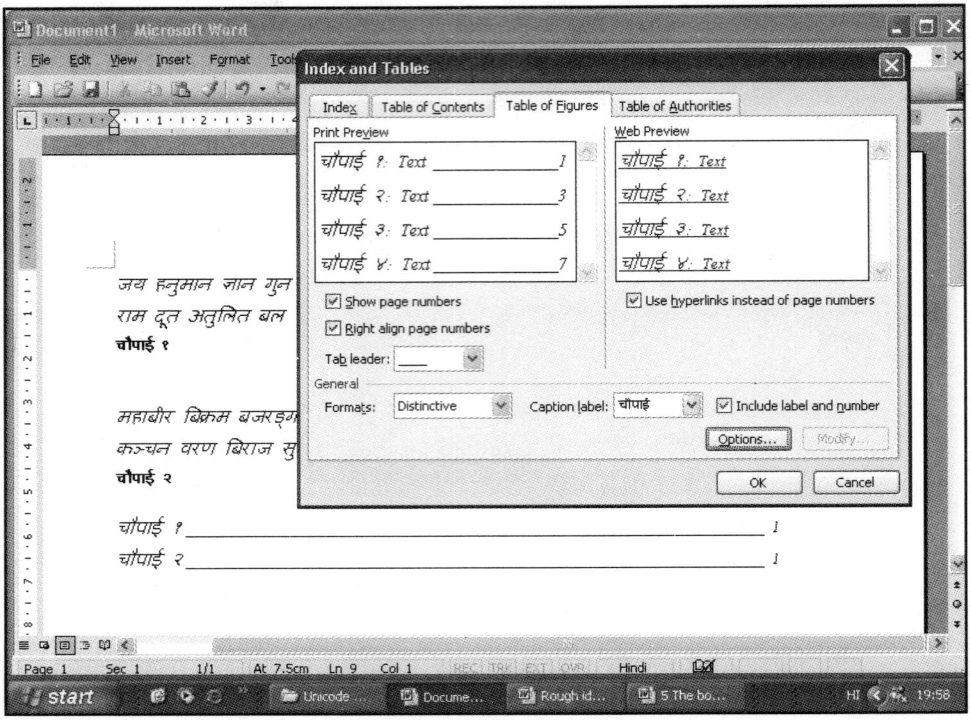

Figure 75: Indexing and tabulating in Indic language

Note: Unusual characters can be typed in Microsoft Word in another way using "Customize Keyboard." This method is especially useful for characters for which there is no specific key, such as for degree sign (°) in QWERTY keyboard layout etc. The method has been illustrated in Figure 76, where "control j" has been customized for the Assamese letter ra (ৰ). Of course, any other shortcut key could be selected, and any character or symbol could be defined. For defining a shortcut key, one will have to click "Assign" button in the window. This window can be reached by clicking the "Shortcut Key" button as shown in Figure 49. "Shortcut Key" should be clicked after selecting the desired character in the font in the frame. (In the illustration at Figure 49, ZWNJ character in Mangal font has been selected.) Of course, one may use some other customized shortcut key combination for the desired character. (The customized key combination can be removed by selecting the character in the font as illustrated in Figure 49, clicking the "Shortcut Key…" button, and then clicking the button "Remove" (see Figure 76, not highlighted in the illustration; "Remove" button can be highlighted by selecting the "Current keys")).

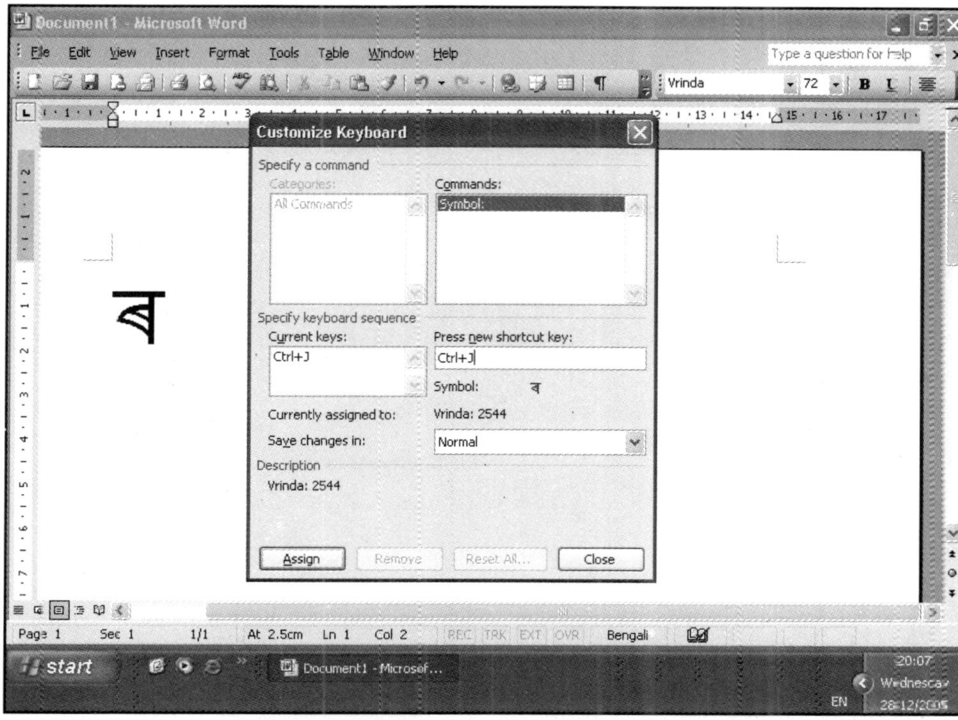

Figure 76: Customization of keyboard

Complex script tab

Microsoft Word has some features specific to complex scripts. It may be worthwhile to have a look at the "Complex Script" tab in the window obtained by the following steps in the menu bar: Tools → Options…. This is especially necessary if a mixture of left-to-right and right-to-left languages are used in the document. Complex Script tab has been shown in Figure 77.

Logical movement of cursor means that in right-to-left languages, the left arrow and the right arrow will move in the opposite directions, that is, towards right and left respectively. However, in visual movement of the cursor, the left cursor will move towards left and the right cursor towards right irrespective of whether it is right-to-left or left-to-right language.

"Use sequence checking" option has already been discussed (see Figure 45).

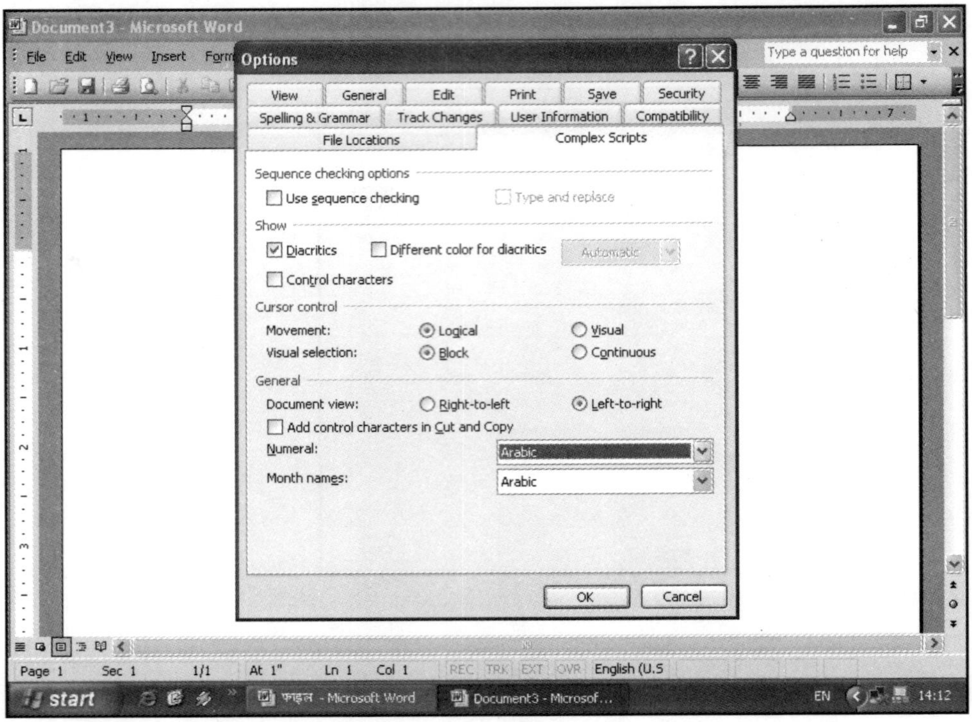

Figure 77: Complex script options in Microsoft Word

Certain features of Microsoft Excel

Figure 78 illustrates the AutoFill in Microsoft Excel, which are available in Hindi also. If one types जनवरी in a cell, the AutoFill action will fill the following months in a sequence in the subsequent cells. After दिसंबर comes जनवरी in a cyclical manner. (One may have to fiddle with the AutoFill Options.)

Similarly, AutoFill fills Hindi weekday names सोमवार, मंगलवार, बुधवार, गुरुवार, शुक्रवार, शनिवार, रविवार in a cyclical manner (see Figure 79).

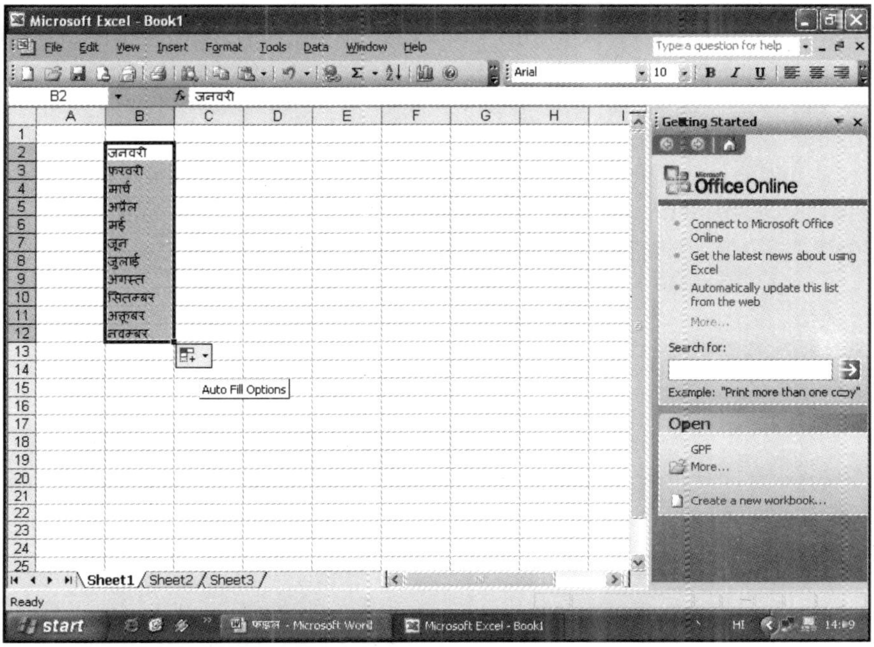

Figure 78: AutoFill in Hindi (months)

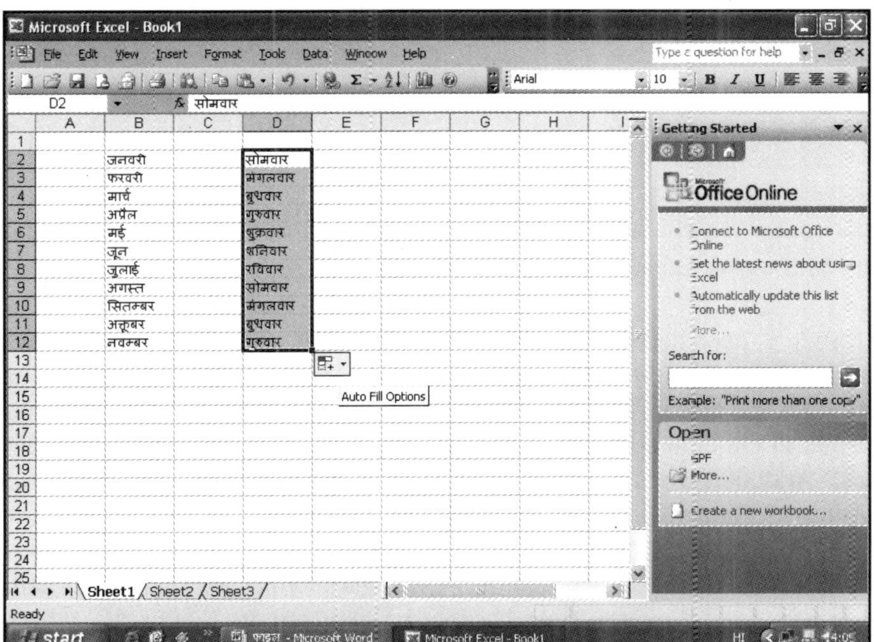

Figure 79: AutoFill in Hindi (weekdays)

It is possible in Microsoft Excel to format numbers not only in bold, italic, underline and font size, but **it is also possible to format numbers in different scripts**! So, apparently, one can do calculations in numbers displayed in different scripts by using the formatting options. One may convert the format of the number appearing in a cell to the script of one's choice by using the following option in the menu bar: Format → Cell → Number → Custom, and selecting or typing the appropriate format from the list (see Figure 80).

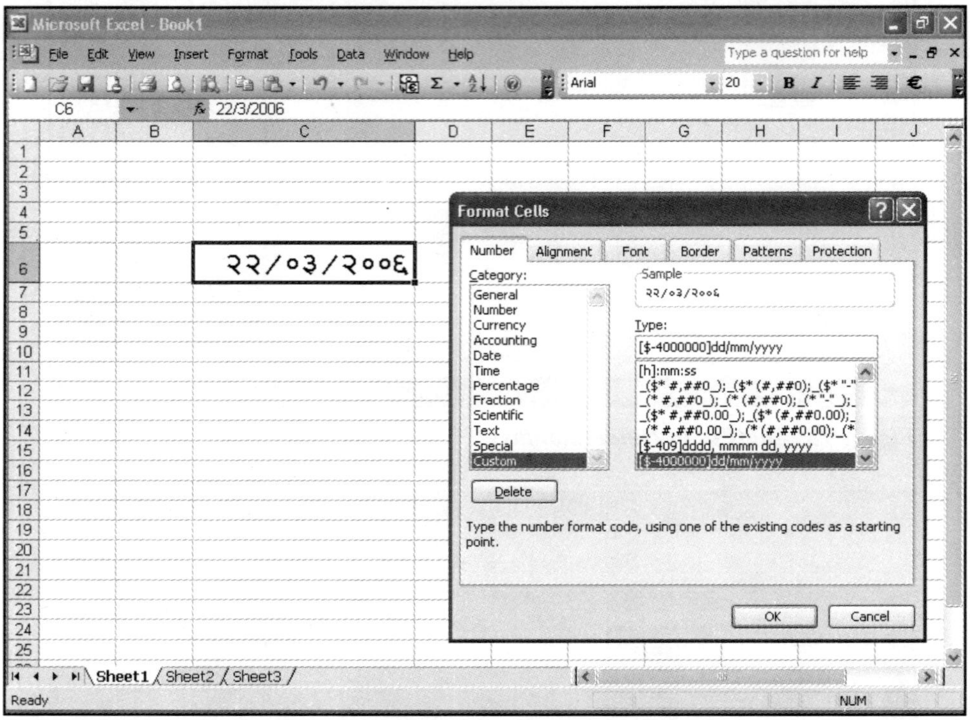

Figure 80: Custom format of cells in Microsoft Excel

The custom format is preceded by [$-1000000] for numerals in Latin script, [$-2000000] for that in Arabic proper script, [$-3000000] for that in Urdu etc, [$-4000000] for that in Devanagari script, [$-5000000] for that in Bengali script, [$-6000000] for that in Gurmukhi script, and [$-7000000] for that in Gujarati script, [$-8000000] for that in Oriya script, [$-9000000] for that in Tamil script, [$-A000000] for that in Telugu script, [$-B000000] for that in Kannada script, [$-C000000] for that in Malayalam script, [$-D000000] for that in Thai script, [$-E000000] for that in Lao script, [$-F000000] for that in Tibetan script, etc. For example, the custom format "[$-4000000]dd/mm/yyyy" will show the date in Devanagari script (see Figure 80). An example for formatting numbers in different scripts has been illustrated in Figure 81, where apparently, numbers in different scripts are added up (i.e., 1 + 2 + 3+4+5 + 6 = 21).

However, a number cannot possibly be written in mixed script. For example, 1 १১௧ (1111 with four digits in English, Devanagari, Bengali and Tamil scripts respectively) will not mean one thousand, one hundred and eleven.

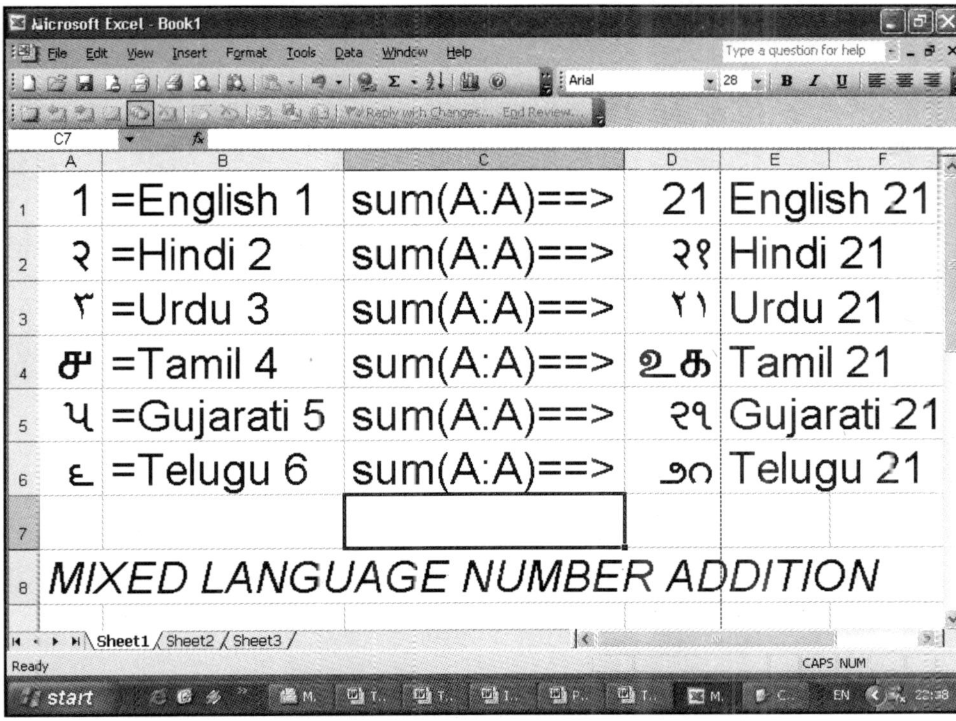

Figure 81: Custom display of numbers in different scripts

Certain features of Microsoft Access

The field names and table names in Microsoft Access can be given in Hindi (or, any other language). In the illustration at Figure 82, the field names are in Hindi. Moreover, the descriptions are in Hindi too. In illustration at Figure 83, the status bar shows the description in Hindi.

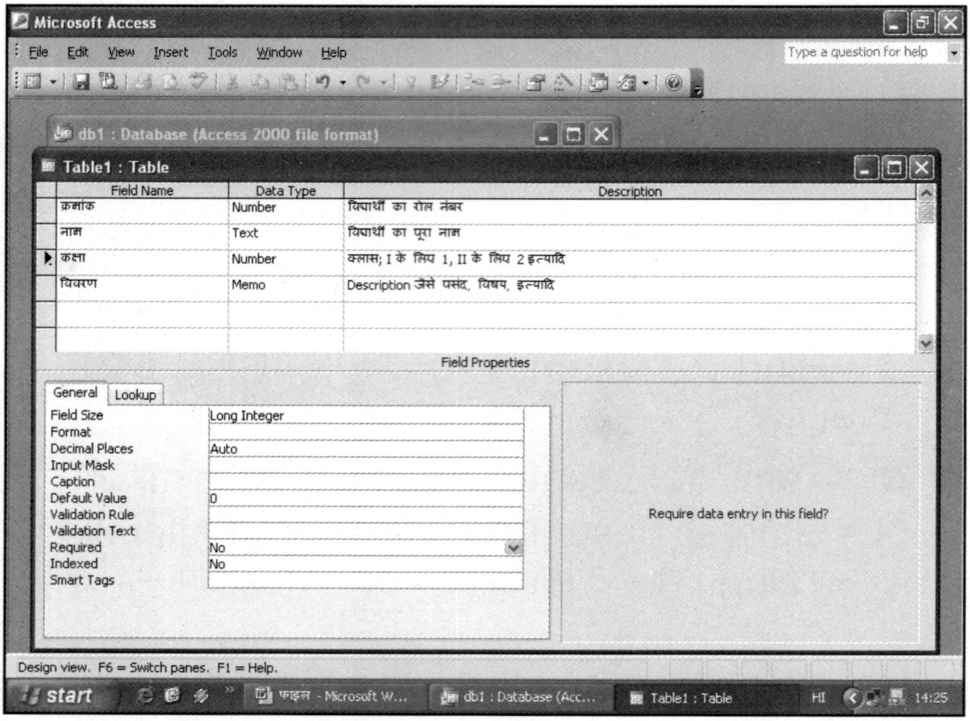

Figure 82: Microsoft Access field names in Hindi

In the illustration at Figure 83, the data have been entered in Hindi. Of course, the data could be in any other language also. Data can be sorted in alphabetical order. Alphabetical sorting is possible even when data are in different scripts. Further description on multilingual sorting is given later in the chapter.

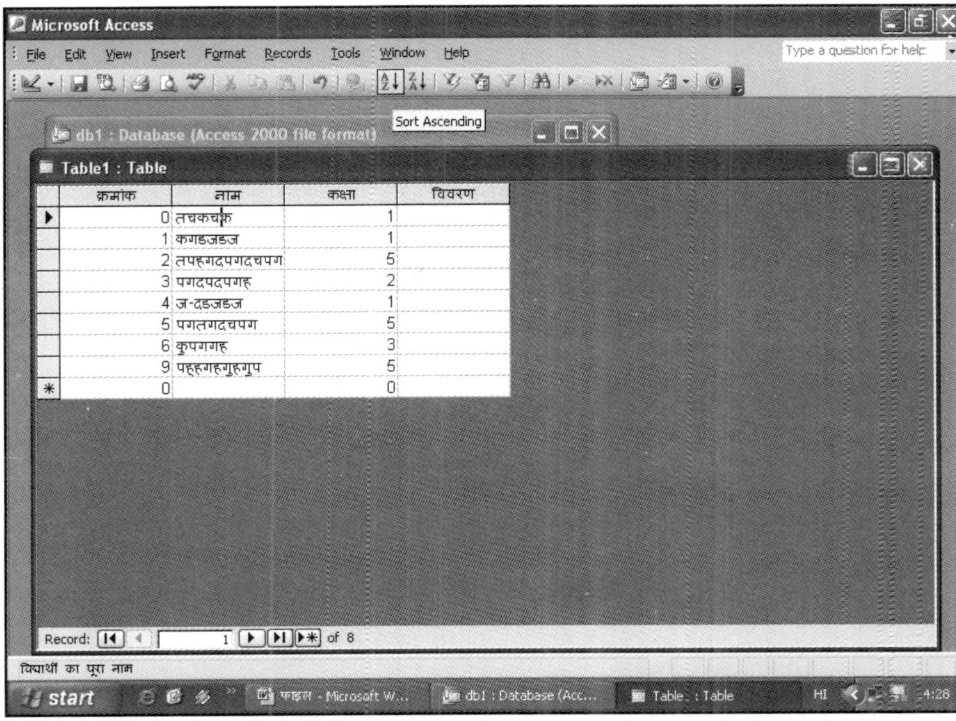

Figure 83: Microsoft Access data in Hindi

Certain features of Microsoft FrontPage

Microsoft FrontPage can be used to design webpage in any language, including a mixture of left-to-right and right-to-left languages. Figure 84 shows designing of a webpage in multiple Indian languages. It may be noted that the decimal numbers prefixed by "&#" and suffixed by ";" in the code pane of the Microsoft FrontPage are the decimal numeric codes of the characters in Unicode.

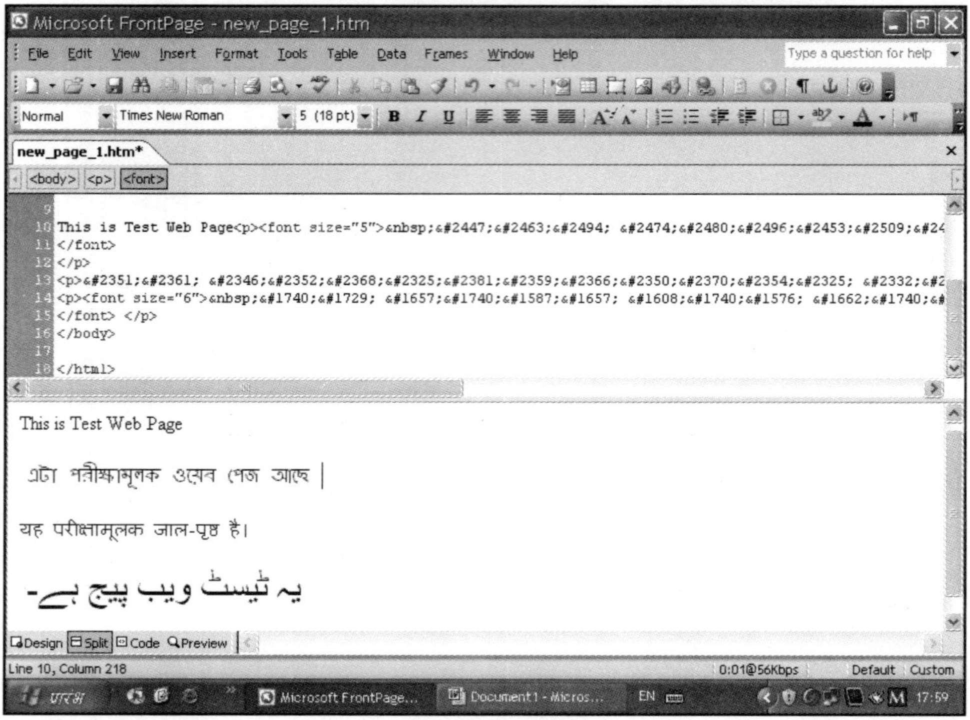

Figure 84: Decimal numeric code of text in Microsoft FrontPage

Figure 85 shows an illustration of marquee in Microsoft FrontPage. For right-to-left languages, the direction of the marquee is better chosen as "right" as illustrated.

Active Server Pages and non-ASCII querystring

Querystring is appended to a URL for sending small amounts of data to the server. Non-ASCII querystring is mapped in ASCII codes. For example, the querystring *first+name=क* is mapped to *first+name=%26%232325%3B*. This is because *first+name=%26%23**2325**%3B* is equivalent to *first+name=क* since *26 hex* is code for the character &, *23 hex* for the character # and *3B hex* for that character ;. And of course, *2325* decimal (i.e., 0915 hex) is the code for character क. Similarly, the querystring *first + name = क ख ग* is actually written as *first+name=%26%232325%3B%26%232326%3B%26%232327%3B* because it is same as *first+name=कखग* and *2325*, *2326* and *2327* are codes for the characters क, ख and ग respectively.

Note: In an input form, if *क* is inputted, it is taken to be क, because *2325* is the decimal code for क. To input the text "*क*", one will have to use codes for characters &, # and ;, that is, the input text will have to be *क*.

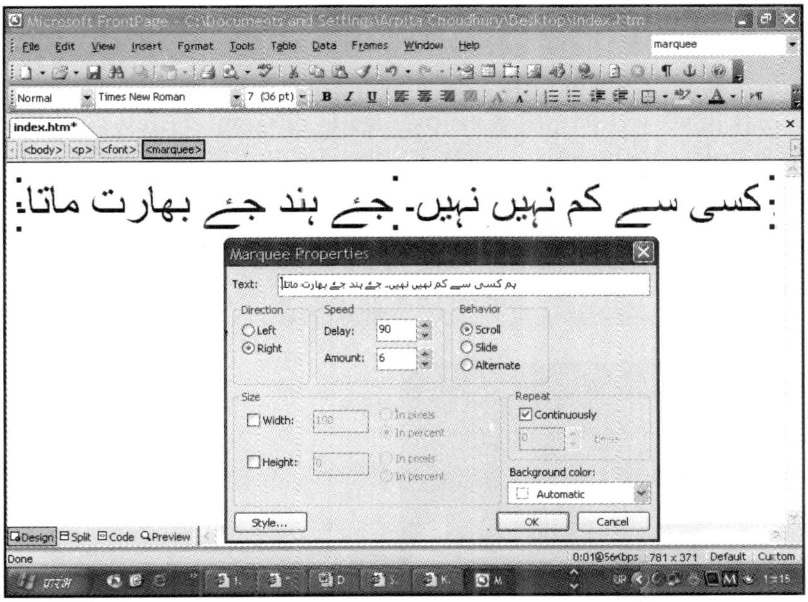

Figure 85: Directionality of marquee

One can also chat over the Internet in Indic and other languages.

OpenOffice

Indic languages can be used in OpenOffice. Figure 86 shows the OpenOffice Writer being used for typing texts in several languages.

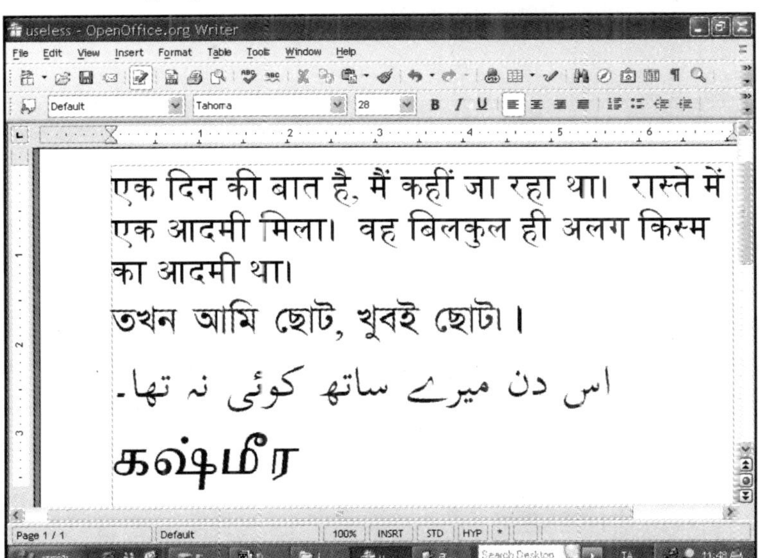

Figure 86: OpenOffice

Multilingual sorting

Alphabetical sorting in a Microsoft Office document can be done not only of a text written in one script, but even texts in several scripts. If the data are in different scripts, then different languages are arranged in the order in which the scripts are encoded in Unicode, and alphabetical sorting is within each script. Figure 87 illustrates this, where the texts are in the following scripts: Latin, Arabic, Devanagari and Bengali. The sorting facility of Microsoft Word (Table → Sort... in menu bar) sorts them as shown on the right side in the figure.

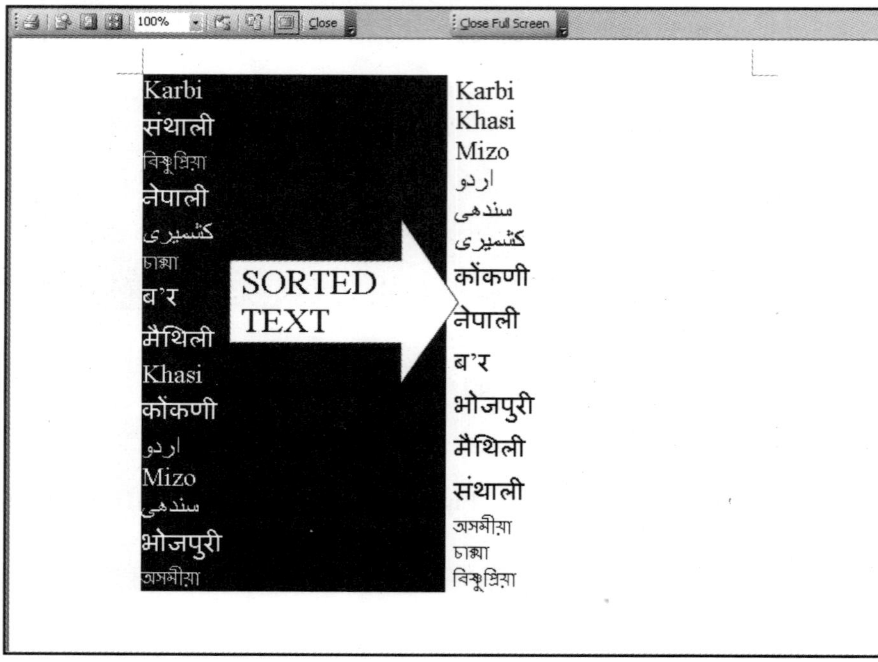

Figure 87: Multilingual sorting

Note: Different languages have different rules for sorting texts. It is possible to sort text according to the rules of another language. For example, Urdu text may be sorted according to Arabic language rule. Moreover, a different variant of the same language may have different sorting rules. For example, Spanish (Spain-Traditional sort) and Spanish (Spain-Modern sort) have different sorting rules as explained by the following table where the same text has been sorted in ascending order according to the rules of two variants of Spanish language and English(US) that yield different results.[27]

---

[27] Double el (LL) is treated as a separate letter of the alphabet [placed between el (L) and em (M)] in traditional Spanish, but it is not treated as a separate letter in modern Spanish. Also, CH is treated as a separate letter after C (cee) but before D (dee) in traditional Spanish. Also, en tilde (Ñ) is treated as a separate letter in Spanish, and is placed between en (N) and oh (O) in the alphabet. But in English, en tilde (Ñ) is treated as the letter en (N) with diacritical mark, and not as a separate letter of the alphabet.

(i) Spanish (Traditional)	(ii) Spanish (Modern)	(iii) English (US)
Libre	Libre	Libre
Lugar	Llamar	Llamar
Llamar	Llover	Llover
Llover	Lugar	Lugar
Más	Más	Más
Nono	Nono	Nono
Norte	Norte	Ñoño
Ñoño	Ñoño	Norte

While sorting in English in Microsoft Word, 'æ' is treated as consisting of two letters 'a' and 'e' in that sequence, but preceding 'ae' in ascending order.

Even though both Hindi and Marathi are written in Devanagari script, the sorting rules are different in the two languages.

If non-default sorting rule is to be selected for sorting the text in Microsoft Word, then the following steps are to be taken:

1. Select the text you want to sort.
2. On the Table menu, click Sort.
3. Click Options… button
4. In the Sorting language list, select the language that has the sorting rules you want Microsoft Word to use.
5. Select any other options you want, and click "OK" button.

This has been illustrated in Figure 88.

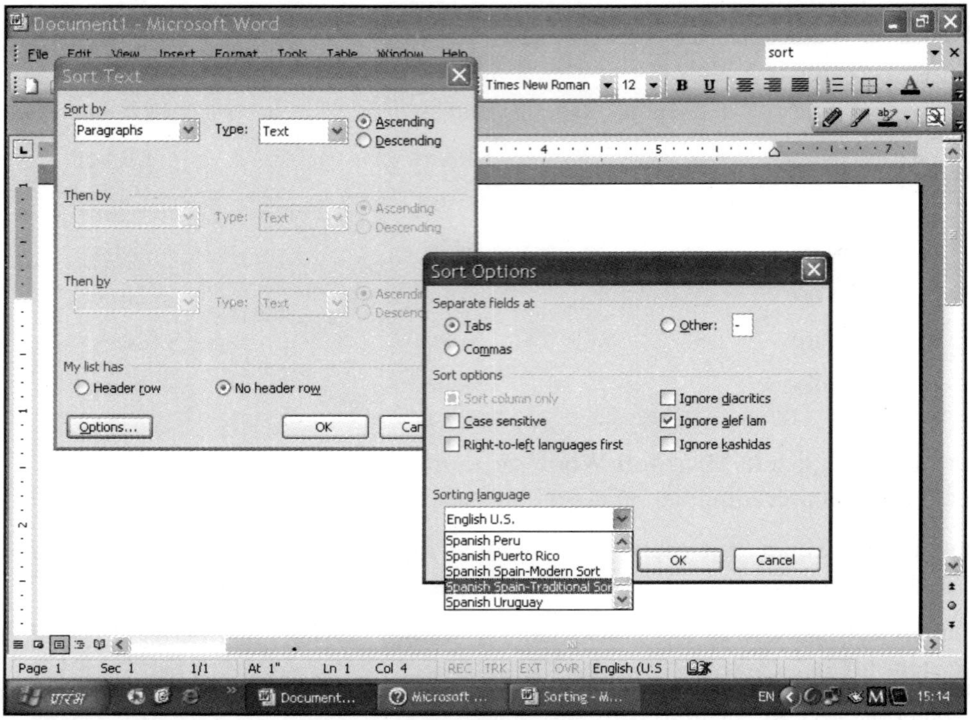

Figure 88: Sorting according to specific language rules

What you have learned

1. Need for language settings in Microsoft Office
2. Language specific features of Microsoft Word
3. Language specific features of Microsoft Excel
4. Language specific features of Microsoft Access
5. Language specific features of Microsoft FrontPage
6. Indian languages in OpenOffice
7. Sorting multilingual texts

7. Indic and other Languages Everywhere

Password in languages

As the password is typed in Yahoo!Mail, one is reminded that password is case-sensitive, i.e., uppercase letters are different from lowercase letters. However, in multi-script situation (which is often inevitable in multilingual environment), it must be kept in mind that password is not just case-sensitive, ***but is also script sensitive***! Many applications and utilities allow passwords in any script. So, for example, the password may be in a combination of Devanagari, Arabic and Latin scripts! In Microsoft Windows and Microsoft Office applications, passwords may be entered in any language supported by the operating system.

The illustration in Figure 89 is the login window of Microsoft Windows with Hindi interface. The computer is password protected, and password is being asked. "HI" next to the textbox for password indicates that the text, i.e., the password, will be entered in Hindi—possibly in Devanagari script—even though what will appear on the screen will be the usual big-sized dots for each character typed. If the password is in Hindi, one can straightaway enter the password. However, if the password is in a different language (i.e., script), one will have to select the script first by selecting the language. This can be done by clicking the arrow next to the "HI" box to select the appropriate language, or by Left-Alt-Shift keys. For example, if the password is "xyz123," then one will have to switch over to English language (Latin script) and then only enter the password in the illustration at Figure 89.

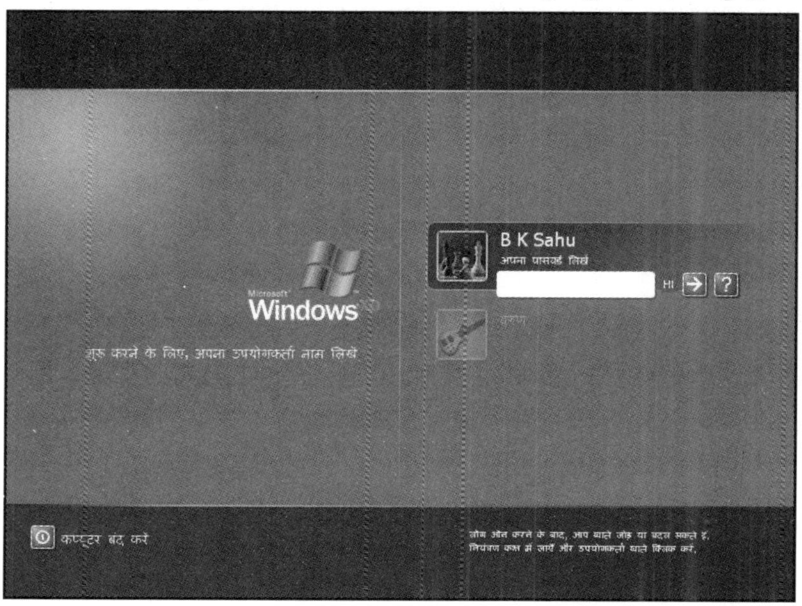

Figure 89: Passwords—not just case-sensitive, but also script-sensitive

Note: In the password box, the number of dots will correspond to the number of characters typed, and not the number of keystrokes or keys pressed. For example, Devanagari conjunct क्ष can be typed in Inscript keyboard layout with only one keystroke together with Shift key. However, क्ष consists of three characters क, ् and ष (codes 0915, 094D, and 0937 hex) in that sequence, and therefore three dots will appear for a single क्ष, and not just one dot. ZWJ, ZWNJ and ZWSP are also one character each, even though these characters do not have any visual shape of their own. Also, ú, æ, ±, Ø, ç and ô consists of only one character each, even though a combination of keys may have to be pressed (i.e., more than one keystroke are needed) to type any one of these characters.

Tips: Password may be in mixed scripts, provided the software permits it. For example, bरु6णकुMव may be a valid password.

Warning: It may not be possible to type in various scripts everywhere and in every computer. Some software may not work well with non-ASCII letters in the password. Therefore, it is advisable to keep password in Latin script (ASCII portion) only.

Webpage in right-to-left languages

Figure 90 illustrates how a webpage in right-to-left language, such as in Arabic language looks like. It may be noted that the vertical scroll bar appears on the left-hand side. (The scroll bar is usually on the right-hand side in the Internet Explorer window in a left-to-right language such as English or Hindi.) Also, the texts are 'left' aligned and not 'right' aligned. Furthermore, the orientation of the combo box is right-to-left. The orientation of the combo box may be selected as either right-to-left or left-to-right from its properties during the design phase.

The directionality of the webpage can be changed in the Internet Explorer by selecting the directionality from the menu bar in Internet Explorer: View → Encoding → Left-To-Right Document/Right-To-Left Document as shown in Figure 91.

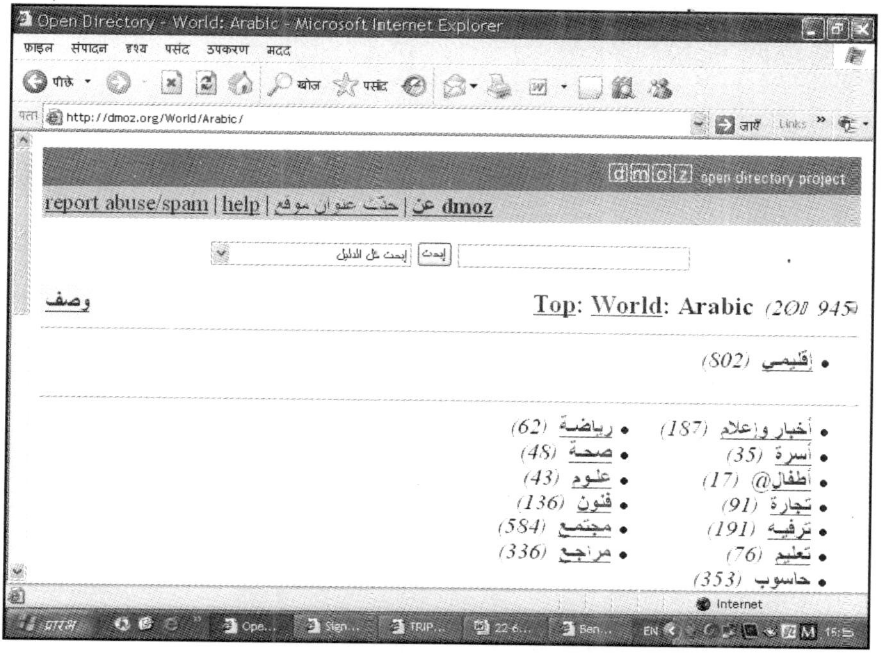

Figure 90: A webpage in Arabic language (right-to-left language)

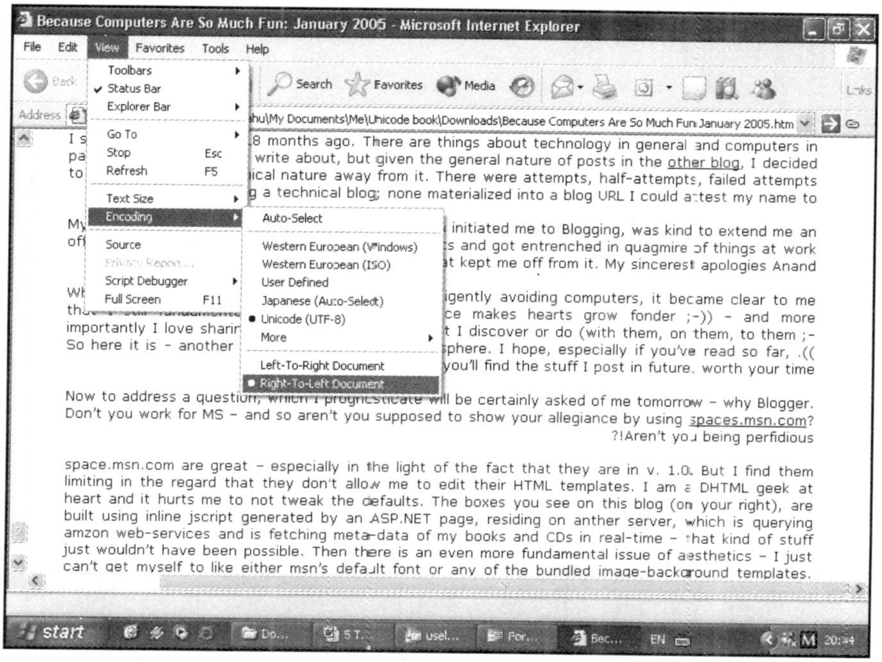

Figure 91: Selecting directionality in Internet Explorer

Figure 92 shows another webpage in Arabic language. This is the screenshot of the official webpage of Microsoft in Arabic.

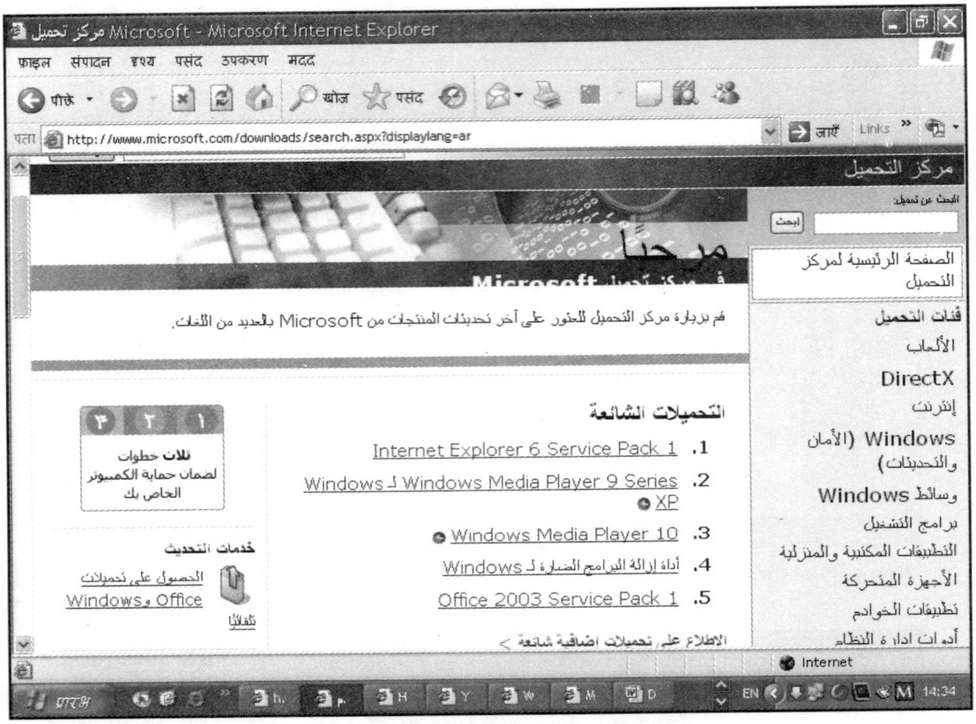

Figure 92: Another webpage in Arabic language (right-to-left language)

Webpage and Internet search in Indic and other languages

Even though English is still the dominant language in the cyberspace, and most websites are in that language, websites are increasingly being written in non-English languages. Websites are available not only in English and European languages, but also in Arabic-script based languages, Indic languages, East-Asian languages, and even in obscure languages of the world. Indic language websites are no longer mostly in non-standard fonts. These are increasingly in Unicode compliant fonts.

Figure 93 shows the homepage of http://www.google.co.in in Tamil language. In the search engines, the search key can be in Devanagari script (or, in another script, or scripts). It is not necessary that one must search only in Tamil script in the Tamil homepage of http://www.google.co.in. One can search in Devanagari script (and other scripts as well) from the Tamil website, as also from websites in other languages. One can perform a single search with search key containing words in different scripts. It may be surprising to see that the cyberspace is crowded with lot many website in all the Indic languages.

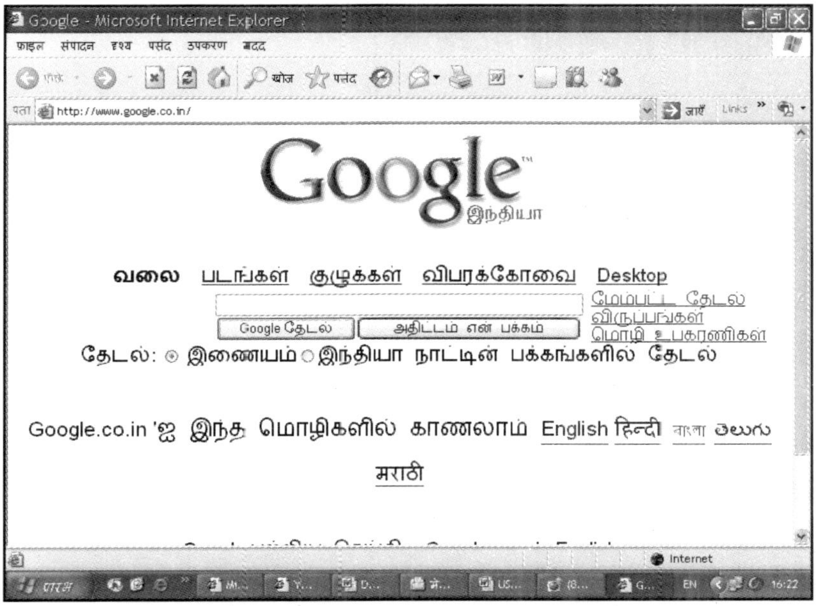

Figure 93: http://www.google.co.in in Tamil

Figure 94 illustrates searching of the Internet with the Hindi word भारत as the search key in the search engine at http://www.msn.com. The key words in the search field need not be in one language or script only. The key words can be in more than one script in a single search, including a mixture of left-to-right and right-to-left scripts.

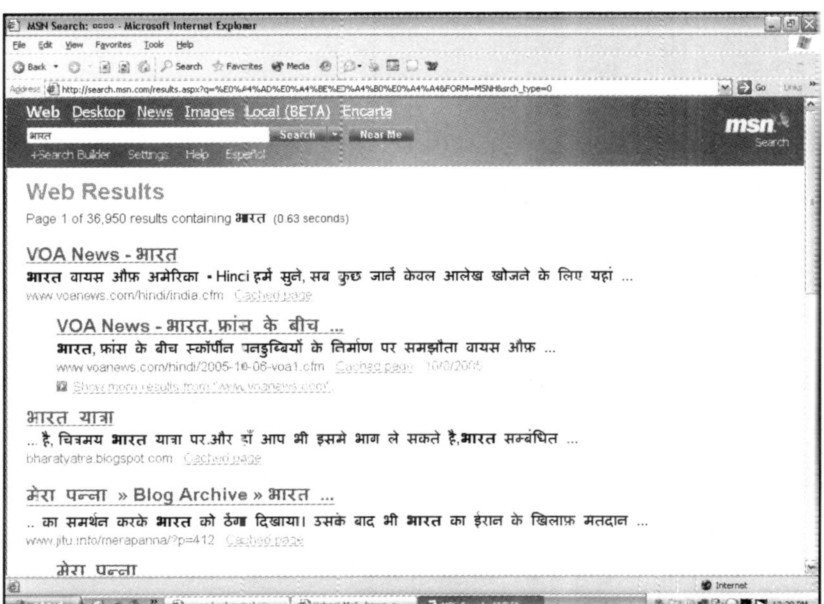

Figure 94: Searching भारत by search engine at http://www.msn.com

URL and e-mail ID in Indic scripts

Internet Explorer allows going to a website with URL in Devanagari (and also other scripts). At the time of writing of this book, not many useful websites with URL in Indic scripts were available. The URL http://www.हिंदी.com served only to redirect to the website http://www.hindi.co.in. The websites with URLs http://www.বাংলা.com and http://www.தமிழ்.com, though accessible, did not offer much useful information.

A webpage is accessed as per the following address format:

```
http://example.com:992/animal/bird?species=seagull#wings
\__/  \_________/ \_/\__________/ \______________/ \___/
 |        |        |    |           /              /
scheme   host    port  path      query    fragment
```

Parts of the address may be in Indic and Arabic scripts. There are several examples where the path, query and fragment etc are in Indic and Arabic scripts.

Note: Certain plug-ins and components may be needed in the Internet Explorer for identification configuration settings, so that website with URL in non-ASCII characters can be browsed. For example, such plug-in components were available in the website http://idn.verisign-grs.com. The plug-in may be needed even to browse websites with URL address in Russian script, and even for the non-ASCII portion of Latin script also.

Internationalized Domain Name (IDN) and Punycode

Internationalized Domain Names (IDNs) are web addresses that are displayed as non-ASCII characters in the web browser address bar. This allows websites to display their address in native language and character set. The IDN, such as ΣΦΩ.net or कखग.com is mapped into punycode format. In punycode, a Unicode character string is mapped into a string of printable ASCII characters. For illustration, Punycode of a few IDNs are as follows: சினிமா.com (xn--hlc4ap8dcb.com), खोज.com (xn--21bm4l.com), भाषा.com (xn--q2buub.com), عربي.com (xn--ngbrx4e.com). One may enter the punycodes in the browser address bar, instead of the IDNs.

IDN and phishing concerns

Because Internationalized Domain Names allow websites to use non-ASCII characters in their name, it is easier for phishers to create a spoofed website. These attacks are because of the fact that different characters in different languages may look the same, or different combination of characters may look the same. The following is a small list of letters in Latin (English), Greek and Cyrillic (Russian) scripts that look the same (hexadecimal Unicode code points are given in parentheses):

Latin letter	Greek letter	Cyrillic letter
A (0041)	A (0391)	A (0410)
B (0042)	B (0392)	B (0412)
C (0043)		C (0421)
E (0045)	E (0395)	E (0415)
H (0048)	H (0397)	H (041D)
I (0049)	I (0399)	I (0406)
J (004A)		J (0408)
K (004B)	K (039A)	K (041A)
M (004D)	M (039C)	M (041C)
N (004E)	N (039D)	
O (004F)	O (039F)	O (041E)
P (0050)	P (03A1)	P (0420)
S (0053)		S (0405)
T (0028)	T (03A4)	T (0422)
X (0028)	X (03A7)	X (0425)
Y (0059)	Y (03A5)	У (0423)
Z (0028)	Z (0396)	

So, unless one has typed it oneself or verified the Unicode characters/punycode of the character string, one cannot be sure that the link looking like *microsoft.com* or *google.com* one is clicking will not take you to a spoofing website, as the letters in the domain name may be not in English, but in Greek, Cyrillic or some other script!

File, folder and e-mail in Indic and other languages

As it may be obvious by now, it is possible to have names of file, folders, icons, shortcuts, networks, drives etc in Indic and other languages. It could even be in a mixture of languages—even a mixture of right-to-left and left-to-right languages. Figure 101 shows an example where file/folder/drive/network names are in Hindi. One can even e-mail in Hindi and other languages, and even in a mixture of several languages, including mixture of left-to-right and right-to-left languages.

Warning: Microsoft Windows 98 did not allow file names even in non-English European languages, not to talk of Arabic and Indic scripts. We have come a long way since then. However, we may still be somewhat away from having Indic language everywhere. For example, Yahoo!Mail did not allow e-mail ID in Devanagari script. Some CD-writers did not work well with file/folder names in non-Latin scripts (such as Devanagari script). Normal Adobe PageMaker 7.0 did not accept Indic and Arabic texts. PDF files could be searched with key in Arabic script, but not in Devanagari script, unless the key was copy-pasted. (These deficiencies might have been removed by now!) As such, Latin script should not be banished from one's computer, at least not in haste or without realizing the consequences!

What you have learned

1. Password in non-English languages
2. Webpage in right-to-left languages
3. Internet search in Indic/Arabic scripts
4. Browsing websites with URL in non-ASCII letters
5. File etc names in Indic/Arabic scripts

8. Indic Version of Microsoft Windows and Office

Non-English versions of Microsoft Windows

So far, we have seen that we can type in, do data processing in and communicate in Indic languages, Arabic-script based languages, European languages, East Asian languages and virtually any language of the world. However, while we could do all these, Microsoft Windows and Microsoft Office etc were themselves in English. All the menu items, property settings and helps were in English. This puts severe handicaps on the populace not well-versed in the language.

Fortunately, today many software applications are available in Indic, East Asian and European etc languages. Microsoft Windows and Office already have versions in several Indian languages. More and more Indian language versions of popular software can only be expected in future.

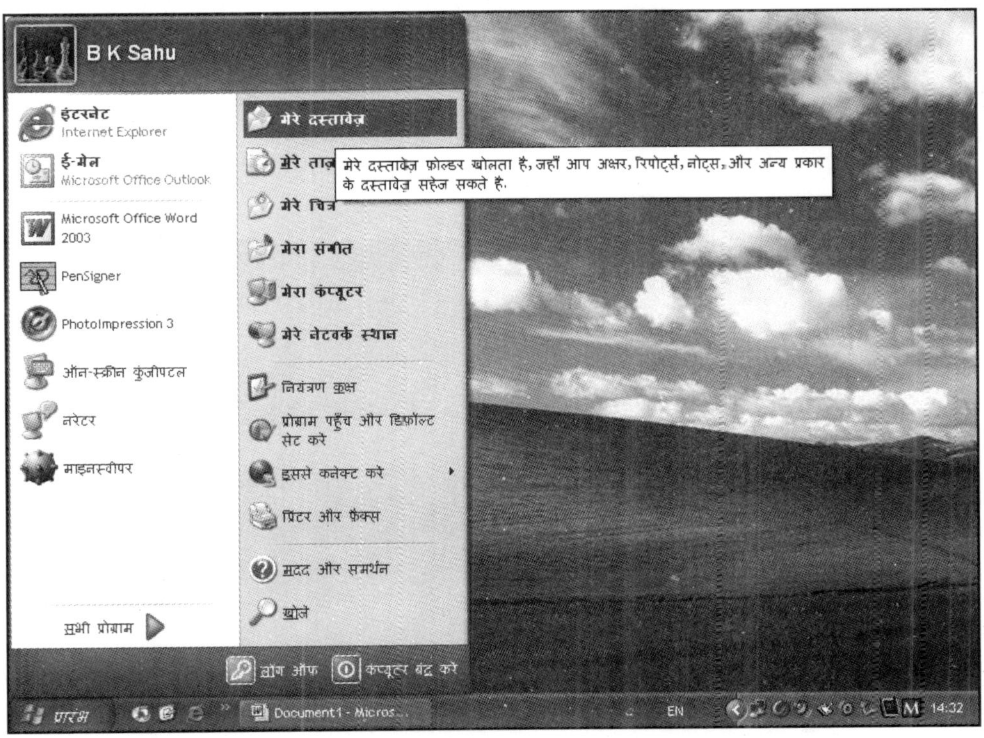

Figure 95: 'Start' becomes 'प्रारंभ' in Hindi version of Microsoft Windows

Figure 95 shows the screenshot from the Hindi version of Microsoft Windows (that is, with Windows Hindi Interface Pack installed). It may be noted that all—or rather, most of—the English words are in Hindi: not just in Devanagari script, but are in real Hindi, and are in Hindi by default. So, 'All Program' is 'सभी प्रोग्राम', 'My Document' is 'मेरे दस्तावेज़', 'Search' is 'खोजें' etc. All the Hindi names are the default names that come with Microsoft Windows operating system.

While Hindi version of Microsoft Windows is a very laudable attempt, there may be scope for improvement in the quality of the translation to Hindi. For example, in the balloon hint on मेरे दस्तावेज़ (My Documents) as shown in Figure 95, 'letter' has been translated to अक्षर (which means a letter of the alphabet) in Hindi, but the contextual meaning of 'letter' is पत्र (epistle or written communication), and not अक्षर (letter of alphabet). The word 'letter' means both अक्षर and पत्र, but the contextual meaning is पत्र, and not अक्षर. One will not store a single letter of the alphabet in a folder, but complete reports. (Also, "Sec" appearing in the status bar of Microsoft Word was translated as सेकंड. Actually, "Sec" is short form of Section, and not second. So, the Hindi translation should have been translated as भाग or अनुभाग, not सेकंड!)

Tips: If a file, folder, icon or shortcut can be renamed, it can be renamed in an altogether different language and script. This is true even for English-language version of Microsoft Windows. For example, on right-clicking a program name appearing in the Start → All Program, if 'Rename' is there in the shortcut menu, one may rename it in Hindi in Devanagari script—or, in other language(s) and/or script(s). This has been illustrated in Figure 96, where "My Document" is being renamed. For example, even in the English version of Microsoft Windows, one may rename 'My Documents' to 'मेरे दस्तावेज़', 'Desktop' to 'डेस्कटॉप' etc.

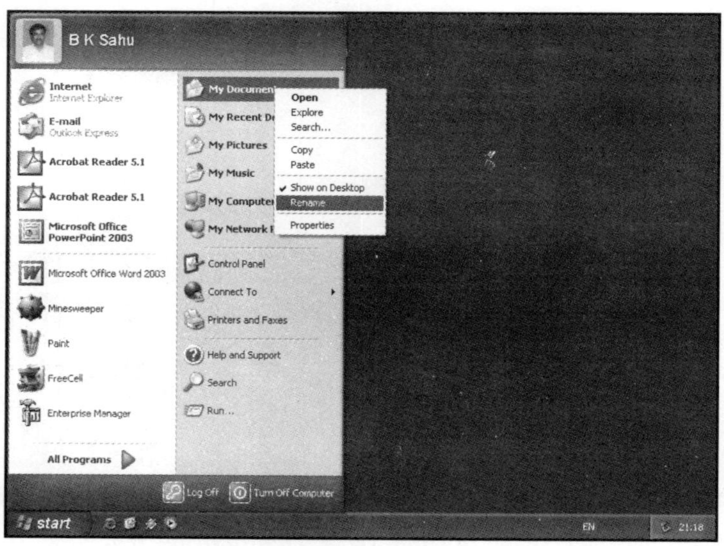

Figure 96: Renaming of "My Document"

Installing language interface packs in Microsoft Windows

One may buy Indian language edition of Microsoft Windows (if available), and install it in one's computer. Microsoft Windows website http:// www.microsoft.com and http://www.bhashaindia.com offered download files for Windows Indian language interface packs (LIPs). The websites may be searched for downloading the desired language interface pack, and then it may be installed on the computer machine. An illustration is at Figure 97, where the link on the appropriate language is to be clicked for downloads in that language.

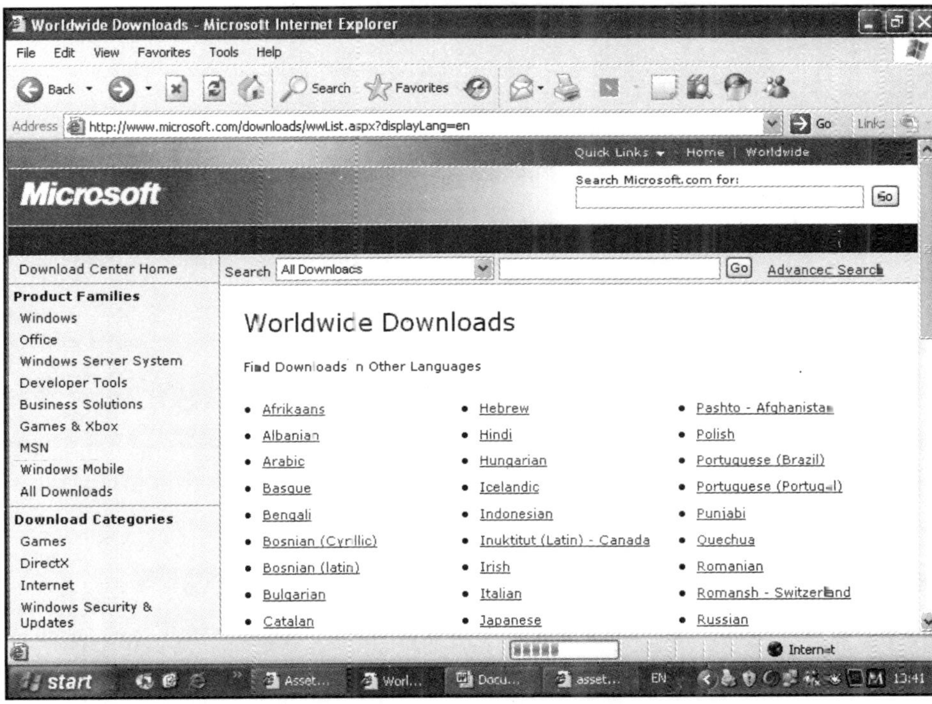

Figure 97: Download in various languages in http://www.microsoft.com

Interface packs for Microsoft Windows and Office are available in several languages now. including many Indian languages. Figure 98 shows two windows of Microsoft webpage that illustrates the hyperlinks to interface pack downloads in Gujarati and Urdu languages.

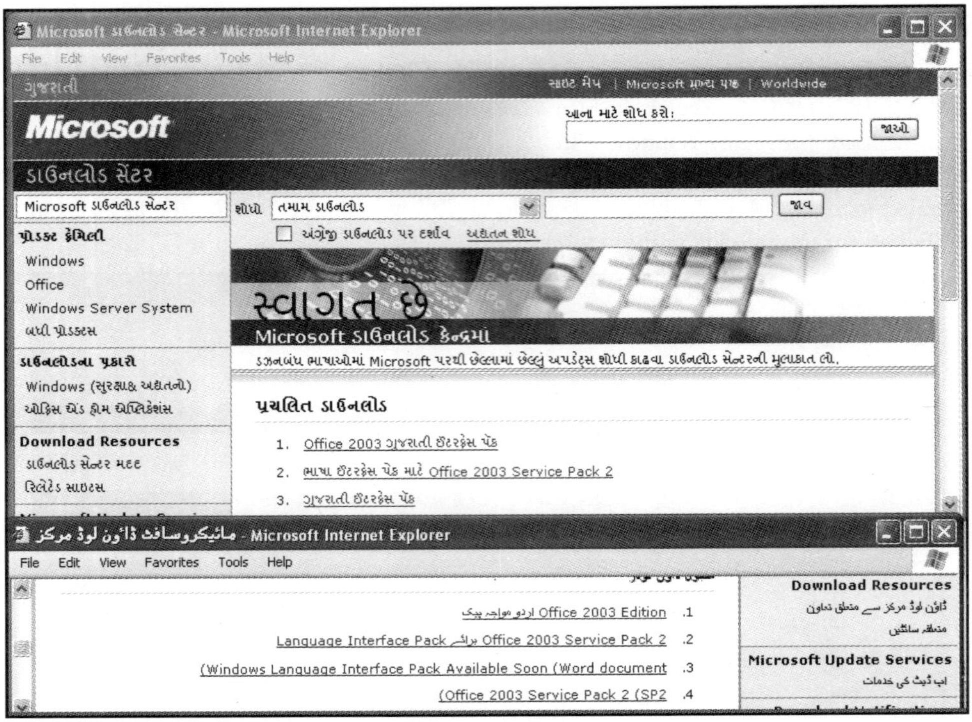

Figure 98: Selecting interfaces in Gujarati and Urdu

The feel of Microsoft Windows in Indian languages

The following pages describe how Microsoft Windows XP with Hindi and Bengali language interface packs installed looks like and feels like, but it could be any other supported language. In the following pages, the familiar icons, options, menus and windows etc in English-language version of Microsoft Windows are shown in Hindi-language interface of the operating system.

Figure 99 shows offline help of Microsoft Windows in Hindi. However, most of the help were still in English. Only a portion of the help files was in Hindi. It may be expected that more and more help files will be available in Hindi in future.

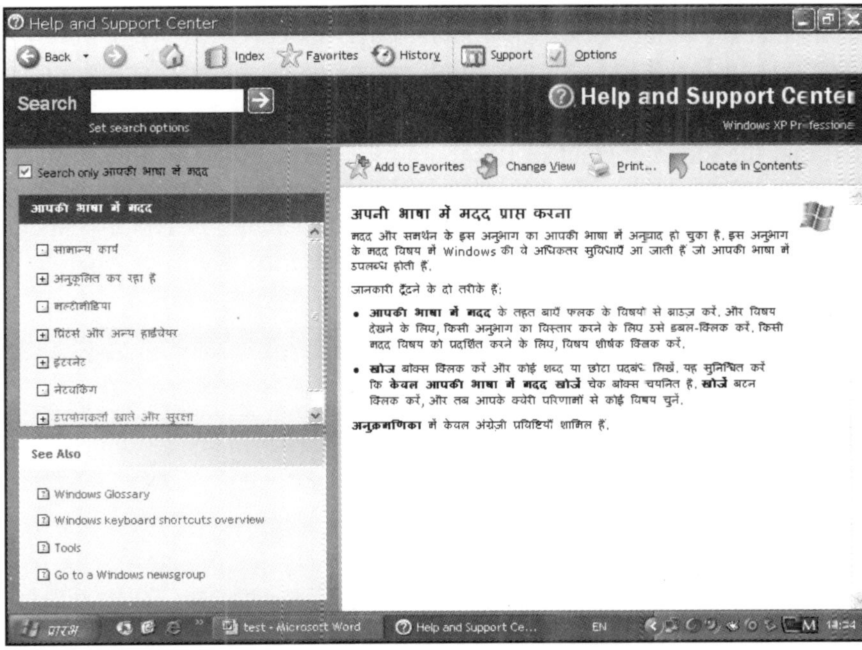

Figure 99: Offline help in Microsoft Windows in Hindi

Right-click of mouse produces shortcut menu in Hindi, or at least partly in Hindi. This has been illustrated in the screenshot at Figure 100.

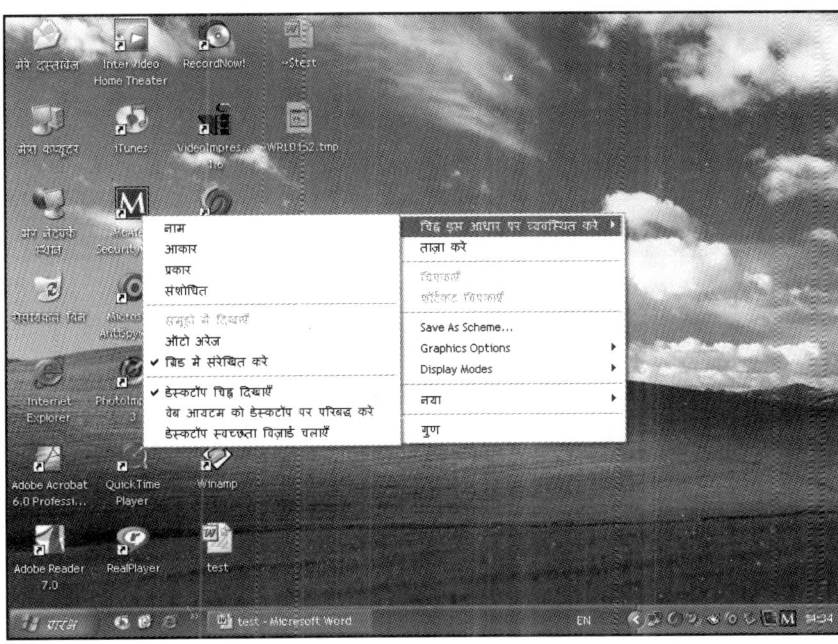

Figure 100: Shortcut menus in Hindi

Figure 101 shows that the names of disks, folders, files, networks etc are in Hindi. The items in the Control Panel are in Hindi too. All the Hindi names in Devanagari script are default names under Microsoft Windows.

It may be noted that the icons in Control Panel are by default sorted in multilingual alphabetical order. The alphabetical order of the names of the icons in English is different from that in Hindi. Therefore, the relative positions of various icons in Control Panel in Hindi-language version of Microsoft Windows are different from that in the English-language version of Microsoft Windows.

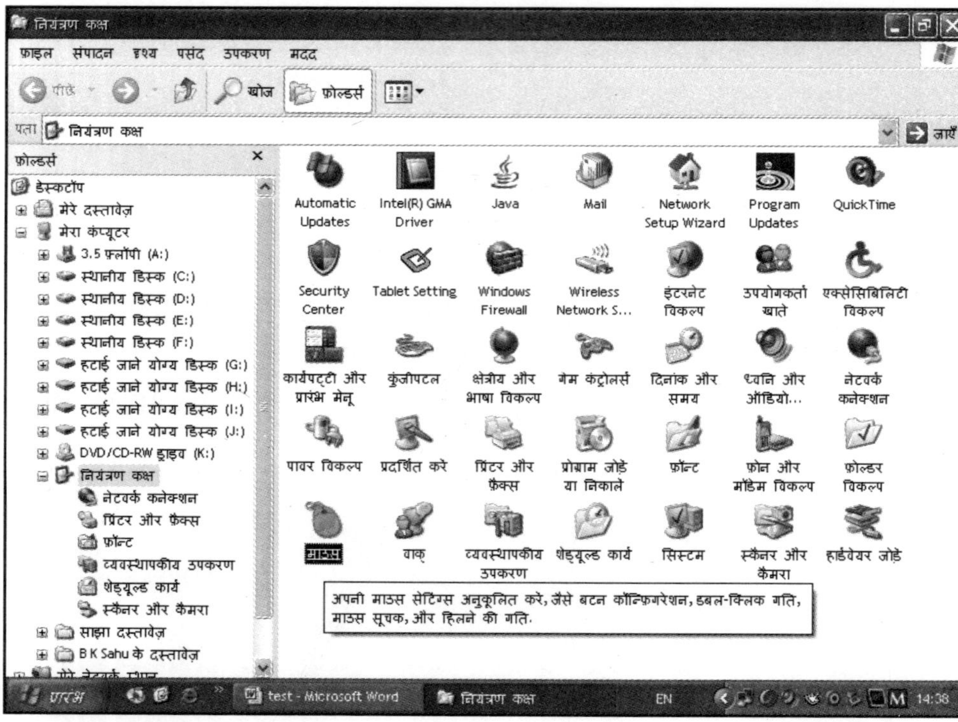

Figure 101: Control Panel in Hindi

Note: With Indian language interface, Indic languages will be automatically selected in Regional and Language Options (क्षेत्रीय और भाषा विकल्प) under Control Panel (नियंत्रण कक्ष) (see Figure 15). Indic and other languages option remains selected by default (and also dimmed, so it cannot be de-selected).

As illustrated in Figure 102, menu bars are in Hindi too!

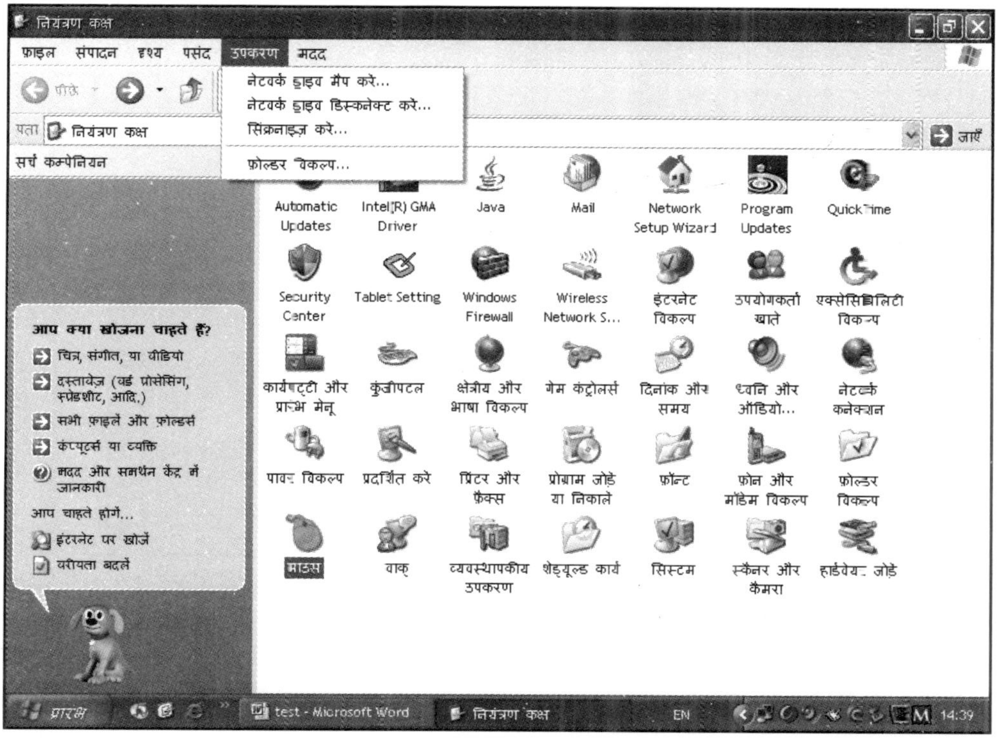

Figure 102: Menu bar in Hindi

Note: In Internet Explorer 7 and Fire-Fox, language setting is important to avoid phishing spoof attack. It is possible for letters and symbols in some languages to be used to impersonate English language websites for phishing scams. If one browses to a website with a non-ASCII language address, but one does not have the language available, a warning message may be displayed.

It is advisable that the number of selected languages in the web browser be kept to a minimum.

For security purposes, web browser may display non-ASCII web address in a standard ASCII text encoding: punycode.

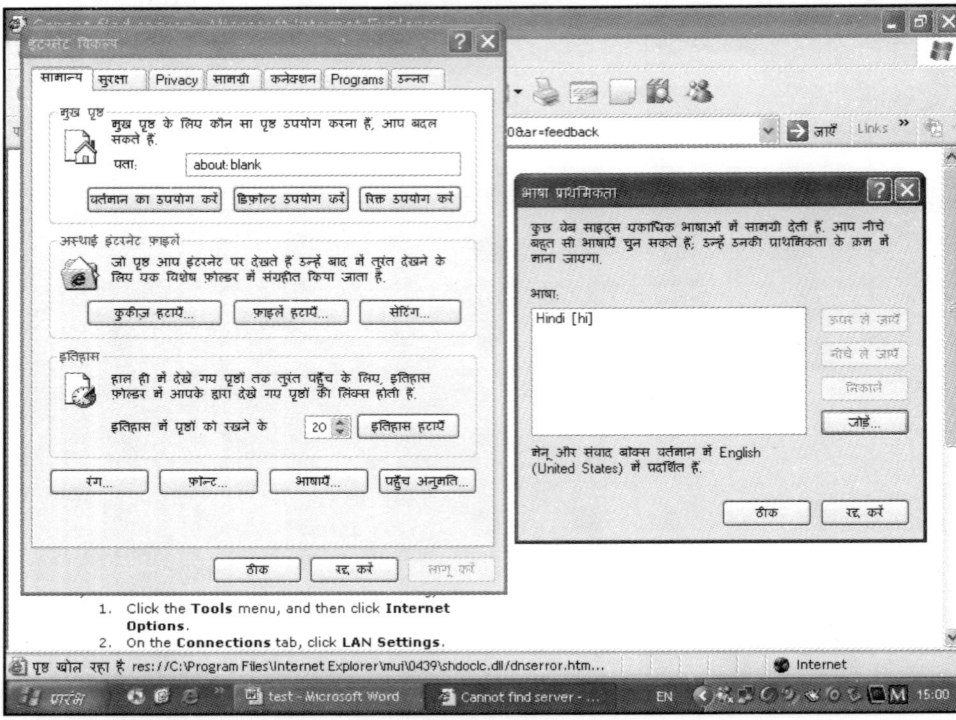

Figure 103: Setting Hindi as the primary language in the Internet Explorer

In "All Programs" in English-language version of Microsoft Windows, the icon Accessories is usually near the top of the list of items (see Figure 50). However, in Hindi-language version of Microsoft Windows, Accessories is named सहायक उपकरण, and it appears almost near the end of the list (see Figure 104). This is possibly because of alphabetical ordering of the items. ('Accessories' almost tops in alphabetical sorting, and सहायक उपकरण almost bottoms in it. Multilingual sorting discussed in Chapter 6 may be referred to.)

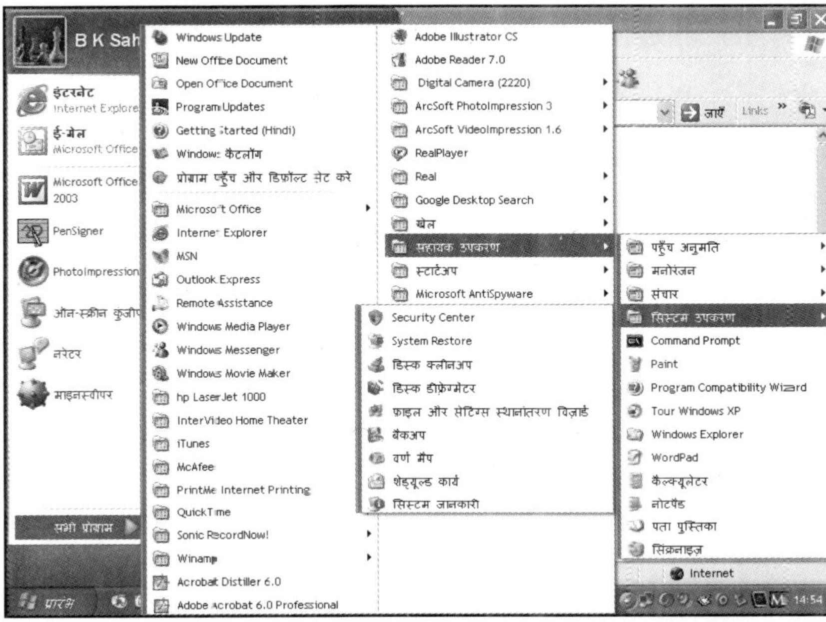

Figure 104: Accessories in "All Programs" is near the bottom of the list of icons

It is not the language interface for Microsoft Windows is available in Hindi only. Indeed, it is available in several languages, including many Indian languages. As an example, Figure 105, Figure 106 and Figure 107 illustrates Microsoft Windows with Bengali language interface pack installed.

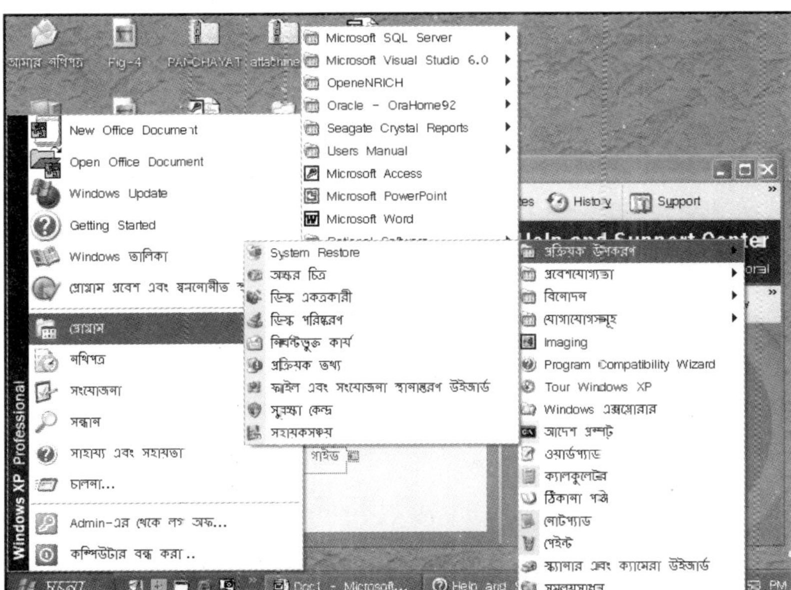

Figure 105: Microsoft Windows in Bengali Interface (Start menu)

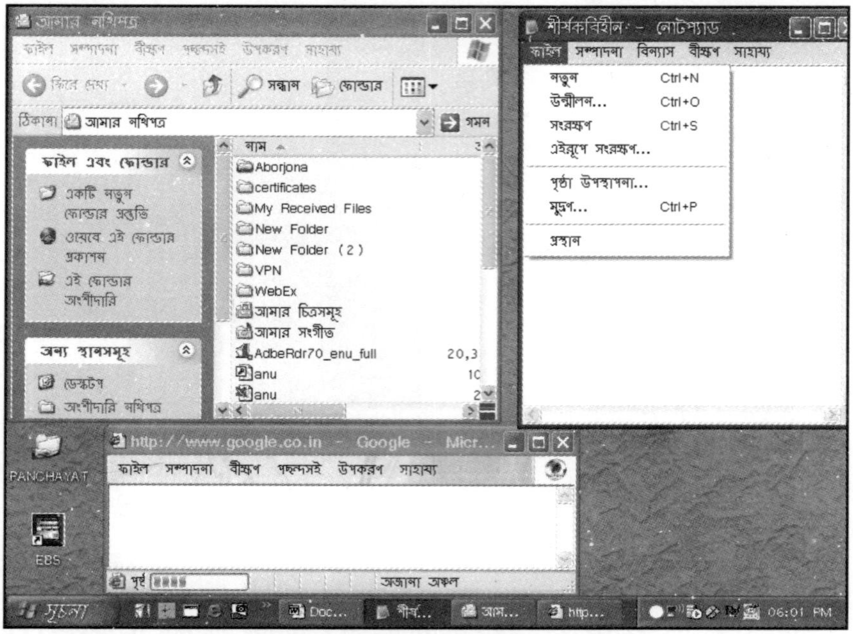

Figure 106: Windows in Bengali Interface (Notepad etc)

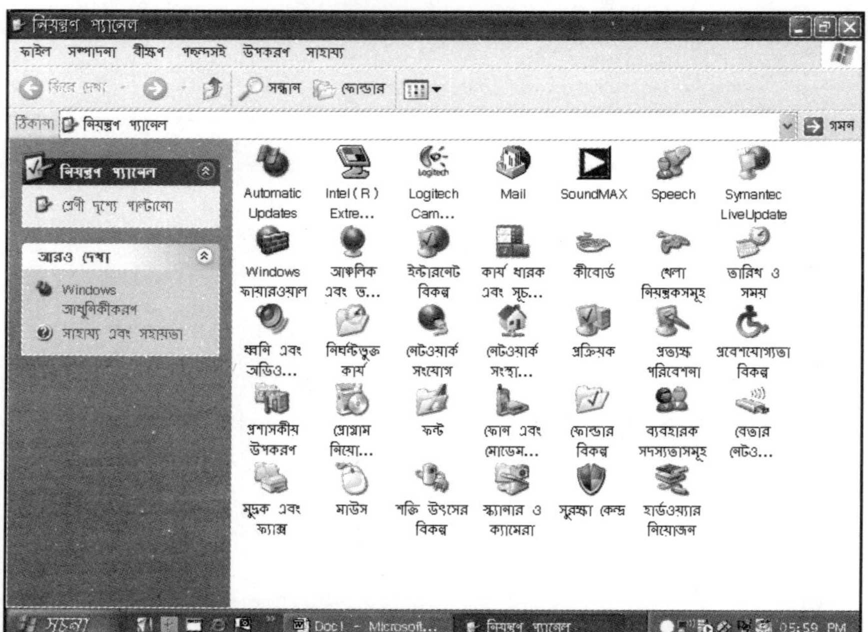

Figure 107: Control Panel in Bengali Interface (Control Panel)

Uninstalling Indian language interface

All said and done—and after working with Indian language interface of Microsoft Windows, one may want to switch over to the English language version of Microsoft Windows. One can switch over to the English version Microsoft Windows by simply uninstalling the Windows Hindi Interface Pack. For uninstalling the Windows Hindi Interface Pack, the following steps may be taken:

1. Open the "Add or Remove Programs" under the "Control Panel."
2. Windows Hindi Interface Pack may be uninstalled as a program is usually uninstalled. This has been illustrated in Figure 108.
3. The system may have to be restarted for the un-installation process to be completed.

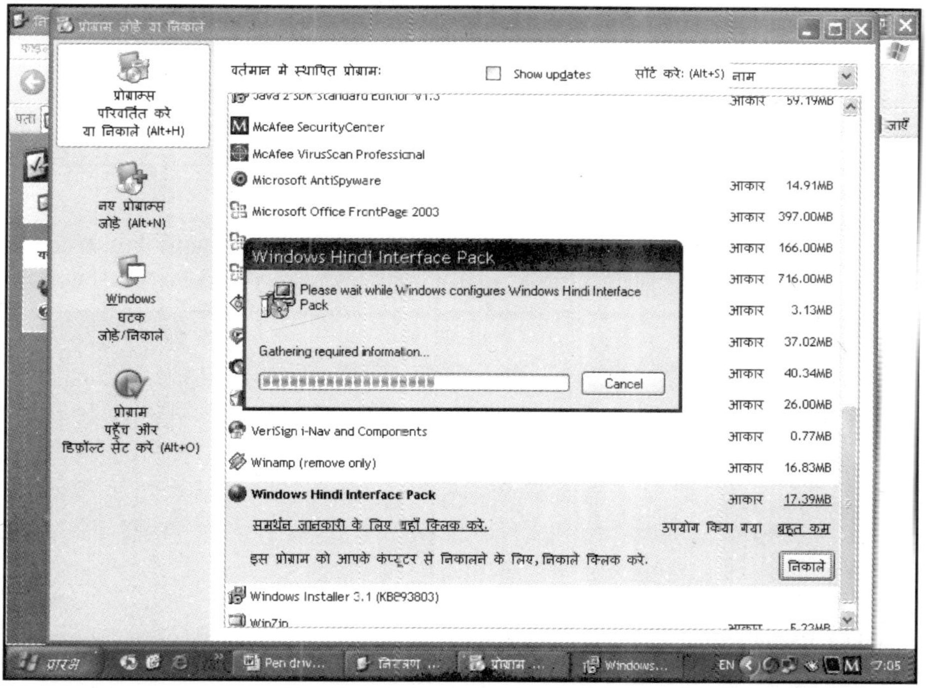

Figure 108: Uninstalling Windows Hindi Interface Pack

Primary language under Linux

The primary language in Linux operating system environment can be changed through the "Control Center" item "Language." This is illustrated in Figure 109, where another primary language is being selected in place of English(US). After selecting the desired primary language, one has to click "Accept" button. The system may have to be restarted for the new primary language to appear.

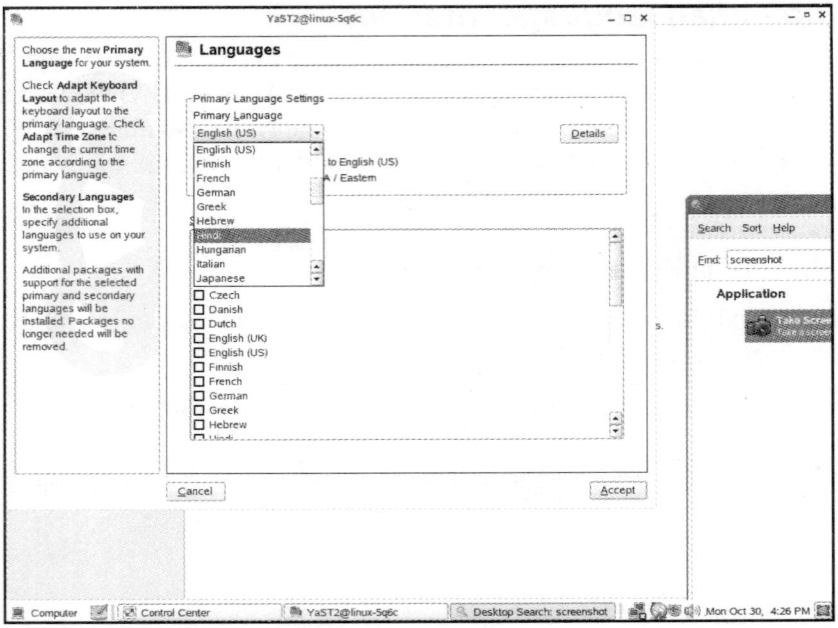

Figure 109: Primary language under Linux

Figure 110 illustrates SUSE Linux operating system environment with Hindi as the primary language. At the time of writing of this book, many features were yet to be translated into Hindi.

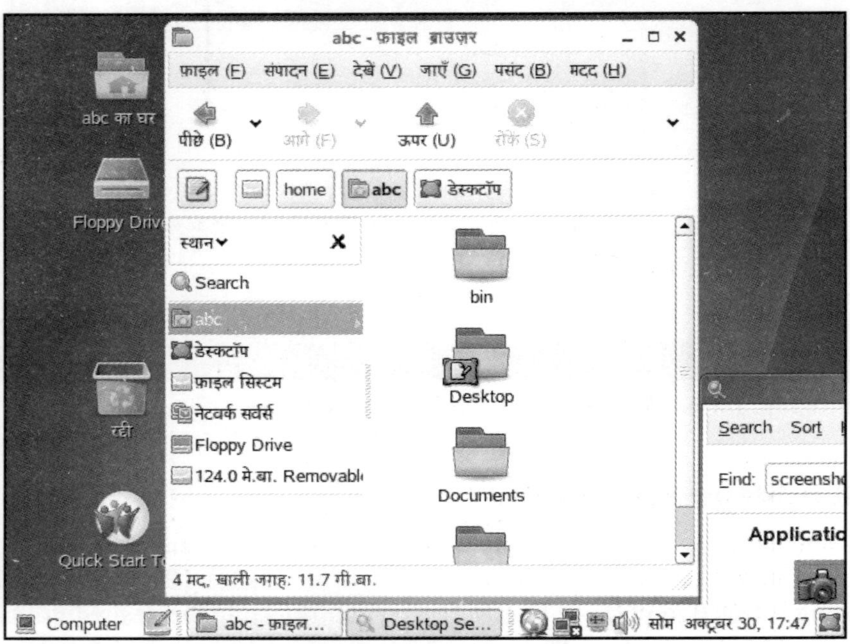

Figure 110: Linux with Hindi as primary language

Language interface for Microsoft Office 2003

Language interface packs are available for Microsoft Office 2003. For example, it may be downloaded from http://www.microsoft.com or http://www.bhashaindia.com. It may be downloaded and installed in the computer machine. Hindi version of Microsoft Office 2003 is available. Proofing tools are available for several Indian languages, including Hindi, Gujarati, Kannada, Marathi, Punjabi, Tamil, Urdu and Telugu etc.

The steps to install language interface is as follows:

1. Install the language interface pack(s) for Microsoft Office for the specific language(s) in the computer machine.
2. Open the Microsoft Office 2003 Language Settings, and select the appropriate language through Microsoft Office 2003 Language Settings, as illustrated earlier in Chapter 6 (see Figure 67).
3. As illustrated in Figure 111, select appropriate languages for Microsoft Office and help from among the languages whose interface packs have been installed. For example, if one wants the Microsoft Office to be in Nepali, then Nepali language may be selected.

The language settings continue to remain the same even after logging off, unless the settings are changed by the user. One can change the language settings anytime. However, settings take effect next time one opens the Microsoft Office application software.

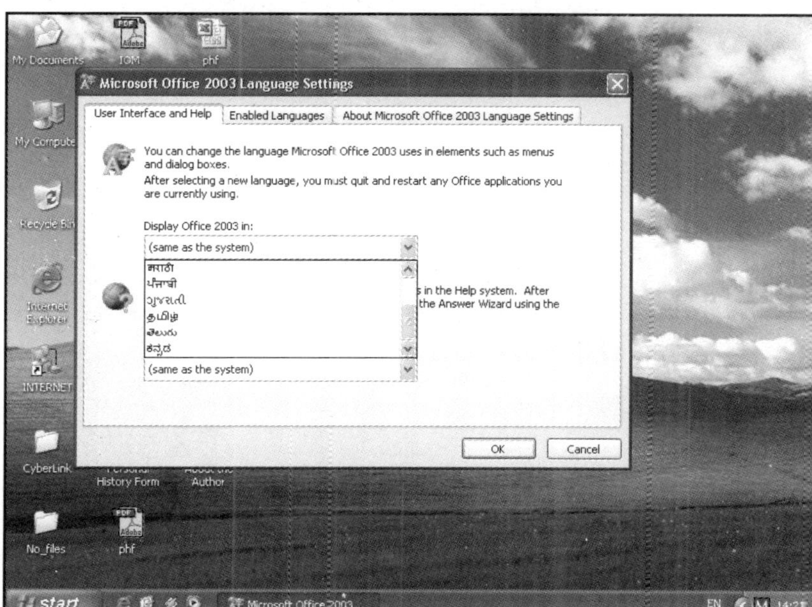

Figure 111: Selecting interface language in Microsoft Office 2003

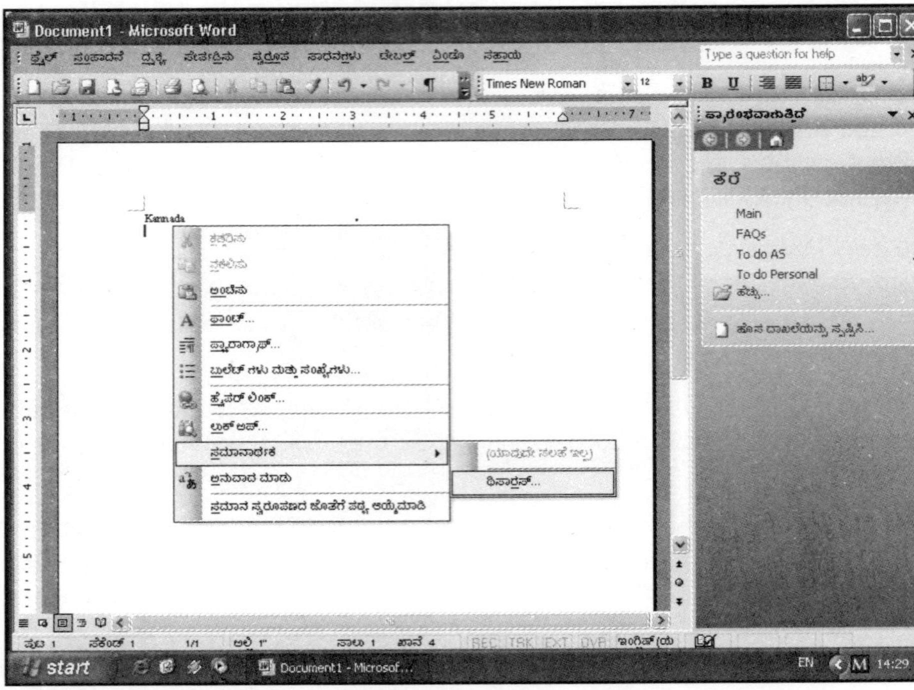

Figure 112: Microsoft Word with Kannada interface pack

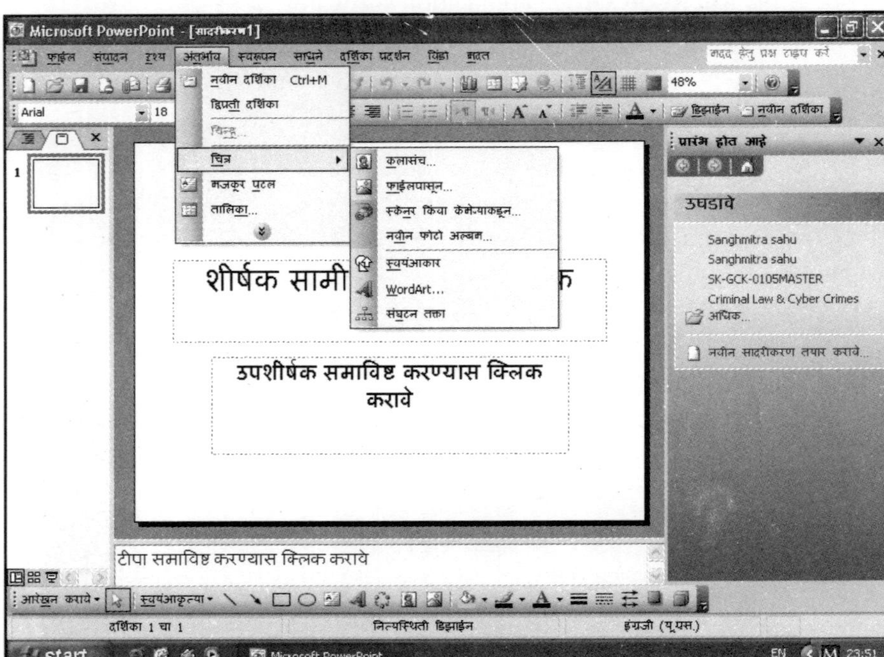

Figure 113: Microsoft PowerPoint with Marathi interface pack

Figure 114 illustrates Microsoft Excel with Urdu interface pack. It may be noted that the columns A, B, C etc are numbered from right to left, and right to left! All—or, rather most—menu bar items are in Urdu.

Indian language versions of Open Office and Fire-Fox may also be available. For example, some of these may be downloaded from the links in the website http://www.ildc.gov.in; see http://www.ildc.gov.in/hindi/hdownloadhindi.htm.

Figure 114: Microsoft Excel with Urdu language interface

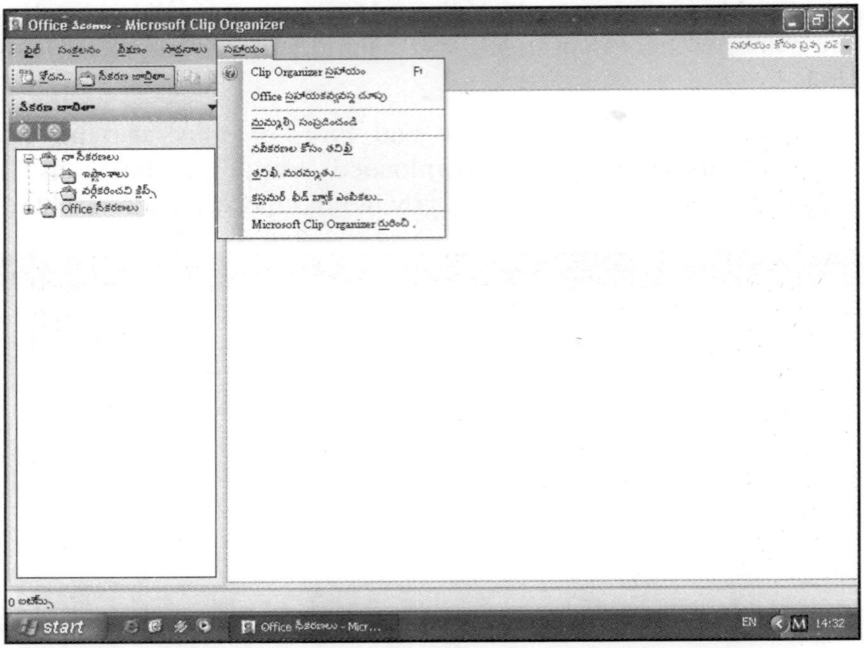

Figure 115: Microsoft Clip Organizer with Telugu language interface

Uninstalling language interface packs

All said and done, one may not want to remove the Microsoft Office language interface pack from one's computer. The language interface pack can be removed by following the under-mentioned steps:

1. Go to Control Panel → Add of Remove Programs, as has been illustrated in case of Microsoft Windows language interface pack.
2. Remove the language interface pack.
3. Restart the application.

What you have learned

1. Software are available in non-English languages, including Indic languages
2. Language interface packs are available for Microsoft Windows and Office for Indian languages
3. How Hindi and Bengali versions of Microsoft Windows feels like
4. How Kannada, Telugu, Marathi and Urdu versions of Microsoft Office feels like
5. How to uninstall Microsoft Windows and Office language interface

9. Thesaurus, Dictionary and Translation

Thesaurus in languages

Spell-checking, grammar checking, thesaurus and translation are important language-specific features of Microsoft Office. Besides, handwriting recognition and speech recognition are important language-specific features of Microsoft Windows. Handwriting and speech recognition have been described briefly (very briefly, actually!) in Chapter 3.

It is possible to perform checking of spelling and grammar only if the relevant proofing tools for the languages have been installed. Proofing tools for English, French and Spanish (including their various variants) are widely available in English version of Microsoft Office. Hindi version of Microsoft Office includes proofing tools for several languages including English, Hindi, Gujarati, Kannada, Marathi, Punjabi, Tamil and Telugu.

Thesaurus gives the meaning of words and phrases, and also words close in meaning to or relevant to the words and phrases. It also gives the antonyms to the words and phrases. One may either look up the synonyms (and in some cases even antonyms) of a word in the thesaurus, or replace the word with the shown synonyms or antonyms.

To use thesaurus, one will have to type the word one wants to look up in the thesaurus, unless an existing word in an open document is to be used. Let us say, one wants to use the thesaurus in Microsoft Word. For this, the word that is to be looked up may be right-clicked. Thereafter, one has to go to 'Synonyms'[28] in the shortcut menu that appears as shown in Figure 116. Alternatively, one may use thesaurus via the main menu bar as follows: Tools → Language → Thesaurus….

Warning: Only a limited number of words and phrases can be looked up in the thesaurus. Even among the listed words, only a few synonyms (and antonyms) may appear, some of which may not even be exact synonyms/antonyms.

Note: Thesaurus is language-specific. The thesaurus specific to the language of the current text is used. For example, if the word 'cow' in the text in Figure 116 were marked Spanish (Spain-Modern Sort), then Microsoft Word would look for the word in Spanish thesaurus even though it is obviously an English word.

[28] However, if the word is marked as having spelling or grammatical error, the option 'Synonyms' may not appear.

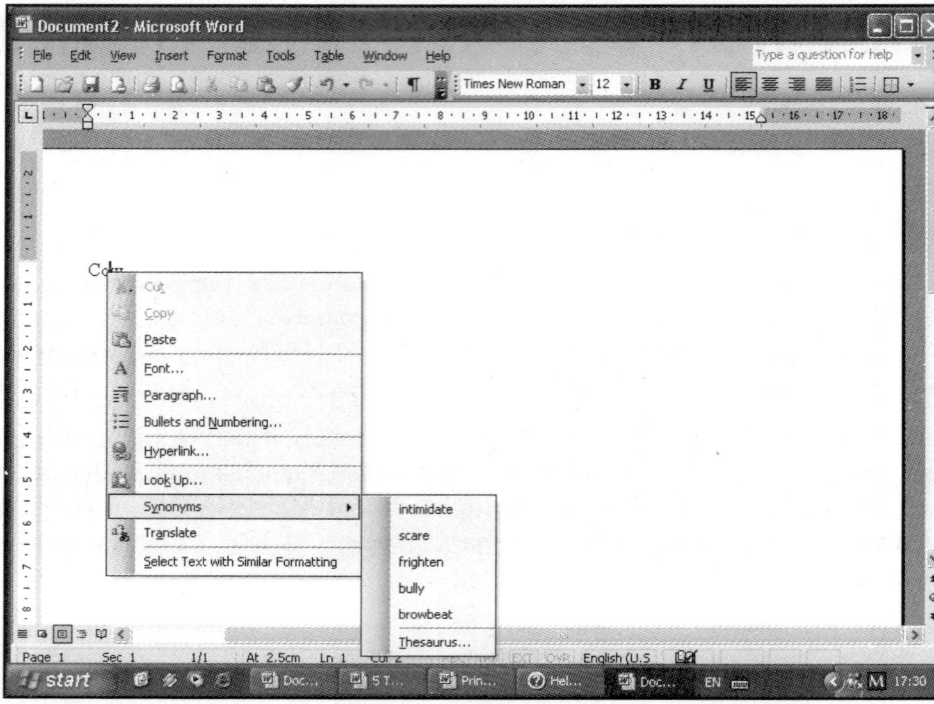

Figure 116: Using thesaurus

Dictionary in languages

If one is working with more than one language, or is working with more than one variant of the language (say, American English and British English), then it is advisable to have custom dictionary for each of the languages one works with, including variants of the same language. This will ensure that the customized words enter into the correct custom dictionaries. For example, *Pervez Musharraf* is spelled as *Pervez Moucharraf* in French; *Kashmir* is spelled as *Cachemire* in French. So, the custom words will be different in different languages.

Creating custom dictionary

1. In the Microsoft Word menu bar, go to Tool → Options…, and then select "Spelling & Grammar" tab.
2. Click the "Custom Dictionaries…" button. See Figure 117.
3. Click the button "Add…" to add a new dictionary
4. Select the appropriate language for the custom dictionary, say, by clicking "Modify…" button.
5. Ensure that the custom dictionary is not de-selected.

Note: If a custom dictionary has been de-selected (by un-checking it, see Figure 117), then that custom dictionary will remain dormant, and will not be used in the current checking of spelling.

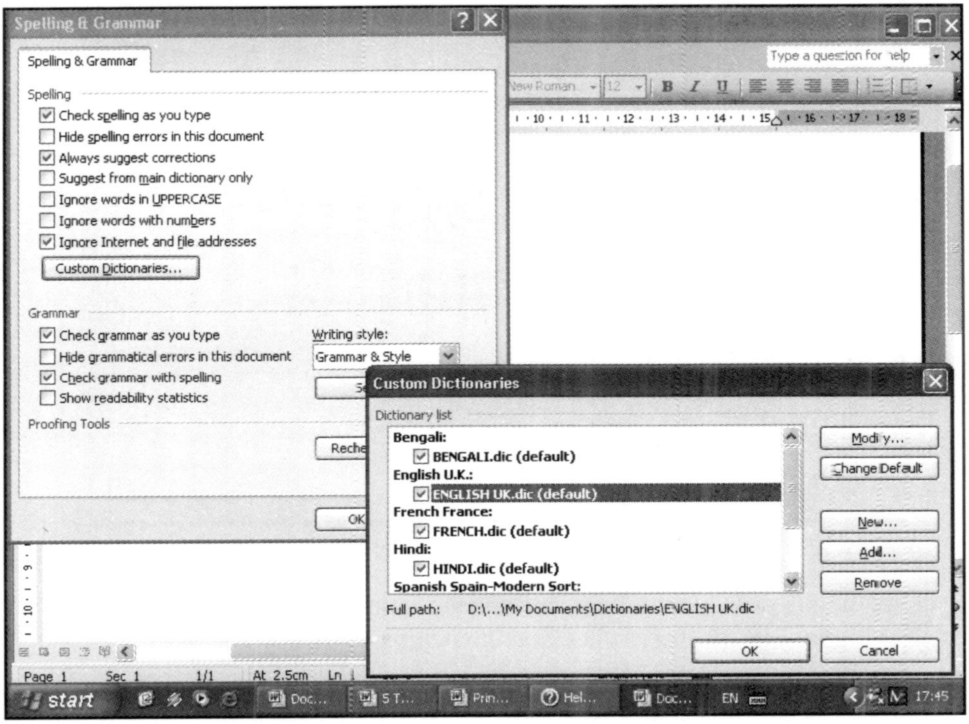

Figure 117: Custom dictionary

One may enter the words directly into the custom dictionary. This has been illustrated in Figure 118. In the illustration, the custom dictionary has been opened by clicking "Modify..." button, and attempt has been made to enter the word "Mahatma" in the custom dictionary. Alternatively, the words may be entered through "Add to Dictionary" option in the shortcut menu that appears on right-clicking the word when it shows spelling error.

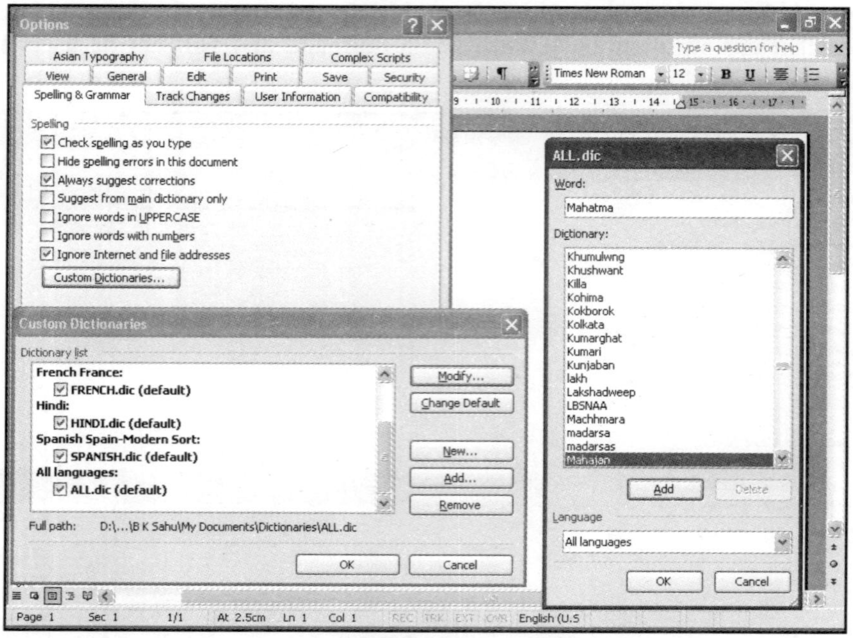

Figure 118: Adding a new word to the custom dictionary

Checking of spelling is possible not only in English, French and Spanish etc, but in many Indian languages also. Figure 119 illustrates checking of spelling in Urdu.

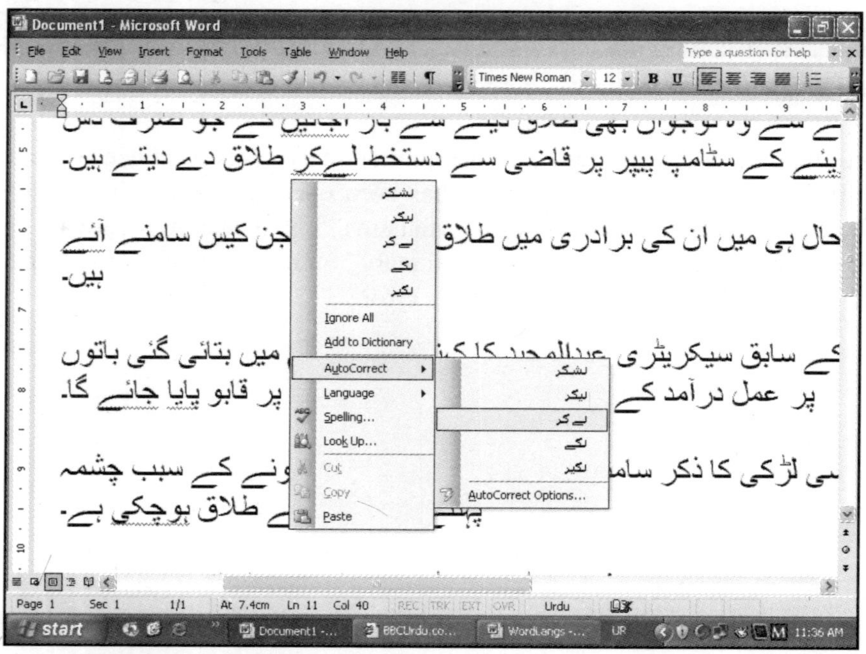

Figure 119: Spelling checking in Urdu

Figure 120 illustrates translation among English, Hindi and Gujarati languages using the Trilingual Smart Tag. Trilingual Smart Tag may be downloaded from the website http://www.bhashaindia.com.

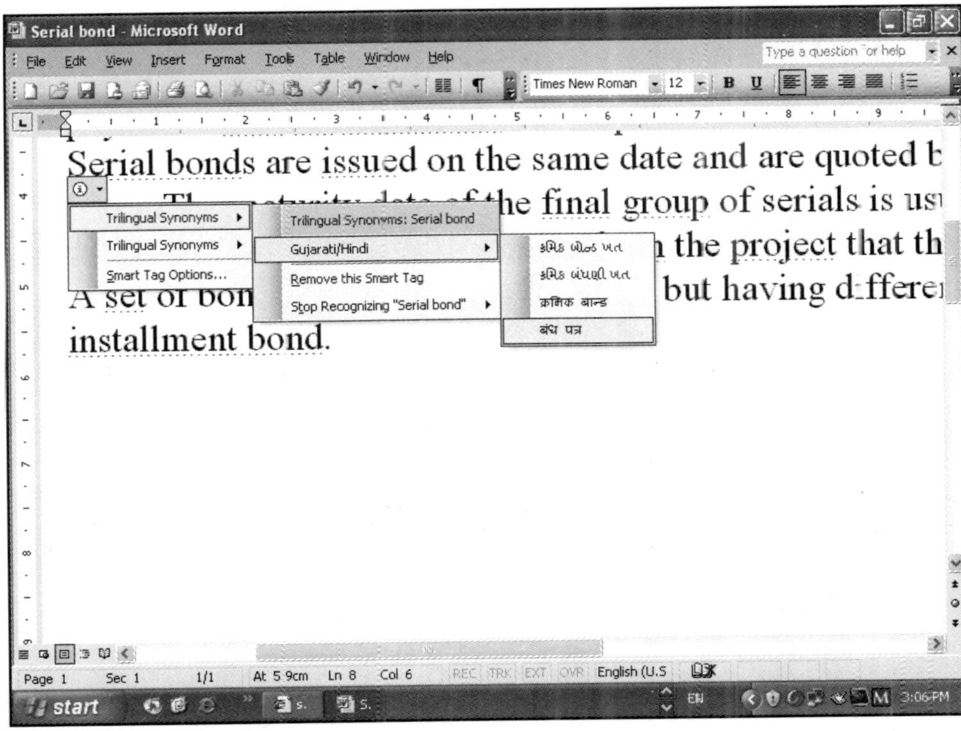

Figure 120: Trilingual smart tag

Offline translation

The English version of Microsoft Office, which is the popular version of Microsoft Office in India, comes with offline translation capabilities between English and Spanish, and between English and French. Offline translation translates a word in one language into another language. However, at the time of writing of this book, it did not appear to translate a complete sentence.

The offline translation gives a host of meanings of a word of a language in another language. It is worth noting that offline translation does not give specific meaning of the word based on the context,[29] but the general meanings of the word.

---

[29] The same word may have several meanings, possibly in different parts of speech. For example, the word 'light' may mean 'not heavy' (adjective), 'illumination' (noun) etc. Notwithstanding the plethora of meanings, a word is generally used in a particular sense is a sentence, even though at times the particular meaning of the word may be uncertain and ambiguous.

Offline translation has been illustrated in Figure 121. The translation task pane can be gotten in Microsoft Word by the following menu bar option: Tools → Language → Translate…. Translation can be done either by clicking "Translate" in the shortcut menu that appears on right-clicking the source word, or by typing the word in the text box in translation task pane. The source and the target languages are to be selected correctly.

Tips: Only word-by-word translation is possible in offline translation.

Note: Offline translation facility will be available only if the files and the programs were installed during installation/updating of Microsoft Office in the computer.

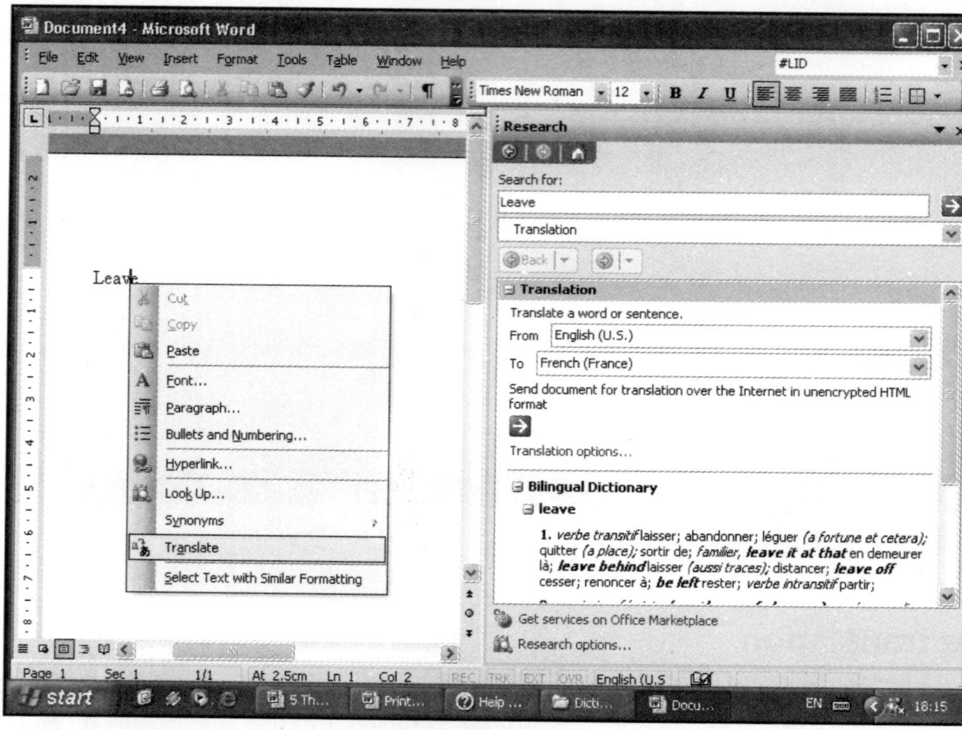

Figure 121: Offline translation in Microsoft Word

Online translation

Online translation translates not just a word, but phrases, sentences, paragraphs, e-mails, web pages, and even whole documents. Online translation gives just one single most appropriate translation.[30] The translation uses the contextual meaning of the words and phrases. It even takes care of grammatical, gender, slang etc issues into account. Notwithstanding the translation being done by machine—and without any human intervention, the accuracy of online translation is very high.

[30] However, some online translation websites also allow manual selection from a limited set of possible translations.

A few of the popular websites offering online translation facilities free of cost are

- http://www.babelfish.altavista.com
- http://www.worldlingo.com
- http://www.google.com

Translation software is also sold as independent application software.

Figure 122 illustrates the translation of text typed in the frame of the webpage from English to Japanese by http://www.babelfish.altavista.com. Figure 123 illustrates the translation of a Chinese website into English. Only the text portion in Unicode have been translated. The Chinese text in the form of pictures (i.e., in .BMP, .JPEG, .GIF etc formats) could not be translated.

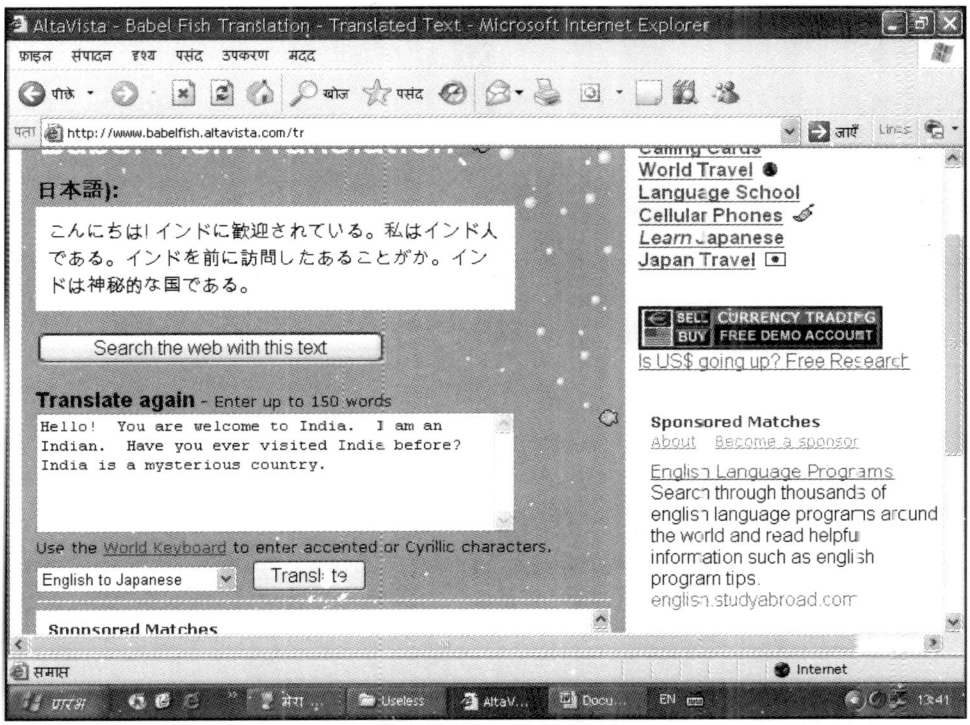

Figure 122: Online translation of typed text

Figure 123: Machine translation of webpage

Facilities for machine-aided translation to and from Indian languages also exist. C-DAC developed software for translation to Hindi and other languages. Anglabharati project of Indian Institute of Technology, Kanpur was a laudable initiative in the realm of online machine-aided translation between English and Hindi.

Figure 124 illustrates the "Translation Support System" software for translation from English to Hindi developed by IIT Kanpur and C-DAC. This is a fairly old software now. The software can be downloaded from the website http://www.tdil.mit.gov.in/download/mat.htm, and possibly also from http://www.ildc.in. One may obtain a copy of the software, and install it in one's computer: installation is somewhat cumbersome, though.

On clicking the "Dictionary" button in Figure 124 in the window of Translation Support System, one may add new English words with meaning, gender, grammatical details etc in Hindi. However, the software comes with enough data on English words for the ordinary users. (It may be noted that the software used non-standard Shusha font for Devanagari text, and not Unicode-compatible font.)

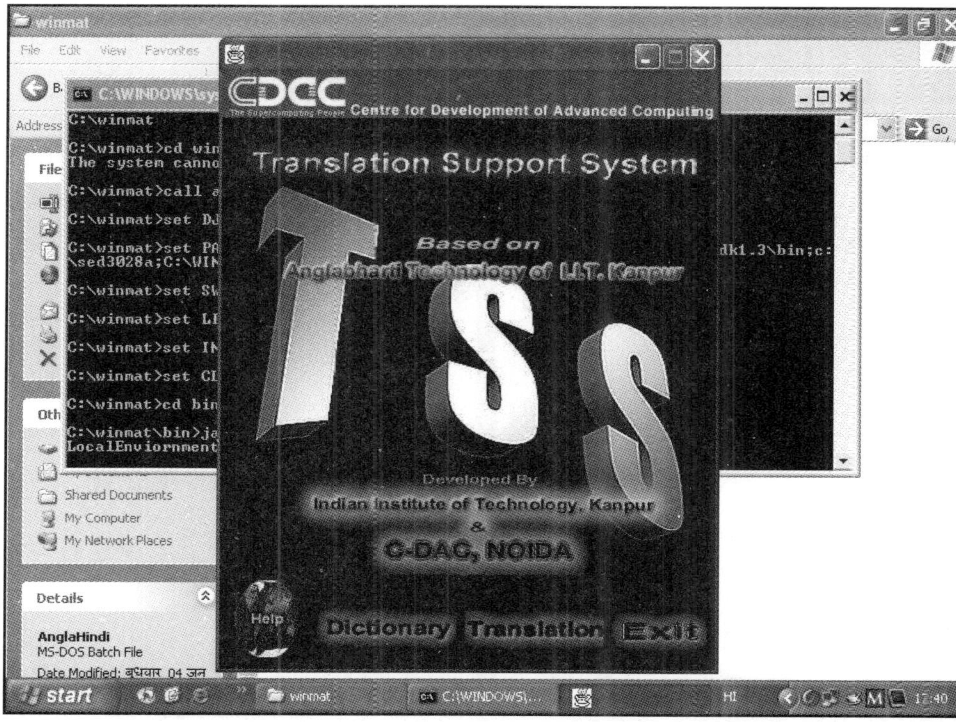

Figure 124: Starting "Translation Support System" software

On clicking "Translation" button in Figure 124, the translation pane as at Figure 125 is obtained, which one may use to translate text (including paragraphs) from English to Hindi. The Hindi text is in non-standard Shusha font. The software also allows one to manually select from a set of possible translations of the text. For all these, the specific helps available with the software may be referred to.

Now it is possible for users to chat online in their own languages in the multilingual scenario. The sender types in message in his language. The message is machine-translated, and the recipient reads the message in his language!

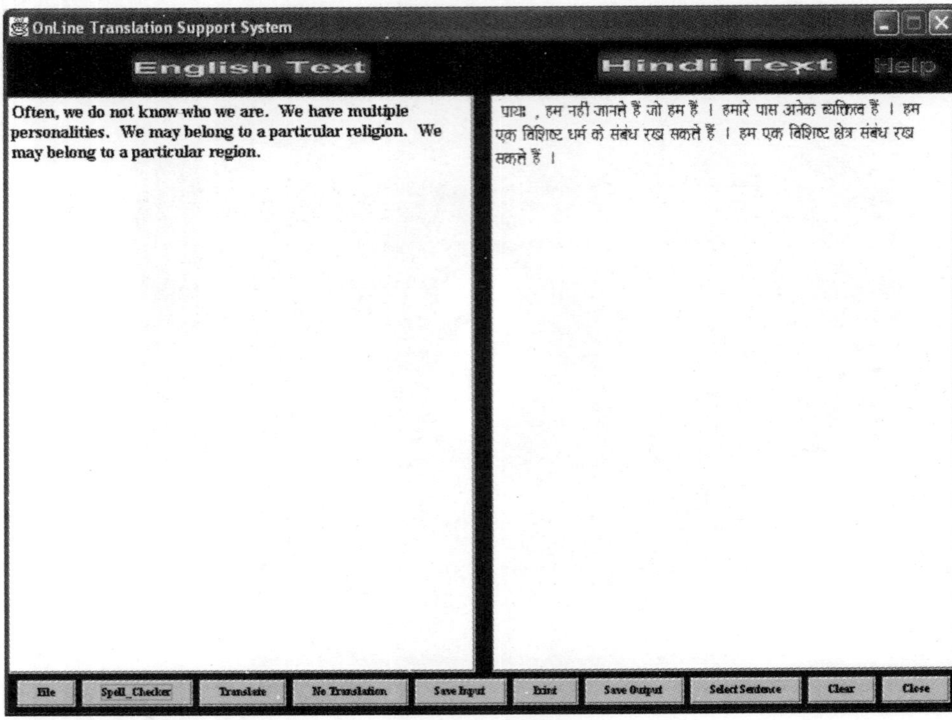

Figure 125: English to Hindi machine-aided translation

One reason for lack of development of machine-aided translation to and from Indian languages was the lack of popular standards in encoding of Indic scripts. With the popularity of Unicode standards, it can be hoped that machine-aided translation to and from Indian languages will only get a boost.

What you have learned

1. Thesaurus in different languages
2. Spelling and grammar checking in different languages
3. Custom dictionary for each of the languages (including variants of a language)
4. Offline translation
5. Online translation

ANNEXURE (A)

Hexadecimal Number System

Decimal number system

We usually write numbers in decimal number system. The radix or base in decimal number system is ten. As a digit in decimal number is promoted towards the left, for each shift towards left, its place value increases to a multiple of ten. Likewise, as the digit is demoted towards the right, for each shift towards right, its place value decreases to one-tenth. For example, "4092" in decimal number system is:

4092 (decimal)=four$\times(\text{ten})^{\text{three}}$ + zero$\times(\text{ten})^{\text{two}}$ + nine$\times(\text{ten})^{\text{one}}$ – two$\times(\text{ten})^{\text{zero}}$.

Also, the value of 40.92 in the same system is:

40.92 (decimal)=four$\times(\text{ten})^{\text{one}}$ + zero$\times(\text{ten})^{\text{zero}}$ + nine$\times(\text{ten})^{\text{minus one}}$ + two$\times(\text{ten})^{\text{minus two}}$.

$(\text{Ten})^{\text{three}}$ denotes ten to the power three, i.e., ten×ten×ten, i.e., one thousand.

We are so familiar with decimal number system that often we fail to realize that there could be number systems with radix or base other than ten. However, in computer science and information technology, it is often convenient to write and represent numbers in binary number system, in which numbers comprise zeros and ones. This is because at the basic level, computer works in binary form: 0/1, On/Off, True/False, Hi/Lo etc. Octal and hexadecimal number systems are closely related to binary number system.

Binary number system

In binary number system, there are only two digits: 0 and 1, and the radix is two. Digits '2', '3' etc are irrelevant, as all numbers can be expressed with zeros and ones only. For illustration, some numbers in the binary number system are given below:

1101 (binary) = one$\times(\text{two})^{\text{three}}$ + one$\times(\text{two})^{\text{two}}$ + zero$\times(\text{two})^{\text{one}}$ + one$\times(\text{two})^{\text{zero}}$ i.e., thirteen

110.1 (binary) = one$\times(\text{two})^{\text{two}}$ – one$\times(\text{two})^{\text{one}}$ + zero$\times(\text{two})^{\text{zero}}$ + one$\times(\text{two})^{\text{minus one}}$ i.e., six and half.

As a digit in the binary number is promoted towards the left, for each shift towards left, its place value increases by a multiple of two (instead of ten as in decimal system). Also, as the digit is demoted towards the right, for each shift towards right, its place value decreases to one-half.

Hexadecimal number system

In hexadecimal number system, there are sixteen digits: 0, 1, 2, 3, 4, 5, 6, 7, 8, 9, A, B, C, D, E and F, and the radix is sixteen. It should be noted that the digit A represents ten, B eleven, C twelve, D thirteen, E fourteen, and F fifteen. For illustration, some numbers in the hexadecimal number system are given below:

30.8 (hex) = three×$(\text{sixteen})^{\text{one}}$ + zero×$(\text{sixteen})^{\text{zero}}$ + eight×$(\text{sixteen})^{\text{minus one}}$ i.e., forty-eight and half

A0F (hex) = ten×$(\text{sixteen})^{\text{two}}$ + zero×$(\text{sixteen})^{\text{one}}$ + fifteen×$(\text{sixteen})^{\text{zero}}$ i.e., two thousand, five hundred and seventy-five.

As a digit is promoted towards left in a hexadecimal number, for each shift towards left, its place value increases to a multiple of sixteen (instead of ten as in decimal system). Also, as the digit is demoted towards right, for each shift towards right, its place value decreases to one-sixteenth.

It is easy to convert a number in binary number system to that in hexadecimal number system and vice versa. A binary number may be converted to hexadecimal number by clubbing together every four bits (i.e., binary digits) on either side of the radix point sign separating the whole part from the fractional part. For example,

11010.01 (binary)

= 00011010.0100 (binary) [by adding valueless preceding and trailing zero digits]

= {0001}{1010}.{0100} (binary) [by clubbing together every four bits on either side of the radix point]

= 1A.4 (hex) [because 0001 binary = 1 hex etc; see the table below]

Decimal number	Binary number	Hexadecimal number
0	0000	0
1	0001	1
2	0010	2
3	0011	3
4	0100	4
5	0101	5
6	0110	6
7	0111	7
8	1000	8
9	1001	9

Decimal number	Binary number	Hexadecimal number
11	1011	B
12	1100	C
13	1101	D
14	1110	E
15	1111	F

A decimal number can be converted to binary (or, hexadecimal) number by (i) division of the whole part of the number by two (or, sixteen), and then repeated division of the whole quotient, and (ii) by repeatedly multiplying the fraction part by two (or, sixteen), as per the following illustration for converting the decimal number 90.8 to binary and hexadecimal numbers:

(i) Whole part:

Whole number	*Division by two*	
	Quotient	*Remainder*
90	45	0
45	22	1
22	11	0
11	5	1
5	2	1
2	1	0
1	0	1

Whole number	*Division by sixteen*	
	Quotient	*Remainder*
90	5	A, i.e., ten
5	0	5

Thus, 90 (decimal) or 90_{10} = 1011010 (binary) = 5A (hex), which may be verified by converting the binary/hex number back to decimal number as follows:

$$1011010 \text{ binary} = \text{two}^{\text{six}} + \text{two}^{\text{four}} + \text{two}^{\text{three}} + \text{two}^{\text{one}}$$

$$5A \text{ hex} = \text{five} \times \text{sixteen}^{\text{one}} + \text{ten} \times \text{sixteen}^{\text{zero}}$$

(ii) Fractional part

Fraction number	*Multiplication by two*	
	Integer part	*Fraction part*
0.8	1	0.6
0.6	1	0.2
0.2	0	0.4
0.4	0	0.8
0.8	1	0.6
0.6	1	0.2
0.2	0	0.4

Fraction number	*Multiplication by sixteen*	
	Integer part	*Fraction part*
0.8	C	0.8
0.8	C	0.8
0.8	C	0.8
0.8	C	0.8
0.8	C	0.8
0.8	C	0.8
0.8	C	0.8

Thus, 0.8 (decimal) = 0.8_{10} = 0.11001100…(binary) [recurring] = 0.CCCC… (hex) [recurring], which may be verified by converting back the binary/hex number to decimal number.

Therefore, 90.8 (decimal) or 90.8_{10} = 1011010.11001100…(binary) [recurring] = 5A.CCC…(hex) [recurring], i.e., whole-part radix point fractional-part

Two binary and hexadecimal numbers may be added just as we add decimal numbers. However, carry of two and sixteen respectively are to be assumed instead of ten. For example,

binary

Carry→		1	1	1			
		1	**0**	**1**	**1**	, i.e.,	**11**
+		**1**	**1**	**0**	**1**	, i.e.,	**13**
	1	*1*	*0*	*0*	*0*	, i.e.,	*24*

Hex

		1			
	1	**2**	**A**	, i.e.,	**298**
+	**9**	**0**	**6**	, i.e.,	**2310**
	A	*3*	*0*	, i.e.,	*2608*

In case of any difficulty, the following functions in Microsoft Excel may be used to convert whole numbers from one base to another:

Function	Conversion from
BIN2DEC()	Binary to decimal
BIN2HEX()	Binary to hexadecimal
DEC2BIN()	Decimal to binary
DEC2HEX()	Decimal to hexadecimal
HEX2BIN()	Hexadecimal to binary
HEX2DEC()	Hexadecimal to decimal

To use the above functions, one may have to add-in Analysis ToolPak from Tools > Add-Ins… in the menu bar in Microsoft Excel. In HEX2BIN and HEX2DEC functions, the hexadecimal number should be within quotes; for example, as HEX2DEC("A3C").

ISCII Codes for Indic Languages

The codes for the ten scripts supported by ISCII standard are given in the following table. A blank in the cell indicates that there is no character corresponding to the code in the script.

Code (decimal)	Unicode	Assamese	Bengali	Devanagari	Gujarati	Kannada	Malayalam	Oriya	Punjabi	Tamil	Telugu
161	¡	ঁ	ঁ	ँ	ઁ			ଁ			
162	¢	ং	ং	ं	ં	ಂ	ം	ଂ	ਂ		ం
163	£	ঃ	ঃ	ः	ઃ	ಃ	ഃ	ଃ		ஃ	ః
164	¤	অ	অ	अ	અ	ಅ	അ	ଅ	ਅ	அ	అ
165	¥	আ	আ	आ	આ	ಆ	ആ	ଆ	ਆ	ஆ	ఆ
166	¦	ই	ই	इ	ઇ	ಇ	ഇ	ଇ	ਇ	இ	ఇ
167	§	ঈ	ঈ	ई	ઈ	ಈ	ഈ	ଈ	ਈ	ஈ	ఈ
168	¨	উ	উ	उ	ઉ	ಉ	ഉ	ଉ	ਉ	உ	ఉ
169	©	ঊ	ঊ	ऊ	ઊ	ಊ	ഊ	ଊ	ਊ	ஊ	ఊ
170	ª	ঋ	ঋ	ऋ	ઋ	ಋ	ഋ	ଋ			ఋ
171	«			ऎ		ಎ	എ			எ	ఎ
172	¬	এ	এ	ए	એ	ಏ	ഏ	ଏ	ਏ	ஏ	ఏ
173	-	ঐ	ঐ	ऐ	ઐ	ಐ	ഐ	ଐ	ਐ	ஐ	ఐ
174	®			ऍ							
175	¯			ऒ		ಒ	ഒ			ஒ	ఒ
176	°	ও	ও	ओ	ઓ	ಓ	ഓ	ଓ	ਓ	ஓ	ఓ
177	±	ঔ	ঔ	औ	ઔ	ಔ	ഔ	ଔ	ਔ	ஔ	ఔ
178	^{2}			ऑ							
179	^{3}	ক	ক	क	ખ	ಕ	ക	କ	ਕ	க	క

Code (decimal)	Unicode	Assamese	Bengali	Devanagari	Gujarati	Kannada	Malayalam	Oriya	Punjabi	Tamil	Telugu
180	´	থ	থ	ख	ખ	ಖ	ഖ	ଖ	ਖ		ఖ
181	µ	গ	গ	ग	ગ	ಗ	ഗ	ଗ	ਗ		గ
182	¶	ঘ	ঘ	घ	ઘ	ಘ	ഘ	ଘ	ਘ		ఘ
183	·	ঙ	ঙ	ङ	ઙ	ಙ	ങ	ଙ	ਙ	ங	ఙ
184	¸	চ	চ	च	ચ	ಚ	ച	ଚ	ਚ	ச	చ
185	¹	ছ	ছ	छ	છ	ಛ	ഛ	ଛ	ਛ		ఛ
186	º	জ	জ	ज	જ	ಜ	ജ	ଜ	ਜ	ஜ	జ
187	»	ঝ	ঝ	झ	ઝ	ಝ	ഝ	ଝ	ਝ		ఝ
188	¼	ঞ	ঞ	ञ	ઞ	ಞ	ഞ	ଞ	ਞ	ஞ	ఞ
189	½	ট	ট	ट	ટ	ಟ	ട	ଟ	ਟ	ட	ట
190	¾	ঠ	ঠ	ठ	ઠ	ಠ	ഠ	ଠ	ਠ		ఠ
191	¿	ড	ড	ड	ડ	ಡ	ഡ	ଡ	ਡ		డ
192	À	ঢ	ঢ	ढ	ઢ	ಢ	ഢ	ଢ	ਢ		ఢ
193	Á	ণ	ণ	ण	ણ	ಣ	ണ	ଣ	ਣ	ண	ణ
194	Â	ত	ত	त	ત	ತ	ത	ତ	ਤ	த	త
195	Ã	থ	থ	थ	થ	ಥ	ഥ	ଥ	ਥ		థ
196	Ä	দ	দ	द	દ	ದ	ദ	ଦ	ਦ		ద
197	Å	ধ	ধ	ध	ધ	ಧ	ധ	ଧ	ਧ		ధ
198	Æ	ন	ন	न	ન	ನ	ന	ନ	ਨ	ந	న
199	Ç			ऩ						ன	
200	È	প	প	प	પ	ಪ	പ	ପ	ਪ	ப	ప
201	É	ফ	ফ	फ	ફ	ಫ	ഫ	ଫ	ਫ		ఫ
202	Ê	ব	ব	ब	બ	ಬ	ബ	ବ	ਬ		బ
203	Ë	ভ	ভ	भ	ભ	ಭ	ഭ	ଭ	ਭ		భ
204	Ì	ম	ম	म	મ	ಮ	മ	ମ	ਮ	ம	మ
205	Í	য়	য়	य	ય	ಯ	യ	ଯ	ਯ	ய	య
206	Î	য	য	य़				ୟ			

Code (decimal)	Unicode	Assamese	Bengali	Devanagari	Gujarati	Kannada	Malayalam	Oriya	Punjabi	Tamil	Telugu
207	Ï	ৰ	র	र	ર	ರ	ര	ର	ਰ	ர	ర
208	Ð			ऱ		ಱ	റ			ற	ఱ
209	Ñ	ল	ল	ल	લ	ಲ	ല	ଲ	ਲ	ல	ల
210	Ò			ळ	ળ	ಳ	ള	ଳ		ள	ళ
211	Ó			ऴ			ഴ			ழ	
212	Ô	ৱ		व	વ	ವ	വ		ਵ	வ	వ
213	Õ	শ	শ	श	શ	ಶ	ശ	ଶ	ਸ਼		శ
214	Ö	ষ	ষ	ष	ષ	ಷ	ഷ	ଷ		ஷ	ష
215	×	স	স	स	સ	ಸ	സ	ସ	ਸ	ஸ	స
216	Ø	হ	হ	ह	હ	ಹ	ഹ	ହ	ਹ	ஹ	హ
217	Ù	INV	INV	INV	INV	INV	INV	INV	INV	INV	INV
218	Ú	◌া	◌া	◌ा	◌ા	◌ಾ	◌ാ	◌ା	◌ਾ	◌ா	◌ా
219	Û	◌ি	◌ি	◌ि	◌િ	◌ಿ	◌ി	◌ି	◌ਿ	◌ி	◌ి
220	Ü	◌ী	◌ী	◌ी	◌ી	◌ೀ	◌ീ	◌ୀ	◌ੀ	◌ீ	◌ీ
221	Ý	◌ু	◌ু	◌ु	◌ુ	◌ು	◌ു	◌ୁ	◌ੁ	◌ு	◌ు
222	Þ	◌ূ	◌ূ	◌ू	◌ૂ	◌ೂ	◌ൂ	◌ୂ	◌ੂ	◌ூ	◌ూ
223	ß	◌ৃ	◌ৃ	◌ृ	◌ૃ	◌ೃ	◌ൃ	◌ୃ			◌ృ
224	à			◌ॆ		◌ೆ	◌െ			◌ெ	◌ె
225	á	◌ে	◌ে	◌े	◌ે	◌ೇ	◌േ	◌େ	◌ੇ	◌ே	◌ే
226	â	◌ৈ	◌ৈ	◌ै	◌ૈ	◌ೈ	◌ൈ	◌ୈ	◌ੈ	◌ை	◌ై
227	ã			◌ॅ							
228	ä			◌ॊ		◌ೊ	◌ൊ				◌ొ
229	å	◌ো	◌ো	◌ो	◌ો	◌ೋ	◌ോ	◌ୋ	◌ੋ	◌ோ	◌ో
230	æ	◌ৌ	◌ৌ	◌ौ	◌ૌ	◌ೌ	◌ൌ	◌ୌ	◌ੌ	◌ௌ	◌ౌ
231	ç			◌ॉ							
232	è	◌্	◌্	◌्	◌્	◌್	◌്	◌୍	◌੍	◌்	◌్
233	é	.	.	.	◌઼				◌਼		

Code (decimal)	Unicode	Assamese	Bengali	Devanagari	Gujarati	Kannada	Malayalam	Oriya	Punjabi	Tamil	Telugu
234	ê			।	।	।			।	.	.
239	ï	ATR	ATR	ATR	ATR	ATR	ATR	ATR	ATR	ATR	ATR
240	ð	EXT	EXT	EXT	EXT	EXT	EXT	EXT	EXT	EXT	EXT
241	ñ	০	০	०	૦	೦	൦	୦	੦	௦	౦
242	ò	১	১	१	૧	೧	൧	୧	੧	௧	౧
243	ó	২	২	२	૨	೨	൨	୨	੨	௨	౨
244	ô	৩	৩	३	૩	೩	൩	୩	੩	௩	౩
245	õ	৪	৪	४	૪	೪	൪	୪	੪	௪	౪
246	ö	৫	৫	५	૫	೫	൫	୫	੫	௫	౫
247	÷	৬	৬	६	૬	೬	൬	୬	੬	௬	౬
248	ø	৭	৭	७	૭	೭	൭	୭	੭	௭	౭
249	ù	৮	৮	८	૮	೮	൮	୮	੮	௮	౮
250	ú	৯	৯	९	૯	೯	൯	୯	੯	௯	౯

Languages and Scripts Supported by Microsoft Windows

The languages supported by Microsoft Windows/Office are listed below. However, more and more languages are getting supported.

Language	Variants[1]
Afrikaans	
Albanian	
Amharic	
Arabic	Yes
Armenian	
Assamese	
Azeri	Yes
Basque	
Belarusian	
Bengali	Yes
Bosnian	Yes
Bulgarian	
Burmese	
Catalan	
Cherokee	
Chinese	Yes
Croatian	Yes
Czech	
Danish	
Divehi	
Dutch	Yes
Edo	
English	Yes
Estonian	Yes
Faeroese	
Farsi/Parsi	

Language	Variants[1]
Filipino	
Finnish	
French	Yes
Frisian	
Fulfulde	
Gaelic	
Galician	
Georgian	
German	Yes
Greek	
Guarani	
Gujarati	
Hausa	
Hawaiian	
Hebrew	
Hindi	
Hungarian	
Ibibio	
Icelandic	
Igbo	
Indonesian	
Inuktitut	Yes
Irish	Yes
Italian	Yes
Japanese	
Kannada	
Kanuri	
Kashmiri	Yes
Kazakh	
Khmer	

[1] A language may have variants depending on script, region etc. All languages have variants, but not all variants have been recognized by Microsoft Windows/Office.

Language	Variants[1]
Konkani	
Korean	
Kyrgyz	Yes
Lao	
Latin	
Latvian	
Lithuanian	
Luxembourgish	
Macedonian (FYROM)	
Malay	Yes
Malayalam	Yes
Maltese	
Manipuri	
Maori	
Mapudungun	Yes
Marathi	
Mohawk	
Mongolian	Yes
Nepali	Yes
Northern Sotho	
Norwegian	Yes
Oriya	
Oromo	
Papiamento	
Pashto	
Polish	
Portuguese	Yes
Punjabi	Yes
Quechua	Yes
Romanian	Yes
Romansh	
Russian	Yes
Sami	Yes
Sanskrit	
Sepedi	

Language	Variants[1]
Serbian	Yes
Sindhi	Yes
Sinhalese	
Slovak	
Slovenian	
Somali	
Sorbian	
Spanish	Yes
Sutu	
Swahili/Kiswahili	
Swedish	Yes
Syriac	
Tajik	
Tamazight	Yes
Tamil	
Tatar	
Telugu	
Thai	
Tibetan	Yes
Tigrinya	Yes
Tsonga	
Tswana	
Turkish	
Turkmen	
Ukrainian	
Urdu	Yes
Uzbek	Yes
Vietnamese	
Welsh	
Xhosa/IsiXhosa	
Yi	
Yiddish	
Yoruba	
Zulu/IsiZulu	

ANNEXURE (D)

Unicode Character Set of Select Languages

The numeric codes in Unicode standard range from 0 through 10FFFF hex (both inclusive). The range of codes for the scripts used in the Indian subcontinent are given in the table below:

Script	Start code		End code	
	In decimal	In hexadecimal	In decimal	In hexadecimal
Latin[2]	*0*	0000	*255*	00FF
Arabic[3]	*1536*	0600	*1791*	06FF
Thaana	*1920*	0780	*1963*	07BF
Devanagari	*2304*	0900	*2431*	097F
Bengali	*2432*	0980	*2559*	09FF
Gurmukhi	*2560*	0A00	*2687*	0A7F
Gujarati	*2688*	0A80	*2815*	0AFF
Oriya	*2816*	0B00	*2943*	0B7F
Tamil	*2944*	0B80	*3071*	0BFF
Telugu	*3072*	0C00	*3199*	0C7F
Kannada	*3200*	0C80	*3327*	0CFF
Malayalam	*3328*	0D00	*3455*	0D7F
Sinhala	*3456*	0D80	*3583*	0DFF
Tibetan	*3840*	0F00	*4095*	0FFF
Myanmar	*4096*	1000	*4255*	109F
Limbu	*6400*	1900	*6479*	194F
Siloti Nagari	*43008*	A800	*43055*	A82F
Old Persian	*66464*	103A0	*66527*	103DF
Kharoshthi	*68096*	10A00	*68191*	10A5F

[2] Excluding Latin Extended-A (0100 to 017F hex) and Latin Extended-B (0180 to 01FF hex) forms.
[3] Excluding Arabic Presentation Forms-A and Arabic Presentation Forms-B.

The likely range of codes for some other scripts are as follows:

Script	Start code		End code	
	In decimal	In hexadecimal	In decimal	In hexadecimal
Avestan	*2048*	0800	*2111*	083F
Pahlavi	*2112*	0840	*2175*	087F
Lepcha	*7168*	1C00	*7247*	1C4F
Ol Chiki	*7248*	1C50	*7295*	1C7F
Meitei Mayek	*7296*	1C80	*7391*	1CDF
Saurashtra	*43136*	A880	*43231*	A8DF
Varang Kshiti	*43776*	AB00	*43839*	AB3F
Sorang Sompeng	*43840*	AB40	*43887*	AB6F
Chakma	*43904*	AB80	*43999*	ABDF

The hexadecimal codes in the Unicode standard for characters of major scripts of the subcontinent are given below.[4] The numeric code of a character is column number + row number in the table. For example, code for Latin letter 'u' is 0000 (column) +0075 (row), i.e., 0075 (hex), that for Devanagari letter 'अ' is 0900 (column) +0005 (row), i.e., 0905 (hex).

	Latin	Latin-1	Arabic	Arabic Extd	Devanagari	Bengali	Gurmukhi	Gujarati	Oriya	Tamil	Telugu	Kannada	Malayalam	Sinhala	Tibetan-1	Tibetan-2
	0000	0080	0600	0680	0900	0980	0A00	0A80	0B00	0B80	0C00	0C80	0D00	0D80	0F00	0F80
0000			؀	ڀ	□	□	□	□	□	□	□	□	□	□	ༀ	ྀ
0001			؁	ځ	ँ	ঁ	□	ઁ	ଁ	□	ఁ	□	□	□	༁	ཱྀ
0002			؂	ڂ	ं	ং	ਂ	ં	ଂ	ஂ	ం	ಂ	ം	ං	༂	ྂ
0003			؃	ڃ	ः	ঃ	□	ઃ	ଃ	ஃ	ః	ಃ	ഃ	ඃ	༃	ྃ
0004			□	ڄ	ऄ	□	□	□	□	□	□	□	□	□	༄	྄
0005			□	څ	अ	অ	ਅ	અ	ଅ	அ	అ	ಅ	അ	අ	༅	྅
0006			□	چ	आ	আ	ਆ	આ	ଆ	ஆ	ఆ	ಆ	ആ	ආ	༆	྆
0007			□	ڇ	इ	ই	ਇ	ઇ	ଇ	இ	ఇ	ಇ	ഇ	ඇ	༇	྇
0008			□	ڈ	ई	ঈ	ਈ	ઈ	ଈ	ஈ	ఈ	ಈ	ഈ	ඈ	༈	ྈ
0009			□	ډ	उ	উ	ਉ	ઉ	ଉ	உ	ఉ	ಉ	ഉ	ඉ	༉	ྉ
000A			□	ڊ	ऊ	ঊ	ਊ	ઊ	ଊ	ஊ	ఊ	ಊ	ഊ	ඊ	༊	ྊ
000B			؋	ڋ	ऋ	ঋ	□	ઋ	ଋ	□	ఋ	ಋ	ഋ	උ	་	ྋ
000C			،	ڌ	ऌ	ঌ	□	□	ଌ	□	ఌ	ಌ	ഌ	ඌ	༌	0F8C

[4] Unicode Consortium website http://www.unicode.org may be referred to for the latest version.

	Latin	Latin-1	Arabic	Arabic Extd	Devanagari	Bengali	Gurmukhi	Gujarati	Oriya	Tamil	Telugu	Kannada	Malayalam	Sinhala	Tibetan-1	Tibetan-2
	0000	0080	0600	0680	0900	0980	0A00	0A80	0B00	0B80	0C00	0C80	0D00	0D80	0F00	0F80
000D			؍	ڍ	ऍ	□	□	ઍ	□	□	□	□	□	ඍ	།	0F8D
000E			؎	ڎ	ऎ	□	□	□	□	எ	ఎ	ಎ	എ	ඎ	༎	0F8E
000F			؏	ڏ	ए	এ	ਏ	એ	ଏ	ஏ	ఏ	ಏ	ഏ	□	༏	0F8F
0010			ؐ	ڐ	ऐ	ঐ	ਐ	ઐ	ଐ	ஐ	ఐ	ಐ	ഐ	□	༐	ྐ
0011			ؑ	ڑ	ऑ	□	□	ઑ	□	□	□	□	□	එ	༑	ྑ
0012			ؒ	ڒ	ऒ	□	□	□	□	ஒ	ఒ	ಒ	ഒ	ඒ	༒	ྒ
0013			ؓ	ړ	ओ	ও	ਓ	ઓ	ଓ	ஓ	ఓ	ಓ	ഓ	ඓ	༓	ྒྷ
0014			ؔ	ڔ	औ	ঔ	ਔ	ઔ	ଔ	ஔ	ఔ	ಔ	ഔ	ඔ	༔	ྔ
0015			ؕ	ڕ	क	ক	ਕ	ક	କ	க	క	ಕ	ക	ඕ	༕	ྕ
0016			□	ږ	ख	খ	ਖ	ખ	ଖ	□	ఖ	ಖ	ഖ	ඖ	༖	ྖ
0017			□	ڗ	ग	গ	ਗ	ગ	ଗ	□	గ	ಗ	ഗ	□	༗	ྗ
0018			□	ژ	घ	ঘ	ਘ	ઘ	ଘ	□	ఘ	ಘ	ഘ	□	༘	0F98
0019			□	ڙ	ङ	ঙ	ਙ	ઙ	ଙ	ங	ఙ	ಙ	ങ	□	༙	ྙ
001A			□	ښ	च	চ	ਚ	ચ	ଚ	ச	చ	ಚ	ച	ක	༚	ྚ
001B			؛	ڛ	छ	ছ	ਛ	છ	ଛ	□	ఛ	ಛ	ഛ	ඛ	༛	ྛ
001C			□	ڜ	ज	জ	ਜ	જ	ଜ	ஜ	జ	ಜ	ജ	ග	༜	ྜ
001D			□	ڝ	झ	ঝ	ਝ	ઝ	ଝ	□	ఝ	ಝ	ഝ	ඝ	༝	ྜྷ
001E			؞	ڞ	ञ	ঞ	ਞ	ઞ	ଞ	ஞ	ఞ	ಞ	ഞ	ඞ	༞	ྞ
001F			؟	ڟ	ट	ট	ਟ	ટ	ଟ	ட	ట	ಟ	ട	ඟ	༟	ྟ
0020			□	ڠ	ठ	ঠ	ਠ	ઠ	ଠ	□	ఠ	ಠ	ഠ	ච	༠	ྠ
0021	!	¡	ء	ڡ	ड	ড	ਡ	ડ	ଡ	□	డ	ಡ	ഡ	ඡ	༡	ྡ
0022	"	¢	آ	ڢ	ढ	ঢ	ਢ	ઢ	ଢ	□	ఢ	ಢ	ഢ	ජ	༢	ྡྷ
0023	#	£	أ	ڣ	ण	ণ	ਣ	ણ	ଣ	ண	ణ	ಣ	ണ	ඣ	༣	ྣ
0024	$	¤	ؤ	ڤ	त	ত	ਤ	ત	ତ	த	త	ತ	ത	ඤ	༤	ྤ
0025	%	¥	إ	ڥ	थ	থ	ਥ	થ	ଥ	□	థ	ಥ	ഥ	ඥ	༥	ྥ
0026	&	¦	ئ	ڦ	द	দ	ਦ	દ	ଦ	□	ద	ದ	ദ	ඦ	༦	ྦ

	Latin	Latin-1	Arabic	Arabic Extd	Devanagari	Bengali	Gurmukhi	Gujarati	Oriya	Tamil	Telugu	Kannada	Malayalam	Sinhala	Tibetan-1	Tibetan-2
	0000	0080	0600	0680	0900	0980	0A00	0A80	0B00	0B80	0C00	0C80	0D00	0D80	0F00	0F80
0027	'	§	ا	ڧ	ध	ধ	ਧ	ધ	ଧ	□	ధ	ಧ	ധ	ට	༧	ྦྷ
0028	(	¨	ب	ڨ	न	ন	ਨ	ન	ନ	ந	న	ನ	ന	ඨ	༨	ྨ
0029	)	©	ة	ک	ऩ	□	□	□	□	ன	□	□	□	ඩ	༩	ྩ
002A	*	ª	ت	ڪ	प	প	ਪ	પ	ପ	ப	ప	ಪ	പ	ඪ	༪	ྪ
002B	+	«	ث	ګ	फ	ফ	ਫ	ફ	ଫ	□	ఫ	ಫ	ഫ	ණ	༫	ྫ
002C	,	¬	ج	ڬ	ब	ব	ਬ	બ	ବ	□	బ	ಬ	ബ	ඬ	༬	ྫྷ
002D	-	-	ح	ڭ	भ	ভ	ਭ	ભ	ଭ	□	భ	ಭ	ഭ	ත	༭	ྭ
002E	.	®	خ	ڮ	म	ম	ਮ	મ	ମ	ம	మ	ಮ	മ	ථ	༮	ྮ
002F	/	¯	د	گ	य	য	ਯ	ય	ଯ	ய	య	ಯ	യ	ද	༯	ྯ
0030	0	°	ذ	ڰ	र	র	ਰ	ર	ର	ர	ర	ರ	ര	ධ	༰	ྰ
0031	1	±	ر	ڱ	ऱ	□	□	□	□	ற	ఱ	ಱ	റ	න	༱	ྱ
0032	2	²	ز	ڲ	ल	ল	ਲ	લ	ଲ	ல	ల	ಲ	ല	□	༲	ྲ
0033	3	³	س	ڳ	ळ	□	ਲ਼	ળ	ଳ	ள	ళ	ಳ	ള	ඳ	༳	ླ
0034	4	´	ش	ڴ	ऴ	□	□	□	□	ழ	□	□	ഴ	ප	༴	ྴ
0035	5	µ	ص	ڵ	व	□	ਵ	વ	□	வ	వ	ವ	വ	ඵ	༵	ྵ
0036	6	¶	ض	ڶ	श	শ	ਸ਼	શ	ଶ	□	శ	ಶ	ശ	බ	༶	ྶ
0037	7	·	ط	ڷ	ष	ষ	□	ષ	ଷ	ஷ	ష	ಷ	ഷ	භ	༷	ྷ
0038	8	¸	ظ	ڸ	स	স	ਸ	સ	ସ	ஸ	స	ಸ	സ	ම	༸	ྸ
0039	9	¹	ع	ڹ	ह	হ	ਹ	હ	ହ	ஹ	హ	ಹ	ഹ	ඹ	༹	ྐྵ
003A	:	º	غ	ں	□	□	□	□	□	□	□	□	□	ය	༺	ྺ
003B	;	»	□	ڻ	□	□	□	□	□	□	□	□	□	ර	༻	ྻ
003C	<	¼	□	ڼ	़	়	਼	઼	଼	□	□	□	□	□	༼	ྼ
003D	=	½	□	ڽ	ऽ	ঽ	□	ઽ	ଽ	□	□	□	□	ල	༽	0FBD
003E	>	¾	□	ھ	ा	া	ਾ	ા	ା	ா	ా	ಾ	ാ	□	༾	྾
003F	?	¿	□	ڿ	ि	ি	ਿ	િ	ି	ி	ి	ಿ	ി	□	༿	྿
0040	@	À	ـ	ۀ	ी	ী	ੀ	ી	ୀ	ீ	ీ	ೀ	ീ	ව	ཀ	࿀

	Latin	Latin-1	Arabic	Arabic Extd	Devanagari	Bengali	Gurmukhi	Gujarati	Oriya	Tamil	Telugu	Kannada	Malayalam	Sinhala	Tibetan 1	Tibetan-2
	0000	0080	0600	0680	0900	0980	0A00	0A80	0B00	0B80	0C00	0C80	0D00	0D80	0F00	0F80
0041	A	Á	ف	ہ	◌ु	◌ু	◌ੁ	◌ુ	◌ୁ	◌ு	◌ు	◌ು	◌ു	ශ	ཁ	࿁
0042	B	Â	ق	ۂ	◌ू	◌ূ	◌ੂ	◌ૂ	◌ୂ	◌ூ	◌ూ	◌ೂ	◌ൂ	ෂ	ག	࿂
0043	C	Ã	ك	ۃ	◌ृ	◌ৃ	□	◌ૃ	◌ୃ	□	◌ృ	◌ೃ	◌ൃ	ස	གྷ	࿃
0044	D	Ä	ل	ۄ	◌ॄ	◌ৄ	□	◌ૄ	□	□	◌ౄ	◌ೄ	□	හ	ང	࿄
0045	E	Å	م	ۅ	◌ॅ	□	□	◌ૅ	□	□	□	□	□	ළ	ཅ	࿅
0046	F	Æ	ن	ۆ	◌ॆ	□	□	□	□	◌ெ	◌ె	◌ೆ	◌െ	ෆ	ཆ	࿆
0047	G	Ç	ه	ۇ	◌े	◌ে	◌ੇ	◌ે	◌େ	◌ே	◌ే	◌ೇ	◌േ	]	ཇ	࿇
0048	H	È	و	ۈ	◌ै	◌ৈ	◌ੈ	◌ૈ	◌ୈ	◌ை	◌ై	◌ೈ	◌ൈ	]	□	࿈
0049	I	É	ى	ۉ	◌ॉ	[	□	◌ૉ	□	□	□	□	□	]	ཉ	࿉
004A	J	Ê	ي	ۊ	◌ॊ	[	□	□	□	◌ொ	◌ొ	◌ೊ	◌ൊ	්	ཊ	࿊
004B	K	Ë	◌ً	ۋ	◌ो	◌ো	◌ੋ	◌ો	◌ୋ	◌ோ	◌ో	◌ೋ	◌ോ	]	ཋ	࿋
004C	L	Ì	◌ٌ	ی	◌ौ	◌ৌ	◌ੌ	◌ૌ	◌ୌ	◌ௌ	◌ౌ	◌ೌ	◌ൌ	]	ཌ	࿌
004D	M	Í	◌ٍ	ۍ	◌्	◌্	◌੍	◌્	◌୍	◌்	◌్	◌್	◌്	]	ཌྷ	0FCD
004E	N	Î	◌َ	ێ	□	□	□	□	□	□	□	□	□	]	ཎ	0FCE
004F	O	Ï	◌ُ	ۏ	□	□	□	□	□	□	□	□	□	◌ා	ཏ	࿏
0050	P	Ð	◌ِ	ې	ॐ	□	□	ૐ	□	□	□	□	□	◌ැ	ཐ	0FD0
0051	Q	Ñ	◌ّ	ۑ	◌॑	□	□	□	□	□	□	□	□	◌ෑ	ད	0FD1
0052	R	Ò	◌ْ	ے	◌॒	□	□	□	□	□	□	□	□	◌ි	དྷ	0FD2
0053	S	Ó	◌ٓ	ۓ	◌॓	□	□	□	□	□	□	□	□	◌ී	ན	0FD3
0054	T	Ô	◌ٔ	۔	◌॔	□	□	□	□	□	□	□	□	◌ු	པ	0FD4
0055	U	Õ	◌ٕ	ە	□	□	□	□	□	□	◌ౕ	◌ೕ	□	□	ཕ	0FD5
0056	V	Ö	◌ٖ	◌ۖ	□	□	□	□	◌ୖ	□	◌ౖ	◌ೖ	□	◌ූ	བ	0FD6
0057	W	×	◌ٗ	◌ۗ	□	◌ৗ	□	□	◌ୗ	◌ௗ	□	□	◌ൗ	□	བྷ	0FD7
0058	X	Ø	◌٘	◌ۘ	क़	□	□	□	□	□	□	□	□	◌ෘ	མ	0FD8
0059	Y	Ù	◌ٙ	◌ۙ	ख़	□	ਖ਼	□	□	□	□	□	□	◌ෙ	ཙ	0FD9
005A	Z	Ú	ٚ	◌ۚ	ग़	□	ਗ਼	□	□	□	□	□	□	◌ේ	ཚ	0FDA

	Latin	Latin-1	Arabic	Arabic Extd	Devanagari	Bengali	Gurmukhi	Gujarati	Oriya	Tamil	Telugu	Kannada	Malayalam	Sinhala	Tibetan-1	Tibetan-2
	0000	0080	0600	0680	0900	0980	0A00	0A80	0B00	0B80	0C00	0C80	0D00	0D80	0F00	0F80
005B	[	Û	ˆ	◌	ज़	▯	ਜ਼	▯	□	▯	□	▯	▯	ෛ	ཛྷ	0FDB
005C	\	Ü	.	ٮ	ड़	ড়	ਗ਼	▯	ଡ଼	▯	□	▯	▯	ො	ཀྵ	0FDC
005D	]	Ý	ˎ	◌	ढ़	ঢ়	▯	▯	ଢ଼	▯	□	▯	▯	ෝ	ཨ	0FDD
005E	^	Þ	˟	✵	फ़	▯	ਫ਼	▯	□	▯	□	ೞ	▯	ෞ	ཊ	0FDE
005F	_	ß	□	◌	य़	য়	▯	▯	ୟ	▯	□	▯	▯	ෟ	ཟ	0FDF
0060	`	à	·	◌	ॠ	ৠ	▯	ૠ	ୠ	▯	ౠ	ೠ	ൠ	▯	ཉ	0FE0
0061	a	á	١	◌	ॡ	ৡ	▯	▯	ୡ	▯	ౡ	ೡ	ൡ	▯	ཡ	0FE1
0062	b	â	٢	◌	ॢ	ৢ	▯	▯	□	▯	□	▯	▯	▯	ར	0FE2
0063	c	ã	٣	◌	ॣ	ৣ	▯	▯	□	▯	□	▯	▯	▯	ལ	0FE3
0064	d	ä	٤	◌	।	▯	▯	▯	□	▯	□	▯	▯	▯	ཤ	0FE4
0065	e	å	٥	ر	॥	▯	▯	▯	□	▯	□	▯	▯	▯	ཥ	0FE5
0066	f	æ	٦	ے	०	০	੦	૦	୦		౦	೦	൦	▯	ས	0FE6
0067	g	ç	٧	◌	१	১	੧	૧	୧	௧	౧	೧	൧	▯	ཧ	0FE7
0068	h	è	٨	◌	२	২	੨	૨	୨	௨	౨	೨	൨	▯	ཨ	0FE8
0069	i	é	٩	ٹ	३	৩	੩	૩	୩	௩	౩	೩	൩	▯	ཀྵ	0FE9
006A	j	ê	٪	◌	४	৪	੪	૪	୪	௪	౪	೪	൪	▯	ཪ	0FEA
006B	k	ë	٫	◌	५	৫	੫	૫	୫	௫	౫	೫	൫	▯	0F6B	0FEB
006C	l	ì	٬	◌	६	৬	੬	૬	୬	௬	౬	೬	൬	▯	0F6C	0FEC
006D	m	í	٭	◌	७	৭	੭	૭	୭	௭	౭	೭	൭	▯	0F6D	0FED
006E	n	î	ٮ	ڈ	८	৮	੮	૮	୮	௮	౮	೮	൮	▯	0F6E	0FEE
006F	o	ï	ٯ	ژ	९	৯	੯	૯	୯	௯	౯	೯	൯	▯	0F6F	0FEF
0070	p	ð	◌	.	॰	ৰ	ੰ	▯	୰	௰	□	▯	▯	▯	0F70	0FF0
0071	q	ñ	ٱ	١	□	ৱ	ੱ	▯	□	௱	□	▯	▯	▯	◌ཱ	0FF1
0072	r	ò	ٲ	٢	□	৲	ੲ	▯	□	௲	□	▯	▯	ෲ	◌ི	0FF2
0073	s	ó	ٳ	٣	□	৳	ੳ	▯	□	▯	□	▯	▯	▯	◌ཱི	0FF3
0074	t	ô	ٴ	٤	□	৴	ੴ	▯	□	▯	□	▯	▯	෴	◌ུ	0FF4

	Latin	Latin-1	Arabic	Arabic Extd	Devanagari	Bengali	Gurmukhi	Gujarati	Oriya	Tamil	Telugu	Kannada	Malayalam	Sinhala	Tibetan-1	Tibetan-2
	0000	0080	0600	0680	0900	0980	0A00	0A80	0B00	0B80	0C00	0C80	0D00	0D80	0F00	0F80
0075	u	õ	ٵ	۵	□	৵	□	□	□	□	□	□	□	□	ཱུ	0FF5
0076	v	ö	ٶ	۶	□	৶	□	□	□	□	□	□	□	□	ྲྀ	0FF6
0077	w	÷	ٷ	۷	□	৷	□	□	□	□	□	□	□	□	ཷ	0FF7
0078	x	ø	ٸ	۸	□	৸	□	□	□	□	□	□	□	□	ླྀ	0FF8
0079	y	ù	ٹ	۹	□	৹	□	□	□	□	□	□	□	□	ཹ	0FF9
007A	z	ú	ٺ	ۺ	□	৺	□	□	□	□	□	□	□	□	ེ	0FFA
007B	{	û	ٻ	ۻ	□	□	□	□	□	□	□	□	□	□	ཻ	0FFB
007C	|	ü	ټ	ۼ	□	□	□	□	□	□	□	□	□	□	ོ	0FFC
007D	}	ý	ٽ	۽	□	□	□	□	□	□	□	□	□	□	ཽ	0FFD
007E	~	þ	پ	۾	□	□	□	□	□	□	□	□	□	□	ཾ	0FFE
007F		Ÿ	ٿ	ۿ	□	□	□	□	□	□	□	□	□	□	ཿ	0FFF

Note: 0000 through 001F, 007F and 0800 through 009F hex are control characters. 0020 hex is the space character, and 00A0 is no-break space (NBSP) character.

Note: Devanagari consonants ऱ, य़, ऩ and ऴ, and the vowels ऍ and ऑ are not used in any major Devanagari script-based language. The consonants ऱ, ऩ and ऴ, and the vowels ऍ and ऑ letters can be used only for transliterating South-Indian scripts, and the consonant य़ can be used for transliterating Bengali and Oriya scripts.

Tips: To know the hexadecimal Unicode of a character in WordPad (2000, XP and higher) and Microsoft Word (2002 and higher), one should select the character and press Alt-x (*but not* Alt-Shift-x).[5] The character will be replaced by its hexadecimal code in Unicode character set. Pressing Alt-x again will toggle the hexadecimal code back to the Unicode character. (Alt-x will not change the hexadecimal code to its corresponding character for the codes zero through thirty-one, and numbers above 10FFFF hex.)

Tips: Certain characters (say upto the code 255) can also be keyed in by pressing Alt key together with code of the character in four-digit decimal number from the numeric keypad (along with preceding zero(es)). Alt key is to be pressed first, then the decimal number[6] is to be entered in consecutive digits while keeping Alt key pressed, and then Alt key is to be released. The numbers are to be keyed in from the numeric keypad only, and not from the main keyboard keys. Also, the NumLock should be in "ON" stat.

[5] In many cases, placing the cursor just after the character, and then pressing Alt-x would produce the same result.

[6] The number will not show up on the screen.

ANNEXURE (E)

Ready Reference for Typist

Typists find it difficult to type in Indic scripts. The difficulties are primarily because of the following reasons whose comprehension will help in typing in Indic scripts. Even though the difficulties have been explained with reference to select Indic scripts, these are also applicable to other Indic and even similar other scripts:

1. Some ligatures are difficult to visualize as a conjunct of consonants. For example, it is difficult to visualize that ज्ञ consists of characters ज, ◌् and ञ, or that क्ष consists of characters क, ◌् and ष in that sequence. One must be conversant with the composition of such conjuncts.
2. Even though Indic languages are written from left-to-right, the formation of ligatures does not strictly follow the left-to-right rule. Formation of ligature in conjunct consonants generally follows top-to-down sequence, left-to-right sequence, or a combination of the two, though not always.[7] Nonetheless, typing must be in the sequence of their spelling (which usually corresponds to the pronunciation), and not visual appearance.
   (a) Certain glyphs appear much before their sound in the word. For example, i-vowel sign is visually the first glyph in स्थि (sthi), even though it is the last sound. In Bengali, Oriya and South Indian scripts, e- and ai-vowel signs precede the consonants they modify.

   (b) Certain glyphs appear on the both sides of consonants and conjuncts. For example, glyphs of o- and au-vowel signs are placed on both the sides of the consonant in some Indic scripts such as Bengali, Oriya and South Indian scripts. They should not be assumed as consisting of two or more vowel signs. For example, கோ (ko in Tamil) is to be typed as க (ka) followed by ◌ோ (vowel sign o), and not க (ka), ெ◌ (vowel sign e), ◌ா (vowel sign aa), or even ெ◌ (vowel sign e), க (ka), ◌ா (vowel sign aa).

---

[7] Similarly, Arabic script texts are written not just in right-to-left pattern. Within a conjunct, the pattern also follows top-to-bottom (and even bottom-to-top). However, unlike Urdu calligraphy, many Arabic script implementations in computers is considerably flattened and linear in form, which reduces the confusion over sequence of characters is considerably less in Arabic script than that in Indic scripts.

(c) Some glyphs appear much later in ligature than their sound. For example, ra-sound is the first sound in र्ध्न्या (rdhnya), even though reph-sign is the rightmost glyph.

(d) Anusvara sign comes a little before its sound in the sequence. For example, even though anusvara appears with letter अ in अंग, it is pronounced as ङ् with the following consonant ग. अंग and अङ्ग are grammatically the same despite different spellings and appearances.

(e) In formation of ligatures, certain prominent sounds get less space. For example, ढ is so prominent in ढ्री (Dhrii) that it appears as if the ii-vowel sign is on letter ढ, even though it is actually on the less prominent letter र!

3. It should be noted that

(a) In certain keyboard layouts, there may be single keys for some frequently used conjuncts (say, for श्र, क्ष, त्र, ज्ञ).

(b) Some ligatures may not appear exactly as shown in the table below, even if the spelling is correct. This is because of font. Change of font changes the formation of ligatures. For example, the sequence of characters ङ, ् and ग produces ङ्ग in Mangal font, but ङ्ग in DVBOTSurekh font.

(c) A few fonts were actually defective!

4. Even though Indic alphabets do not list *halant* (also called *hasant*, *virama* etc), it is the most important character for typing in Indic scripts. As the conjunct consonants have not been coded separately in Unicode, the conjunct consonants are to be formed with the help of *halant*.

Some conjucnt syllables and sequence of characters for typing them are given below. This sequence is to be used for typing texts using telephone keypads. The sequence of typing is left-to-right.

Syllable	Character sequence
Devanagari	
ॐ	ॐ (*not* ऊ ◌ँ)
ऊँट	ऊ ◌ँ ट
एवं	ए व ◌ं
क्	क ◌्
क्क	क ◌् क
क्त	क ◌् त
क़्त	क ◌़ ◌् त
क्ति	क ◌् त ि◌[8]
क्तिं	क ◌् त ि◌ ◌ं
क्ते	क ◌् त ◌े
क्त्व	क ◌् त ◌् व
क्न	क ◌् न
क्र	क ◌् र
क्रॄ	क ◌् र ◌ॄ
क्व	क ◌् व
क्ष	क ◌् ष
क्षे	क ◌् ष ◌े
क्ष्मि	क ◌् ष ◌् म ि◌
क्ष्र	क ◌् ष ◌् र
क्ष्व	क ◌् ष ◌् व
ख्न	ख ◌् न
ग्नि	ग ◌् न ि◌
ग्र	ग ◌् र
ग्रैः	ग ◌् र ◌ै ◌ः
घ्न	घ ◌् न
ङ्क	ङ ◌् क
ङ्क्त	ङ ◌् क ◌् त
ङ्क्ति	ङ ◌् क ◌् त ि◌
ङ्क्षे	ङ ◌् क ◌् ष ◌े
ङ्ख	ङ ◌् ख
ङ्गे	ङ ◌् ग ◌े
ङ्गो	ङ ◌् ग ◌ो
ङ्घ	ङ ◌् घ
ङ्म	ङ ◌् म
च्च	च ◌् च
च्छृं	च ◌् छ ◌ृ ◌ं
च्छ्रु	च ◌् छ ◌् र ◌ु
च्छ्रे	च ◌् छ ◌् र ◌े
छ्व	छ ◌् व
ज़ि	ज ◌़ ि◌ *or* ज़ ि◌
ज्ज	ज ◌् ज
ज्ज्व	ज ◌् ज ◌् व
ज्ञ	ज ◌् ञ
ज्ञि	ज ◌् ञ ि◌
ज्ञै	ज ◌् ञ ◌ै
ज्ञ्र	ज ◌् ञ ◌् र
ज्र	ज ◌् र
ञ्च	ञ ◌् च
ञ्छ	ञ ◌् छ
ञ्ज	ञ ◌् ज
ञ्झ	ञ ◌् झ
ट्क	ट ◌् क
ट्ग	ट ◌् ग

[8] Vowel letter cannot be treated as a sequence of अ and the vowel sign. Also, a vowel sign cannot be treated as a sequence of halant and vowel letter. Thus, आ ≠ अ + ◌ा, ई ≠ अ + ◌ी, and कि ≠ क + ◌् + इ.

Syllable	Character sequence
ट्ट	ट ◌् ट
ट्ठ	ट ◌् ठ
ट्न	ट ◌् न
ट्य	ट ◌् य
ट्र	ट ◌् र
ट्विं	ट ◌् व ि ं
ठ्ठ	ठ ◌् ठ
ठ्न	ठ ◌् न
ठ्य	ठ ◌् य
डॉ	ड ◌ॉ
ड्ग	ड ◌् ग
ड्ड	ड ◌् ड
ड्ढ	ड ◌् ढ
ड्न	ड ◌् न
ड्य	ड ◌् य
ड्रं	ड ◌् र ◌ं
ड्व	ड ◌् व
ढ्ढ	ढ ◌् ढ
ढ्न	ढ ◌् न
ढ्य	ढ ◌् य
तृ	त ◌ृ
त्त	त ◌् त
त्त्व	त ◌् त ◌् व
त्न	त ◌् न
त्र	त ◌् र
त्रि	त ◌् र ि
त्र्य	त ◌् र ◌् य
त्वि	त ◌् व ि
थ्न	थ ◌् न
दुः	द ◌ु ◌ः

Syllable	Character sequence
दृ	द ◌ृ
द्ग	द ◌् ग
द्ग्र	द ◌् ग ◌् र
द्घ	द ◌् घ
द्दे	द ◌् द ◌े
द्ध	द ◌् ध
द्धि	द ◌् ध ि
द्ध्य	द ◌् ध ◌् य
द्न	द ◌् न
द्ब	द ◌् ब
द्ब्र	द ◌् ब ◌् र
द्भ	द ◌् भ
द्भि	द ◌् भ ि
द्भ्य	द ◌् भ ◌् य
द्म	द ◌् म
द्मि	द ◌् म ि
द्य	द ◌् य
द्यौ	द ◌् य ◌ौ
द्य्भ	द ◌् य ◌् भ
द्य्र	द ◌् य ◌् र
द्य्व	द ◌् य ◌् व
द्र	द ◌् र
द्र्य	द ◌् र ◌् य
द्व	द ◌् व
द्वि	द ◌् व ि
द्वै	द ◌् व ◌ै
ध्न	ध ◌् न
न्द्रि	न ◌् द ◌् र ि
न्द्वै	न ◌् द ◌् व ◌ै
न्धि	न ◌् ध ि

Syllable	Character sequence
न्ध्रि	न ◌् ध ◌् र ◌ि
न्नि	न ◌् न ◌ि
न्नै	न ◌् न ◌ै
न्न्य	न ◌् न ◌् य
न्वि	न ◌् व ◌ि
प्त	प ◌् त
प्न	प ◌् न
प्र	प ◌् र
फ्न	फ ◌् न
फ़्रि	फ ◌़ ◌् र ◌ि *or* फ़ ◌् र ◌ि
फ्र्क	फ ◌् र ◌् क
बॅंक	ब ◌ॅ ◌ं क
ब्न	ब ◌् न
भ्न	भ ◌् न
में	म ◌े ◌ं
म्न	म ◌् न
म्मा	म ◌् म ◌ा
यूँ	य ◌ू ◌ँ
य्न	य ◌् न
रु	र ◌ु
रू	र ◌ू
र्क	र ◌् क
र्ग	र ◌् ग
र्गा	र ◌् ग ◌ा
र्ग्य	र ◌् ग ◌् य
र्जि	र ◌् ज ◌ि
र्ज्यो	र ◌् ज ◌् य ◌ो
र्णों	र ◌् ण ◌ो ◌ं
र्ता	र ◌् त ◌ा
र्तिं	र ◌् त ◌ि ◌ं
र्त्रे	र ◌् त ◌् र ◌े
र्थी	र ◌् थ ◌ी
र्थ्य	र ◌् थ ◌् य
र्दे	र ◌् द ◌े
र्द्ध	र ◌् द ◌् ध
र्द्र	र ◌् द ◌् र
र्द्व	र ◌् द ◌् व
र्ध्न्या	र ◌् ध ◌् न ◌् य ◌ा
र्ध्रु	र ◌् ध ◌् र ◌ु
र्ध्व	र ◌् ध ◌् व
र्प	र ◌् प
र्बु	र ◌् ब ◌ु
र्ब्र	र ◌् ब ◌् र
र्भा	र ◌् भ ◌ा
र्भु	र ◌् भ ◌ु
र्मा	र ◌् म ◌ा
र्मि	र ◌् म ◌ि
र्म्नो	र ◌् म ◌् न ◌ो
र्म्य	र ◌् म ◌् य
र्यु	र ◌् य ◌ु
र्यों	र ◌् य ◌ो ◌ं
र्रे	र ◌् र ◌े
र्वं	र ◌् व ◌ं
र्वि	र ◌् व ◌ि
र्शी	र ◌् श ◌ी
र्श्व	र ◌् श ◌् व
र्षि	र ◌् ष ◌ि
र्षों	र ◌् ष ◌ो ◌ं
र्ष्णे	र ◌् ष ◌् ण ◌े
र्ष्म	र ◌् ष ◌् म

Syllable	Character sequence
र्हृ	र ◌् ह ◌ृ
ल्ल	ल ◌् ल
ल्वि	ल ◌् व ◌ि
ळ्क	ळ ◌् क
व्द्य	व ◌् द ◌् य
व्न	व ◌् न
श्च	श ◌् च
श्चै	श ◌् च ◌ै
श्न	श ◌् न
श्मि	श ◌् म ◌ि
श्र	श ◌् र
श्रि	श ◌् र ◌ि
श्ल	श ◌् ल
श्व	श ◌् व
ष्ट	ष ◌् ट
ष्टं	ष ◌् ट ◌ं
ष्टुं	ष ◌् ट ◌ु ◌ं
ष्ट्र	ष ◌् ट ◌् र
ष्ट्वे	ष ◌् ट ◌् व ◌े
ष्ठि	ष ◌् ठ ◌ि
ष्ठ्र	ष ◌् ठ ◌् र
स्ट्रि	स ◌् ट ◌् र ◌ि
स्ट्रॉं	स ◌् ट ◌् र ◌ॉ ◌ं
स्ट्रो	स ◌् ट ◌् र ◌ो
स्ति	स ◌् त ◌ि
स्त्रि	स ◌् त ◌् र ◌ि
स्थि	स ◌् थ ◌ि
स्थ्म्र्यिँ	स ◌् थ ◌् म ◌् र ◌् य ◌ि ◌ँ
स्नि	स ◌् न ◌ि
स्र	स ◌् र

Syllable	Character sequence
स्वि	स ◌् व ◌ि
हूँ	ह ◌ू ◌ँ
हृ	ह ◌ृ
ह्क	ह ◌् क
ह्ण	ह ◌् ण
ह्न	ह ◌् न
ह्म	ह ◌् म
ह्य	ह ◌् य
ह्रिं	ह ◌् र ◌ि ◌ं
ह्रु	ह ◌् र ◌ु
ह्ल	ह ◌् ल
ह्ळ	ह ◌् ळ
ह्व	ह ◌् व
ह्वृ	ह ◌् व ◌ृ
Bengali	
অ্যঁ	অ ◌্ য ◌ঁ
অ্যাঁ	অ ◌্ য ◌া ◌ঁ
এ্যাঁ	এ ◌্ য ◌া ◌ঁ
ক্	ক ◌্
কৃ	ক ◌ৃ
কৄ	ক ◌ৄ
ক্ক	ক ◌্ ক
ক্ট্র	ক ◌্ ট ◌্ ৰ *or* ক ◌্ ট ◌্ র[9]
ক্ত	ক ◌্ ত
ক্ত্র	ক ◌্ ত ◌্ র
ক্ন	ক ◌্ ন
ক্ব	ক ◌্ ব
ক্ম	ক ◌্ ম
ক্যা	ক ◌্ য ◌া
ক্যিঁ	ক ◌্ য ◌ি ◌ঁ
ক্যীঁ	ক ◌্ য ◌ী ◌ঁ
ক্যূঁ	ক ◌্ য ◌ূ ◌ঁ
ক্যৈঁ	ক ◌্ য ◌ৈ ◌ঁ
ক্যৌঁ	ক ◌্ য ◌ৌ ◌ঁ
ক্র	ক ◌্ র

[9] Bengali letter র may be replaced by corresponding Assamese letter ৰ everywhere in the table.

Syllable	Character sequence
ক্ল	ক ◌্ ল
ক্ষ	ক ◌্ ষ
ক্ষ্ণ	ক ◌্ ষ ◌্ ণ
ক্ষ্ব	ক ◌্ ষ ◌্ ব
ক্ষ্ম	ক ◌্ ষ ◌্ ম
ক্ষ্র	ক ◌্ ষ ◌্ র
ক্ষ্র্যৌঁ	ক ◌্ ষ ◌্ র ◌্ য ◌ৌ ◌ঁ
ক্স	ক ◌্ স
কি	ক ◌ি
কে	ক ◌ে
কৈ	ক ◌ৈ
কো	ক ◌ো
কৌ	ক ◌ৌ
কৗ	ক ◌ৗ
ক্ব	ক ◌্ ব
খ্রু	খ ◌্ র ◌ু
খ্রূ	খ ◌্ র ◌ূ
গ্দ	গ ◌্ দ
গ্ধ	গ ◌্ ধ
গ্ম	গ ◌্ ম
গ্রু	গ ◌্ র ◌ু
গ্রূ	গ ◌্ র ◌ূ
ঘ্র	ঘ ◌্ র
ঘ্রু	ঘ ◌্ র ◌ু
ঘ্রূ	ঘ ◌্ র ◌ূ
ঙ্ক	ঙ ◌্ ক
ঙ্ক্র	ঙ ◌্ ক ◌্ র
ঙ্ক্ষ্র	ঙ ◌্ ক ◌্ ষ ◌্ র
ঙ্গ	ঙ ◌্ গ
ঙ্ঘ্র	ঙ ◌্ ঘ ◌্ র
ঙ্ম	ঙ ◌্ ম
চ্ছ্ব	চ ◌্ ছ ◌্ ব
চ্ছ্র	চ ◌্ ছ ◌্ র
চ্ঞ	চ ◌্ ঞ
জ্জ্ব	জ ◌্ জ ◌্ ব
জ্ঞ	জ ◌্ ঞ
জ্রু	জ ◌্ র ◌ু
জ্রূ	জ ◌্ র ◌ূ
ঞ্চ	ঞ ◌্ চ
ঞ্চ্ব	ঞ ◌্ চ ◌্ ব
ঞ্ছ	ঞ ◌্ ছ
ঞ্জ	ঞ ◌্ জ
ঞ্ঝ	ঞ ◌্ ঝ
ট্ট	ট ◌্ ট
ট্ট্র	ট ◌্ ট ◌্ র
ট্বি	ট ◌্ ব ◌ি
ট্ম	ট ◌্ ম
ট্র	ট ◌্ র
ড্ড	ড ◌্ ড
ড্ম	ড ◌্ ম
ণ্ট্রি	ণ ◌্ ট ◌্ র ◌ি
ণ্ঠে	ণ ◌্ ঠ ◌ে
ণ্ড	ণ ◌্ ড
ণ্ড্র	ণ ◌্ ড ◌্ র
ণ্ণ	ণ ◌্ ণ
ণ্ন	ণ ◌্ ন
ণ্ম	ণ ◌্ ম
ত্ত	ত ◌্ ত
ত্ত্ব	ত ◌্ ত ◌্ ব
ত্থ	ত ◌্ থ
ত্ন	ত ◌্ ন
ত্র	ত ◌্ র
ত্রু	ত ◌্ র ◌ু
ত্রূ	ত ◌্ র ◌ূ
থ্রু	থ ◌্ র ◌ু
থ্রূ	থ ◌্ র ◌ূ
দ্দ	দ ◌্ দ
দ্দ্ব	দ ◌্ দ ◌্ ব
দ্ধ	দ ◌্ ধ
দ্ব	দ ◌্ ব
ধ্ব্র	ধ ◌্ ব ◌্ র
ধ্রু	ধ ◌্ র ◌ু
ধ্রূ	ধ ◌্ র ◌ূ
ন্ত্ব	ন ◌্ ত ◌্ ব
ন্ত্র	ন ◌্ ত ◌্ র
ন্থ	ন ◌্ থ
ন্দ্রু	ন ◌্ দ ◌্ র ◌ু
ন্দ্রূ	ন ◌্ দ ◌্ র ◌ূ
ন্ধ্র	ন ◌্ ধ ◌্ র
প্ত	প ◌্ ত
প্ত্র	প ◌্ ত ◌্ র
প্রু	প ◌্ র ◌ু
প্রূ	প ◌্ র ◌্ ◌ূ
প্লু	প ◌্ ল ◌ু
প্লূ	প ◌্ ল ◌ূ
ফ্ট	ফ ◌্ ট
ব্জ	ব ◌্ জ
ব্দ্রু	ব ◌্ দ ◌্ র ◌ু
ব্দ্রূ	ব ◌্ দ ◌্ র ◌ূ
ব্রু	ব ◌্ র ◌ু
ব্রূ	ব ◌্ র ◌ূ
ম্ব্র	ম ◌্ ব ◌্ র

Syllable	Character sequence
ম্রু	ম ◌্ র ◌ু
ম্রূ	ম ◌্ র ◌ূ
ম্স্র	ম ◌্ স ◌্ র
র্ক	র ◌্ ক
র্য	র ◌্ য
র্য্য	র ◌্ য ◌্ য
র্য্যা	র ◌্ য ◌্ য ◌া
ল্গু	ল ◌্ গ ◌ু
ল্গূ	ল ◌্ গ ◌ূ
ল্ত	ল ◌্ ত
শ্রি	শ ◌্ র ি
ষ্ক্র	ষ ◌্ ক ◌্ র
ষ্ট্রি	ষ ◌্ ট ◌্ র ি
ষ্ঠ্র	ষ ◌্ ঠ ◌্ র
ষ্ণ	ষ ◌্ ণ
স্ক্র	স ◌্ ক ◌্ র
স্ট্রি	স ◌্ ট ◌্ র ি
স্ট্রো	স ◌্ ট ◌্ র ◌ো
স্ত্ব	স ◌্ ত ◌্ ব
স্ফ্র	স ◌্ ফ ◌্ র
স্রু	স ◌্ র ◌ু
স্রূ	স ◌্ র ◌ূ
স্লু	স ◌্ ল ◌ু
স্লূ	স ◌্ ল ◌ূ
হ্ন	হ ◌্ ন
হ্ব	হ ◌্ ব
হ্র	হ ◌্ র
ৰ্য	ৰ ◌্ য
ৰ্ৰ	ৰ ◌্ ৰ
Gurmukhi	
ਕੱ	ਕ ◌ੱ
ਕ੍ਹ	ਕ ◌੍ ਹ
ਕ੍ਹ੍ਰਿੰ	ਕ ◌੍ ਹ ◌੍ ਰ ਿ ◌ੰ
ਕ੍ਯ	ਕ ◌੍ ਯ
ਕ੍ਯਿੱ	ਕ ◌੍ ਯ ਿ ◌ੱ
ਕ੍ਯਿੰ	ਕ ◌੍ ਯ ਿ ◌ੰ
ਕ੍ਰ	ਕ ◌੍ ਰ
ਕ੍ਰਿੱ	ਕ ◌੍ ਰ ਿ ◌ੱ
ਕ੍ਵ	ਕ ◌੍ ਵ
ਕ੍ਵੈੰ	ਕ ◌੍ ਵ ◌ੈ ◌ੰ
ਕਾਂ	ਕ ◌ਾ ◌ਂ
ਕਿੰ	ਕ ਿ ◌ੰ
ਕੀੱ	ਕ ◌ੀ ◌ੱ
ਕੀਂ	ਕ ◌ੀ ◌ਂ
ਕੁ	ਕ ◌ੁ
ਕੁੱ	ਕ ◌ੁ ◌ੱ
ਕੂ	ਕ ◌ੂ
ਕੇ	ਕ ◌ੇ
ਕੈ	ਕ ◌ੈ
ਕੋ	ਕ ◌ੋ
ਕੌ	ਕ ◌ੌ
ੜ	ੜ *or* ਡ ◌਼
Gujarati	
ક્ક	ક ◌્ ક
ક્ક્ર	ક ◌્ ક ◌્ ર
ક્ય	ક ◌્ ય
ક્ય્ર	ક ◌્ ય ◌્ ર
ક્ય્ર	ક ◌્ ય ◌્ ર
ક્ષ્ર	ક ◌્ ષ ◌્ ર
ઙ્ક	ઙ ◌્ ક
ઙ્ક્ષ	ઙ ◌્ ક ◌્ ષ
ઙ્ગ	ઙ ◌્ ગ
ઙ્ઘ	ઙ ◌્ ઘ
છ્વ	છ ◌્ વ
જી	જ ◌ી
જ્ઞ્ર	જ ◌્ ઞ ◌્ ર
ઞ્ચ્ર	ઞ ◌્ ચ ◌્ ર
ઞ્જ્ર	ઞ ◌્ જ ◌્ ર
ટ્ટ્ર	ટ ◌્ ટ ◌્ ર
ટ્ઠ્ર	ટ ◌્ ઠ ◌્ ર
ઠ્ઠ	ઠ ◌્ ઠ
ઠ્ઠ્ર	ઠ ◌્ ઠ ◌્ ર

Syllable	Character sequence
ડ્ડ્ર	ડ ્ ડ ્ ર
ડ્રૃ	ડ ્ ર ૃ
ઢ્ઢ્ર	ઢ ્ ઢ ્ ર
ણ્ર	ણ ્ ર
ત્ત્ર	ત ્ ત ્ ર
દ્ગ્ર	દ ્ ગ ્ ર
દ્ઘ	દ ્ ઘ
દ્ઘ્ર	દ ્ ઘ ્ ર
દ્દ	દ ્ દ
દ્દ્ર	દ ્ દ ્ ર
દ્ધ	દ ્ ધ
દ્ધ્ર	દ ્ ધ ્ ર
દ્ન્ર	દ ્ ન ્ ર
દ્બ	દ ્ બ
દ્બ્ર	દ ્ બ ્ ર
દ્મ્ર	દ ્ મ ્ ર
દ્ય્ર	દ ્ ય ્ ર
દ્ર્ય	દ ્ ર ્ ય
દ્ર્ય્ર	દ ્ ર ્ ય ્ ર
દ્વ	દ ્ વ
દ્વ્ર	દ ્ વ ્ ર
ન્ન્ર	ન ્ ન ્ ર
ફ્ર	ફ ્ ર
રૂ	ર ૂ
ર્કિં	ર ્ ક િ ં
ર્ક્કિઁ	ર ્ ક ્ ક િ ઁ

Syllable	Character sequence
ર્સ્ટ્ય્રિ	ર ્ સ ્ ટ ્ ય ્ ર િ
શ્ચ્ર	શ ્ ચ ્ ર
શ્ર્ન	શ ્ ર ્ ન
શ્વ્ર	શ ્ વ ્ ર
હ્ણ	હ ્ ણ
હ્ણ્ર	હ ્ ણ ્ ર
હ્ન	હ્ન
હ્ન્ર	હ ્ ન ્ ર
હ્મ્ર	હ ્ મ ્ ર
હ્ય	હ ્ ય
હ્ય્ર	હ ્ ય ્ ર
હ્ર	હ ્ ર
હ્લ	હ ્ લ
હ્લ્ર	હ ્ લ ્ ર
હ્વ	હ ્ વ
હ્વ્ર	હ ્ વ ્ ર
Oriya	
କୗ	କ ୗ
କି	କ ି
କୁଂ	କ ୁ ଂ
କ୍ଟ	କ ୍ ଟ
କ୍ଟ୍ରୁ	କ ୍ ଟ ୍ ର ୁ
କ୍ତ	କ ୍ ତ
କ୍ନ	କ ୍ ନ
କ୍ବ	କ ୍ ବ
କ୍ୟ	କ ୍ ୟ

Syllable	Character sequence
କ୍ରୁ	କ ◌୍ ର ◌ୁ
କ୍ଲ	କ ◌୍ ଲ
କ୍ଲ୍ରିଂ	କ ◌୍ ଲ ◌୍ ର ◌ି ◌ଂ
କ୍ମ	କ ◌୍ ମ
କ୍ଷ	କ ◌୍ ଷ
କ୍ଷ୍ଣ	କ ◌୍ ଷ ◌୍ ଣ
କ୍ସ	କ ◌୍ ସ
କା	କ ◌ା
କୀ	କ ◌ୀ
କେ	କ ◌େ
କୈ	କ ◌ୈ
କୋ	କ ◌ୋ
କୌ	କ ◌ୌ
କ◌ୗ	କ ◌ୗ
ଗ୍ଦ	ଗ ◌୍ ଦ
ଗ୍ଧ	ଗ ◌୍ ଧ
ଙ୍କ	ଙ ◌୍ କ
ଙ୍କ୍ତିଂ	ଙ ◌୍ କ ◌୍ ତ ◌ି ◌ଂ
ଙ୍କ୍ଷ	ଙ ◌୍ କ ◌୍ ଷ
ଙ୍ଖ	ଙ ◌୍ ଖ
ଙ୍ଗ	ଙ ◌୍ ଗ
ଙ୍ଘ	ଙ ◌୍ ଘ
ଚ୍ଚ	ଚ ◌୍ ଚ
ଚ୍ଛ	ଚ ◌୍ ଛ
ଜ୍ଜ	ଜ ◌୍ ଜ
ଜ୍ଝ	ଜ ◌୍ ଝ

Syllable	Character sequence
ଜ୍ଞ	ଜ ◌୍ ଞ
ଞ୍ଚ	ଞ ◌୍ ଚ
ଞ୍ଛ	ଞ ◌୍ ଛ
ଞ୍ଜ	ଞ ◌୍ ଜ
ଞ୍ଝ	ଞ ◌୍ ଝ
ଟ୍ଟ	ଟ ◌୍ ଟ
ଡ୍ଡ	ଡ ◌୍ ଡ
ଣ୍ଟ	ଣ ◌୍ ଟ
ଣ୍ଠ	ଣ ◌୍ ଠ
ଣ୍ଡ	ଣ ◌୍ ଡ
ଣ୍ଢ	ଣ ◌୍ ଢ
ଣ୍ଣ	ଣ ◌୍ ଣ
ତ୍ତ	ତ ◌୍ ତ
ତ୍ଥ	ତ ◌୍ ଥ
ତ୍ପ	ତ ◌୍ ପ
ତ୍ମ	ତ ◌୍ ମ
ତ୍ର	ତ ◌୍ ର
ତ୍ସ	ତ ◌୍ ସ
ତ୍ସ୍ନ	ତ ◌୍ ସ ◌୍ ନ
ଦ୍ଘ	ଦ ◌୍ ଘ
ଦ୍ଦ	ଦ ◌୍ ଦ
ଦ୍ଭ	ଦ ◌୍ ଭ
ଦ୍ୟ	ଦ ◌୍ ଯ
ଧ୍ୟ	ଧ ◌୍ ଯ
ନ୍ତ	ନ ◌୍ ତ
ନ୍ତ୍ର	ନ ◌୍ ତ ◌୍ ର

Syllable	Character sequence
ନ୍ଥ	ନ ◌୍ ଥ
ନ୍ଦ	ନ ◌୍ ଦ
ନ୍ଧ	ନ ◌୍ ଧ
ନ୍ନ	ନ ◌୍ ନ
ପ୍ତ	ପ ◌୍ ତ
ପ୍ପ	ପ ◌୍ ପ
ପ୍ସ	ପ ◌୍ ସ
ବ୍ଦ	ବ ◌୍ ଦ
ବ୍ଧ	ବ ◌୍ ଧ
ବ୍ବ	ବ ◌୍ ବ
ବ୍ୟ	ବ ◌୍ ଯ
ମ୍ପ	ମ ◌୍ ପ
ମ୍ଫ	ମ ◌୍ ଫ
ମ୍ବ	ମ ◌୍ ବ
ମ୍ବ୍ବ	ମ ◌୍ ବ ◌୍ ବ
ମ୍ଭ	ମ ◌୍ ଭ
ମ୍ମ	ମ ◌୍ ମ
ର୍ତ୍ୟି	ର ◌୍ ତ ◌୍ ଯ ◌ି
ର୍ଯ	ର ◌୍ ଯ
ର୍ଷ୍ୟେଂ	ର ◌୍ ଷ ◌୍ ଯ ◌େ ◌ଂ
ଲ୍କ	ଲ ◌୍ କ
ଲ୍ଗ	ଲ ◌୍ ଗ
ଲ୍ପ	ଲ ◌୍ ପ
ଲ୍ଫ	ଲ ◌୍ ଫ
ଲ୍ଲ	ଲ ◌୍ ଲ
ଳ୍କ	ଳ ◌୍ କ

Syllable	Character sequence
ଳ୍ଳ	ଳ ◌୍ ଳ
ଶ୍ଚ	ଶ ◌୍ ଚ
ଶ୍ଛ	ଶ ◌୍ ଛ
ଷ୍କ	ଷ ◌୍ କ
ଷ୍ଟ	ଷ ◌୍ ଟ
ଷ୍ଟ୍ୟୌଁ	ଷ ◌୍ ଟ ◌୍ ଯ ◌ୌ ◌ଁ
ଷ୍ଠ	ଷ ◌୍ ଠ
ଷ୍ଣ	ଷ ◌୍ ଣ
ଷ୍ପ	ଷ ◌୍ ପ
ଷ୍ଫ	ଷ ◌୍ ଫ
ସ୍କ	ସ ◌୍ କ
ସ୍ଖ	ସ ◌୍ ଖ
ସ୍ତ	ସ ◌୍ ତ
ସ୍ତ୍ର	ସ ◌୍ ତ ◌୍ ର
ସ୍ତ୍ର୍ୟୌଂ	ସ ◌୍ ତ ◌୍ ର ◌୍ ଯ ◌ୌ ◌ଂ
ସ୍ଥ	ସ ◌୍ ଥ
ସ୍ଥିଁଃ	ସ ◌୍ ଥ ◌ି ◌ଁ ଃ
ସ୍ପ	ସ ◌୍ ପ
ସ୍ଫ୍ରୌ	ସ ◌୍ ଫ ◌୍ ର ◌ୌ
ସ୍ବୈ	ସ ◌୍ ବ ◌ୈ
ହଁର୍କୀଁ	ହ ◌ଁ ର ◌୍ କ ◌ୀ ◌ଁ
Tamil	
க்	க ◌்
க்ஷ	க ◌் ஷ
கா	க ◌ா
கி	க ◌ி

Syllable	Character sequence
கீ	க ◌ீ
கு	க ◌ு
கெ	க ெ◌
கே	க ே◌
கை	க ை◌
கொ	க ெ◌ா
கோ	க ே◌ா
கௌ	க ெ◌ள
ஙு	ங ◌ு
ஙூ	ங ◌ூ
சு	ச ◌ு
சூ	ச ◌ூ
ஞு	ஞ ◌ு
ஞூ	ஞ ◌ூ
டி	ட ◌ி
டீ	ட ◌ீ
டு	ட ◌ு
டூ	ட ◌ூ
ணு	ண ◌ு
ணூ	ண ◌ூ
து	த ◌ு
தூ	த ◌ூ
நு	ந ◌ு
நூ	ந ◌ூ
பு	ப ◌ு
பூ	ப ◌ூ
மு	ம ◌ு
மூ	ம ◌ூ
யு	ய ◌ு

Syllable	Character sequence
யூ	ய ◌ூ
ரி	ர ◌ி
ரீ	ர ◌ீ
ரு	ர ◌ு
ரூ	ர ◌ூ
லு	ல ◌ு
லூ	ல ◌ூ
வு	வ ◌ு
வூ	வ ◌ூ
ளு	ள ◌ு
ளூ	ள ◌ூ
று	ற ◌ு
றூ	ற ◌ூ
னு	ன ◌ு
னூ	ன ◌ூ
Telugu	
కా	క ◌ా
కి	క ◌ి
కీ	క ◌ీ
కు	క ◌ు
కూ	క ◌ూ
కృ	క ◌ృ
కౄ	క ◌ౄ
కె	క ◌ె
కే	క ◌ే
కై	క ◌ై
కొ	క ◌ొ

Syllable	Character sequence
కో	క ◌ో
కౌ	క ◌ౌ
క్	క ◌్
క్కో	క ◌్ క ◌ో
క్ఖౌం	క ◌్ ఖ ◌ౌ ◌ం
క్య	క ◌్ య
క్ర	క ◌్ ర
క్ష	క ◌్ ష
జ్క	జ ◌్ క
జ్క్తి	జ ◌్ క ◌్ త ◌ి
జ్క్ష	జ ◌్ క ◌్ ష
జ్గ	జ ◌్ గ
జ్ఘ	జ ◌్ ఘ
జ్జ	జ ◌్ జ
జ్మ	జ ◌్ మ
జ్జ్వై	జ ◌్ జ ◌్ వ ◌ై
జ్ఞ	జ ◌్ ఞ
ఞ్చ	ఞ ◌్ చ
ఞ్ఛ	ఞ ◌్ ఛ
ఞ్జ	ఞ ◌్ జ
ఞ్ఝ	ఞ ◌్ ఝ
ట్య	ట ◌్ య
డ్డ	డ ◌్ డ
ణ్ట	ణ ◌్ ట
ణ్ఠ	ణ ◌్ ఠ

Syllable	Character sequence
ణ్డ	ణ ◌్ డ
ణ్డ	ణ ◌్ డ
ణ్ఢ	ణ ◌్ ఢ
ణ్ణ	ణ ◌్ ణ
త్త	త ◌్ త
త్ర	త ◌్ ర
ద్దే	ద ◌్ ద ◌ే
ద్ధ్య	ద ◌్ ధ ◌్ య
ద్న	ద ◌్ న
ద్బ్ర	ద ◌్ బ ◌్ ర
ద్య	ద ◌్ య
ద్యి	ద ◌్ య ◌ి
ద్వ	ద ◌్ వ
ద్వి	ద ◌్ వ ◌ి
న్త	న ◌్ త
న్థ	న ◌్ థ
న్ద	న ◌్ ద
న్ధ	న ◌్ ధ
న్ధ్రి	న ◌్ ధ ◌్ ర ◌ి
న్న	న ◌్ న
న్వి	న ◌్ వ ◌ి
ప్తి	ప ◌్ త ◌ి
మ్ప	మ ◌్ ప
మ్ఫ	మ ◌్ ఫ
మ్బ	మ ◌్ బ

Syllable	Character sequence
మ్భ	మ ◌్ భ
మ్మ	మ ◌్ మ
ర్	ర ◌్
ర్ణో	ర ◌్ ణ ◌ో
ర్తా	ర ◌్ త ◌ా
ర్త్రై	ర ◌్ త ◌్ ర ◌ై
ర్థీ	ర ◌్ థ ◌ీ
ర్థ్యై	ర ◌్ థ ◌్ య ◌ై
ర్ద్ధి	ర ◌్ ద ◌్ ధ ◌ి
ర్ద్యో	ర ◌్ ద ◌్ య ◌ో
ర్ధ్రు	ర ◌్ ధ ◌్ ర ◌ు
ర్రో	ర ◌్ ర ◌ో
ళ్క	ళ ◌్ క
ళ్ళ	ళ ◌్ ళ
వి	వ ◌ి
శ్చ	శ ◌్ చ
శ్న	శ ◌్ న
శ్ర	శ ◌్ ర
శ్లో	శ ◌్ ల ◌ో
శ్వి	శ ◌్ వ ◌ి
ష్ట	ష ◌్ ట
ష్ణ	ష ◌్ ణ
ష్య	ష ◌్ య
స్త్రి	స ◌్ త ◌్ ర ◌ి
హ్ఖ	హ ◌్ ఖ

Syllable	Character sequence
హ్ణ	హ ◌్ ణ
హ్మ	హ ◌్ మ
హ్య	హ ◌్ య
హ్ల	హ ◌్ ల
హ్వ	హ ◌్ వ
Kannada	
ಕಾ	ಕ ◌ಾ
ಕಿ	ಕ ◌ಿ
ಕೀ	ಕ ◌ೀ
ಕು	ಕ ◌ು
ಕೂ	ಕ ◌ೂ
ಕೃ	ಕ ◌ೃ
ಕೄ	ಕ ◌ೄ
ಕೆ	ಕ ◌ೆ
ಕೇ	ಕ ◌ೇ
ಕೈ	ಕ ◌ೈ
ಕೊ	ಕ ◌ೊ
ಕೋ	ಕ ◌ೋ
ಕೌ	ಕ ◌ೌ
ಕ್	ಕ ◌್
ಕ್ಕೋ	ಕ ◌್ ಕ ◌ೋ
ಕ್ಖೌಂ	ಕ ◌್ ಖ ◌ೌ ◌ಂ
ಕ್ಯ	ಕ ◌್ ಯ
ಕ್ರ	ಕ ◌್ ರ
ಕ್ಷ	ಕ ◌್ ಷ
ಜ್ಕ	ಜ ◌್ ಕ
ಜ್ಕ್ತ್	ಜ ◌್ ಕ ◌್ ತ ◌್

Syllable	Character sequence
ಙ್ಕ್ಷ	ಙ ◌್ ಕ ◌್ ಷ
ಙ್ಗ	ಙ ◌್ ಗ
ಙ್ಘ	ಙ ◌್ ಘ
ಙ್ಙ	ಙ ◌್ ಙ
ಙ್ಮ	ಙ ◌್ ಮ
ಜ್ಜ್ವೈ	ಜ ◌್ ಜ ◌್ ವ ◌ೈ
ಜ್ಞ	ಜ ◌್ ಞ
ಞ್ಚ	ಞ ◌್ ಚ
ಞ್ಛ	ಞ ◌್ ಛ
ಞ್ಜ	ಞ ◌್ ಜ
ಞ್ಝ	ಞ ◌್ ಝ
ಟ್ಯ	ಟ ◌್ ಯ
ಡ್ಡ	ಡ ◌್ ಡ
ಣ್ಟ	ಣ ◌್ ಟ
ಣ್ಠ	ಣ ◌್ ಠ
ಣ್ಡ	ಣ ◌್ ಡ
ಣ್ಡ	ಣ ◌್ ಡ
ಣ್ಢ	ಣ ◌್ ಢ
ಣ್ಣ	ಣ ◌್ ಣ
ತ್ತ	ತ ◌್ ತ
ತ್ರ	ತ ◌್ ರ
ದ್ದೇ	ದ ◌್ ದ ◌ೇ
ದ್ಧ್ಯ	ದ ◌್ ಧ ◌್ ಯ
ದ್ನ	ದ ◌್ ನ
ದ್ಬ್ರ	ದ ◌್ ಬ ◌್ ರ
ದ್ಯ	ದ ◌್ ಯ
ದ್ಯಿ	ದ ◌್ ಯ ◌ಿ

Syllable	Character sequence
ದ್ವ	ದ ◌್ ವ
ದ್ವಿ	ದ ◌್ ವ ◌ಿ
ನ್ತ	ನ ◌್ ತ
ನ್ಥ	ನ ◌್ ಥ
ನ್ದ	ನ ◌್ ದ
ನ್ಧ	ನ ◌್ ಧ
ನ್ಧ್ರಿ	ನ ◌್ ಧ ◌್ ರ ◌ಿ
ನ್ನ	ನ ◌್ ನ
ನ್ವಿ	ನ ◌್ ವ ◌ಿ
ಪ್ತಿ	ಪ ◌್ ತ ◌ಿ
ಮ್ಪ	ಮ ◌್ ಪ
ಮ್ಫ	ಮ ◌್ ಫ
ಮ್ಬ	ಮ ◌್ ಬ
ಮ್ಭ	ಮ ◌್ ಭ
ಮ್ಮ	ಮ ◌್ ಮ
ರ್	ರ ◌್
ರ್ಣೋ	ರ ◌್ ಣ ◌ೋ
ರ್ತಾ	ರ ◌್ ತ ◌ಾ
ರ್ತ್ರೈ	ರ ◌್ ತ ◌್ ರ ◌ೈ
ರ್ಥೀ	ರ ◌್ ಥ ◌ೀ
ರ್ಥ್ಯೈ	ರ ◌್ ಥ ◌್ ಯ ◌ೈ
ರ್ದ್ಧಿ	ರ ◌್ ದ ◌್ ಧ ◌ಿ
ರ್ದ್ಯೋ	ರ ◌್ ದ ◌್ ಯ ◌ೋ
ರ್ಧ್ರು	ರ ◌್ ಧ ◌್ ರ ◌ು
ರ್ರೋ	ರ ◌್ ರ ◌ೋ
ವಿ	ವ ◌ಿ
ಶ್ಚ	ಶ ◌್ ಚ

Syllable	Character sequence
ಶ್ನ	ಶ ◌್ ನ
ಶ್ರ	ಶ ◌್ ರ
ಶ್ಲೋ	ಶ ◌್ ಲ ◌ೋ
ಶ್ವಿ	ಶ ◌್ ವ ◌ಿ
ಷ್ಟ	ಷ ◌್ ಟ
ಷ್ಣ	ಷ ◌್ ಣ
ಷ್ಯ	ಷ ◌್ ಯ
ಸ್ತ್ರಿ	ಸ ◌್ ತ ◌್ ರ ◌ಿ
ಹ್ಖ	ಹ ◌್ ಖ
ಹ್ಣ	ಹ ◌್ ಣ
ಹ್ಮ	ಹ ◌್ ಮ
ಹ್ಯ	ಹ ◌್ ಯ
ಹ್ಲ	ಹ ◌್ ಲ
ಹ್ವ	ಹ ◌್ ವ
ಳ್ಕ	ಳ ◌್ ಕ
ಳ್ಳ	ಳ ◌್ ಳ
Malayalam	
ക്ക	ക ◌് ക
ക്ട	ക ◌് ട
ക്ത	ക ◌് ത
ക്യ	ക ◌് യ
ക്ര	ക ◌് ര
ക്ല	ക ◌് ല
ക്വ	ക ◌് വ
ക്ഷ	ക ◌് ഷ
ക്ഷൌ	ക ◌് ഷ ◌ൌ
കെ	ക ◌െ
കേ	ക ◌േ
കൈ	ക ◌ൈ
കൊ	ക ◌ൊ
കോ	ക ◌ോ
കൌ	ക ◌ൌ
കൗ	ക ◌ൗ
ഖ്ല	ഖ ◌് ല
ഗ്ഗ	ഗ ◌് ഗ
ഗ്ന	ഗ ◌് ന
ഗ്മ	ഗ ◌് മ
ഗ്ല	ഗ ◌് ല
ങ്ക	ങ ◌് ക
ങ്ങ	ങ ◌് ങ
ച്ച	ച ◌് ച
ച്ഛ	ച ◌് ഛ
ച്ല	ച ◌് ല
ജ്ജ	ജ ◌് ജ
ജ്ഞ	ജ ◌് ഞ
ജ്ല	ജ ◌് ല
ഞ്ഞ	ഞ ◌് ഞ
ട്ട	ട ◌് ട
ട്ല	ട ◌് ല
ഠ്ല	ഠ ◌് ല
ഡ്ഡ	ഡ ◌് ഡ
ഡ്ല	ഡ ◌് ല
ഢ്ല	ഢ ◌് ല
ണ്ഡ	ണ ◌് ഡ
ണ്ണ	ണ ◌് ണ
ണ്മ	ണ ◌് മ
ത്ത	ത ◌് ത
ത്ഥ	ത ◌് ഥ
ത്ഭ	ത ◌് ഭ
ത്മ	ത ◌് മ
ത്സ	ത ◌് സ
ദ്ദ	ദ ◌് ദ
ദ്ധ	ദ ◌് ധ
ദ്ല	ദ ◌് ല
ന്ത	ന ◌് ത
ന്ഥ	ന ◌് ഥ
ന്ദ	ന ◌് ദ
ന്ധ	ന ◌് ധ
ന്ന	ന ◌് ന
പ്പ	പ ◌് പ
പ്ല	പ ◌് ല
ഫ്ല	ഫ ◌് ല
ബ്ദ	ബ ◌് ദ
ബ്ധ	ബ ◌് ധ
ബ്ബ	ബ ◌് ബ
ബ്ല	ബ ◌് ല
ഭ്ല	ഭ ◌് ല
മ്പ	മ ◌് പ
മ്മ	മ ◌് മ
മ്ല	മ ◌് ല
യ്യ	യ ◌് യ
റ്റ	റ ◌് റ
ല്ല	ല ◌് ല
ള്ള	ള ◌് ള
വ്വ	വ ◌് വ
ശ്ല	ശ ◌് ല
ശ്ശ	ശ ◌് ശ
ഷ്ട	ഷ ◌് ട

Syllable	Character sequence
സ്ഥ	സ ◌് ഥ
സ്റ്റ	സ ◌് റ ◌് റ
സ്റ്റേ	സ ◌് റ ◌് റ േ◌
സ്ല	സ ◌് ല

Syllable	Character sequence
സ്സ	സ ◌് സ
ഹ്ന	ഹ ◌് ന
ഹ്മ	ഹ ◌് മ
ഹ്ല	ഹ ◌് ല

Note: If formatting is changed within the sequence of characters, then the ligatures may not be formed correctly.

Certain ligatures using ZWJ and ZWNJ characters:

Syllable	Character sequence
क्‍	क ◌् ZWJ
द्‌य	द ◌् ZWNJ य
द्‌व	द ◌् ZWNJ व
र्‍य	र ◌् ZWJ य
र्‍ह	र ◌् ZWJ ह
ा	ZWJ ◌ा[10]
ि	ZWJ ि◌
ी	ZWJ ◌ी
ु	ZWJ ◌ु
ू	ZWJ ◌ू
ृ	ZWJ ◌ृ
ॅ	ZWJ ◌ॅ
े	ZWJ ◌े
ै	ZWJ ◌ै
ॉ	ZWJ ◌ॉ
ो	ZWJ ◌ो
ौ	ZWJ ◌ौ
्	ZWJ ◌्
कि	ZWJ ि◌ *formatting*[11] क

Syllable	Character sequence
अि	ZWJ ि◌ अ
अु	अ ZWJ ◌ु
ia	ZWJ ि◌ a
au	a ZWJ ◌ु
iaी	ZWJ ि◌ a ZWJ ◌ी
ৎ	ত্ ZWJ[12]
ৎত	ত্ ZWJ ত
ত্‌ত	ত্ ZWNJ ত
র‍্য	র ZWSP ZWJ ্য[13]
স্য	স্ ZWJ য
হু	হ ZWJ[14] ু
গু	গ ZWJ ু
রু	র ZWJ ু
রৃ	র ZWJ ৃ
্যঁ	ZWJ ্য ঁ
্যাঁ	ZWJ ্য া ঁ

[10] In Microsoft Word, ZWJ character should be typed when the desired language is select as the input language (which is Hindi in the present example).
[11] To have formatting of the vowel sign different from that of the letter.

[12] Now, *khanda ta* is a separate character in Unicode.
[13] As per the standard, ZWSP is unnecessary. Also note that র্ য without ZWJ character produces র্য.
[14] Ideally, ZWJ should not be needed here and the next few items, and also in গু.

Note: Letters of Indic scripts join to form ligatures in so many ways that it is not possible to cover all of them with only ZWJ, ZWNJ and ZWSP characters.

Note: Things also depend on the font. For example, there is a Unicode based Devanagari font by the name *Gargi* (http://www.tdil.mit.go.in/download/gargi.htm). If one types ि क ी in the font, it becomes किी, and not िकी! Of course typing क ि ी also produces the same visual look किी! Typing a ु produces aु, and not a◌ु! One can type कि in two ways: (i) ि क and (ii) क ि, of which the former is technically wrong notwithstanding the same visual look.

Use of combining characters:

Appearance	**Character sequence: base letter followed by diacritical marks in any sequence**
a̰̔	a ̔ ̰ *or*, a ̰ ̔
अ॒॑	अ ॑ ॒ *or*, अ ॒ ॑
ङ़̃	ङ ̃ " ़[15]
அ̭̊	அ ̭ ̊ *or*, அ ̊ ̭

Word = Sequence of one or more conjunct syllables;
Conjunct syllable = one or more grapheme

[15] In Microsoft Word, ZWJ character should be typed when the desired language is select as the input language (which is Hindi in the present example).

Note: Bengali vowel letters অ (a) and এ (e) can also be followed by *hasant* (্) and য (ya), and the conjunct is treated as if it were a consonant letter. However, in normal Bengali writing, অ্য and এ্য is always followed by aa-vowel sign (া), and an optional vowel modifier sign.

Note: The above sequence of characters is to be used for typing Indic text using telephone keypads.

Typing in Arabic Script

The following table illustrates how to type in Arabic script based languages, such as Urdu in Microsoft Windows/Office environments.

For this	Type this in right-to-left sequence
یومِ آزادی	ی و م ِ ZWNJ آ ز ا د ی
یومِآزادی	ی و م ِ آ ز ا د ی
نعمت	ن ع م ت
مکھّی	م ک ھ ّ ی
مکّھی	م ک ّ ھ ی
العراق	ا ل ع ر ا ق
ایران	ا ی ر ا ن
عید مبارک	ع ی د Space م ب ا ر ک
محمد	م ح م د
اکبر	ا ک ب ر
باً	ب ا ً
ہندوستاں	ہ ن د و س ت ا ں
پاکستان	پ ا ک س ت ا ن
ہم دم	ہ م Space/ZWNJ د م
بَروُنْ کُمار	ب َ ر و ُ ن ْ Space ک ُ م ا ر
سِر	س ِ ر
سَیّد	س َ ی ّ د
اللہ	ا ل ل ہ
اللہ	ا ل ل ZWJ ہ
جائیں	ج ا ئ ی ں
ہوئی	ہ و ئ ی
کہ	ک ہ
کھ	ک ھ
کھ	ک ھ ZWJ[16]
کھا	ک ھ ا

[16] In some fonts, ZWJ character is not required!

For this	Type this in right-to-left sequence
کہا	ک ہ ا
گی	گ ی
گئ	گ ئ
گیی	گ ی ی
گے	گ ے
گیں	گ ی ں
گئں	گ ئ ں
گئے	گ ئے
گریڈیہہ	گ ر ی ڈ ی ہ ہ
یہ	ی ہ
١،٢٣٤,٥	٥ , ٤ ٣ ٢ ، ١
؀۱۲۳۴	؀ ۱ ۲ ۳ ۴

Note: A space character (0020 hex) is used between two words in Urdu. The space character is used even if the two adjoining letters do not join form ligature. For example, space will have to be used between کر and چکا, even though ر do not join to form ligature with the چ following it in کر چکا. ZWNJ character can be used to break formation of ligature within a word, if the two adjoining letters are such that they will join to form ligature.

Note: Specific software uses different key sequence for typing in Arabic script. For example, for typing in INPAGE software (see Chapter 1), a slightly different character sequence was used. The letter ء (hamza) is to be used wherever the letter ئ (yeh with hamza) appears in the above table.

Note: Formation of the ligature will be affected if the fonts are changed within a word. This is true not only for Arabic script, but also for Indic scripts. For example, کک will become ک‌ک if two different fonts are used to write the word; क्क becomes क्‌क, if the first क is in one font and the subsequent ् and क are in another font.

Note: An older version of the popular "Times New Roman" font formed a few defective ligatures in Arabic. One may need to obtain a newer version of the font.

Inscript Keyboard Layout

Inscript keyboard layout for Devanagari script is shown below. Inscript keyboard layout is same or similar for other Indic scripts. If a letter/conjunct is not there in an Indic script, then that key may not be used; e.g., Bengali alphabet does not have any letter equivalent to South Indian letter ऎ.

Devanagari inscript keyboard layout

Legend:

English key with Shift	*Devanagari with shift*
English key	*Devanagari normal*

(1) Standard keyboard layout

~ ऑ	! ऍ	@ ◌ॅ	# ^	$ र्	% ज्ञ	^ त्र	& क्ष	* श्र	((	))	_ ◌ः	+ ऋ	| ऑ
` ◌ॊ	1 1	2 2	3 3	4 4	5 5	6 6	7 7	8 8	9 9	0 0	- -	= ◌ृ	\ ◌ॉ

Tab	Q औ	W ऐ	E आ	R ई	T ऊ	Y भ	U ङ	I घ	O ध	P झ	{ ढ	} ञ
	q ◌ौ	w ◌ै	e ◌ा	r ◌ी	t ◌ू	y ब	u ह	i ग	o द	p ज	[ड	] ◌़

Symbol Lock	A ओ	S ए	D अ	F इ	G उ	H फ	J ऱ	K ख	L थ	: छ	" ठ	Enter
	a ◌ो	s ◌े	d ◌्	f ि◌	g ◌ु	h प	j र	k क	l त	; च	' ट	

Shift	Z ऎ	X ◌ँ	C ण	V ऩ	B ऴ	N ळ	M श	< ष	> ।	? य़	Shift
	z ◌ॆ	x ◌ं	c म	v न	b व	n ल	m स	, ,	. .	/ य	

Ctrl		LeftAlt	SPACE BAR	Rt Alt			Ctrl

(2) Keyboard layout with right-alt key

~	! ¡	@	#	$	%	^	&	*	(	)	_	+ ॠ	|
`	1 १	2 २	3 ३	4 ४	5 ५	6 ६	7 ७	8 ८	9 ९	0 ०	-	= ◌ॄ	\

Tab	Q	W	E	R ॡ	T	Y	U	I	O	P	{ ढ़	}
	q	w	e	r ◌ॣ	t	y	u	i ग़	o	p ज़	[ड़	]

Symbol Lock	A a	S s	D d	F ऌ f ॢ	G g	H फ़ h	J j	K ख़ k क़	L l	: ; ॄ	" ॅ '	Enter
Shift	Z z ॆ	X ॐ x	C c ॅ	V v	B b ह़	N n	M m	< , ॰	> ऽ . ॥	? ॽ /	Shift	
Ctrl		LeftAlt	SPACE BAR					Rt Alt			Ctrl	

Traditional Hindi keyboard layout

(1) Standard keyboard layout

~ `	! ऍ 1 1	@ ॅ 2 2	# ^ 3 3	$ र् 4 4	% ज्ञ 5 5	^ त्र 6 6	& क्ष 7 7	* श्र 8 8	((9 9	)) 0 0	_ ः - -	+ ऋ = -	| ऑ \ ॉ
Tab	Q औ q ौ	W ऐ w ै	E आ e ा	R ई r ी	T ऊ t ू	Y भ y ब	U ङ u ह	I घ i ग	O ध o द	P झ p ज	{ ढ [ड	} ञ] ़	
Symbol Lock	A ओ a ो	S ए s े	D अ d ्	F इ f ि	G उ g ु	H फ h प	J ऱ j र	K ख k क	L थ l त	: छ ; च	" ठ ' ट	Enter	
Shift	Z z	X ँ x ं	C ण c म	V v न	B b व	N ळ n ल	M श m स	< ष , ,	> । . .	? य़ / य	Shift		
Ctrl		LeftAlt	SPACE BAR					Rt Alt			Ctrl		

(2) Keyboard layout with right-alt key

~ ~ ` `	! ! 1 १	@ @ 2 २	# # 3 ३	$ $ 4 ४	% % 5 ५	^ ^ 6 ६	& & 7 ७	* * 8 ८	((9 ९	)) 0 ०	_ _ - -	+ + = =	| | \ \
Tab	Q q	W w	E e	R r	T t	Y y	U u	I i	O o	P p	{ { [[	} }]]	
Symbol Lock	A a	S s	D D	F f	G g	H h	J j	K k	L l	: : ; ;	" " ' '	Enter	
Shift	Z Z	X ॐ x	C c	V v	B b	N n	M m	< < , ,	> > . .	? ? / /	Shift		
Ctrl		LeftAlt	SPACE BAR					Rt Alt		Ctrl			

***Standard Gurmukhi keyboard layout*:**

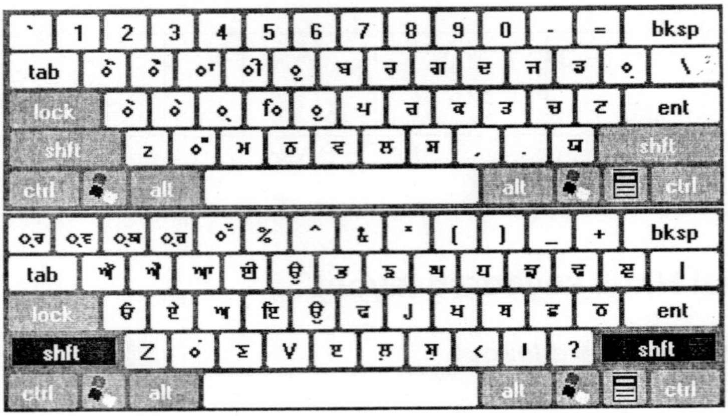

***Special features of Bengali Inscript keyboard*:**

Key sequence	**Bengali/Assamese letter/symbol**
Right-Alt-x	ঁ (Isshar)
Right-Alt-j	ৰ (Assamese ra)
Right-Alt-Shift-j	ৱ (Assamese wa/va)

Building Customized Keyboard Layout

Many keyboard layouts for different languages have been described in Chapter 4 and *Annexure (F)*. Microsoft Windows comes with plenty of keyboard layouts and input method editors (IMEs). Many others can be downloaded from the Internet. Normally, these should be sufficient. Nonetheless, one may want to create customized keyboard layouts to cater to one's specific needs. For example, say, one is designing the keyboard layout for a tribal language that uses letters like ङ, ञ, ऽ etc very frequently. However, in normal Devanagari keyboard layouts, it is cumbersome to type these letters. Evidently, the normal Devanagari keyboard layouts will not be very handy, and one may desire to create one's own customized keyboard layout. As another example, one may want to change QWERTY keyboard layout to ABCDEF keyboard layout. Maybe, one is very ingenious, and desires to design a new keyboard layout that one believes is better than the existing keyboard layouts, or a keyboard layout that will become the standard in future!

Microsoft Keyboard Layout Creator program can be used to design and create customized keyboard layout. Microsoft Keyboard Layout Creator program may be obtained from friends, or downloaded from the Internet. Microsoft website also allowed free download of the software. One may install the program in one's computer. .NET Framework Files are needed for proper installation of the program. As such, appropriate .NET Framework Files should be installed before installing the layout creator program.

The following figure shows how Microsoft Keyboard Layout Creator program looks like when opened.

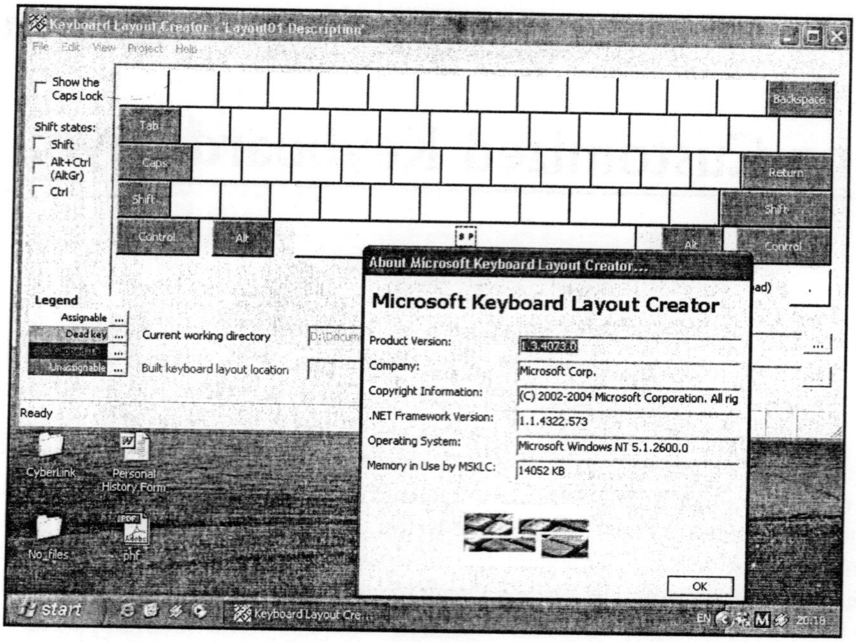

To understand how to use the program to design and create keyboard layout, it is recommended that one may go through the helps available in the application software.

The keyboard layouts are specific to the language and even the variant of the language. For example, a keyboard layout for Hindi will have to be specified as a keyboard layout for Hindi (India) language. The language is to be set through the action Project → Properties… under the menu bar in the Keyboard Layout Creator window.

One can define most of the keys in the keyboard using the keyboard layout creator program. The keys may be programmed for different behavior of keys depending on the status of the virtual keys: Shift, Control, CapsLock, and Alt etc. The following pictures illustrate an example, where different keys have been defined to generate a keyboard layout, when the "Shift status" is ON.

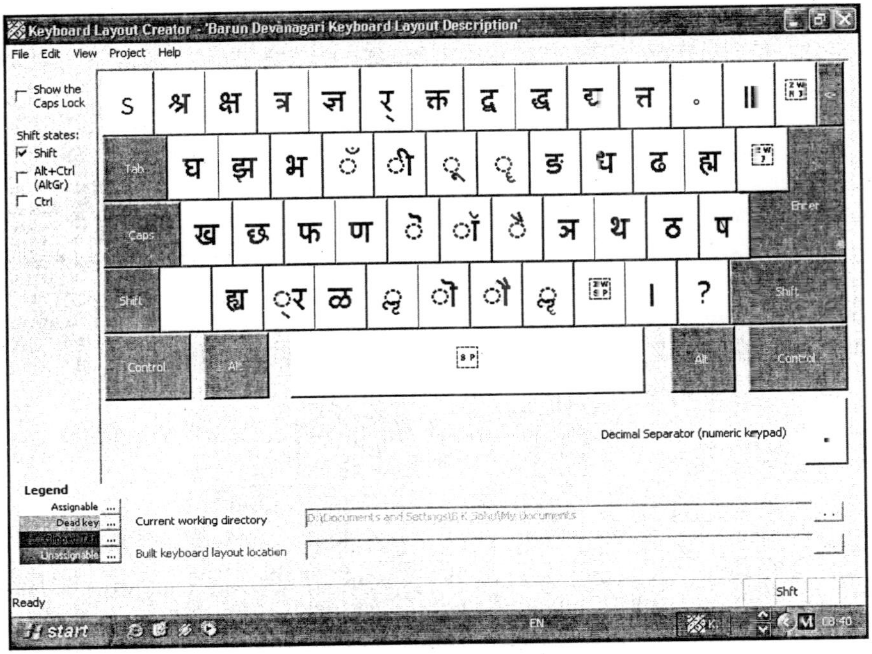

The following screenshot illustration illustrates "Dead Key View" and "Advanced View" in the design of a keyboard layout.

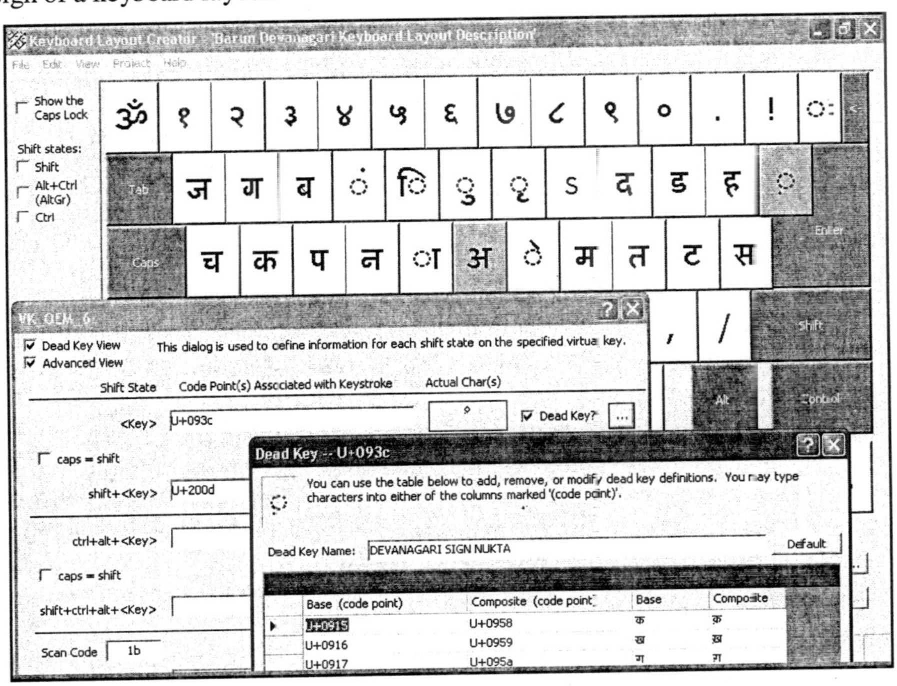

A key may be defined as a single character. Alternatively, a key may be defined as an ordered sequence of two or more characters. The number of characters in the sequence of characters is subject to an upper limit. The keys may be defined to visible, quasi-visible or invisible character, or a mix of visible, quasi-visible and invisible characters. For example, keys may be defined to denote ZWJ, ZWNJ, ZWSP, *halant* etc characters. Keys may be defined as one character each, such as for क, ख, ग... अ, आ, इ... etc. Keys may be defined as a sequence of more than one character, such as for the conjuncts क्ष (U+0915 U+094D U+0937), क्त (U+0915 U+094D U+0924), and क्‍त (U+0915 U+094D U+200D U+0924). If a key in a particular state of the virtual keys has been defined as a "Dead Key," then the character(s) inputted depends on the subsequent key that is pressed. If a key has not been defined, then pressing that key will not cause inputting of any character.

Some keys may be defined in another script. For example, in the design of keyboard layout of a Devanagari script based language (say, Hindi), some keys may be defined as being in another script/subset (such as, Latin, general punctuations, currency symbols etc).

How to install the customized keyboard layout

1. Design the keyboard layout using Microsoft Keyboard Layout Creator program.
2. Use Project → "Build DLL and Setup Package" menu bar option of the keyboard layout creator program to build DLL ("Application Extension") and Setup Package ("Windows Installer Package") for the designed keyboard layout.
3. Run the Setup Package produced by the keyboard layout creator program to install the Setup Package.
4. The keyboard layout will figure in the list of keyboard layouts/IMEs as explained in Chapter 3 (see Figure 19 and 20). The keyboard layout may be selected for inputting the text in the desired language as explained in that chapter.
5. The desired language and the keyboard layout may be selected, and used to input text.

How to uninstall the keyboard layout

All said and done, one may want to uninstall the keyboard layout one has designed and installed in the computer machine. To uninstall a customized keyboard layout, one has to execute the following steps:

1. Ensure from Control Panel → "Regional and Language Options" → Languages → Details that no language is using the keyboard layout to be uninstalled (see Chapter 3). If the keyboard layout has been specified for input text in any language, then the keyboard layout should be removed from the list of keyboard layouts specified for the language.
2. Go to Control Panel → Add/Remove Programs, and remove keyboard layout.
3. The keyboard has been uninstalled!

Frequently Asked Questions and their Answers

QUESTION	*ANSWER*
1. Do I have to buy any software for Indian and other languages?	No! Microsoft Windows (2000 version or later) operating system is the least you need.
2. Can I use Indic language in other operating systems?	Microsoft Windows supports Indic languages in Unicode. Many other operating systems also support Indic languages in Unicode, examples being Linux, Unix, Mac and GNU. However, this book has been written primarily for Microsoft Windows environment. There are some illustrations in Linux also.
3. Do I have to buy new keyboards for the different languages?	No, you will use the same keyboard to input text in all languages. Though, you may prefer to buy stickers for pasting on the keys on the keyboard—assuming that they have not yet invented keyboard where the letters printed on the keys change with change of keyboard layout.
4. Do I require any computer skill to learn using computer in Hindi/other languages?	No, except familiarity with the language and the computers (equivalent to standard V student).
5. Which languages can I use?	Almost all languages across the world! Including European, Indic, Arabic, East Asian and even many obscure languages! More and more languages are being made available. However, some software may still not perform well with certain languages. For example, some CD- writers did not work well with file and folder names in Devanagari script.
6. How do I install Hindi and other languages in my computer?	See Chapter 3.
7. How many languages can I install in one computer?	Any number or combination of languages your operating system supports!
8. What is the keyboard layout I am using for Hindi or other languages?	See Chapters 3 and 4. It is also possible to design customized keyboard—for example, by Microsoft Keyboard Layout Creator program.

	QUESTION	*ANSWER*
9.	Will my friend have to install the language to read my e-mails/documents in the language?	For Indic and Arabic languages: Maybe, yes! Font may not be enough to write, or in a few cases even to read text in complex scripts.
10.	How do I write in a new script I have invented?	See Chapter 1. However, you will have to read books on font designing.
11.	How do I type complex conjuncts of Indic and Arabic languages?	See Chapter 4 and *Annexure (E)*.
12.	Can I write one language in another script: Urdu in Devanagari script? Tamil in English script? Sanskrit in Arabic script?	Yes, though it is not recommended. Most supports may be available in the popular script only.
13.	How do I write in French? Spanish? German? Russian?	See Chapter 4.
14.	Can I use Indic numerals? Mixture of numerals in different languages?	Yes! Yes! You can also switch between Indic and international numerals!
15.	Can I make Hindi (or another language) as the default input language?	Yes! But probably not at the BIOS level right now, as options at BIOS level may be only among English, French and Spanish.
16.	Can I give name to a file or folder in two different scripts? In ten different scripts?	Yes, in any combination! You may even mix left-to-right scripts with right-to-left scripts in the file names, anywhere! سمجھے या नहीं?
17.	Can I sort a table of data written in Hindi (or another language)? Even if it has data in more than one language/script?	Yes! Yes!
18.	Can I search the Internet in Hindi? Tamil? Bengali? Nepali? Urdu? Russian? Chinese? Arabic?	Yes! But probably not in the language you have invented, or that is very obscure—and that is still not supported.
19.	How do I open a website with URL like http://www.कखग.gov.in, http://www.αβγ.com, http://www.ГДЖШ.net, http://www.éçρäñøl.org?	See Chapter 7.
20.	How do I install Hindi, Tamil, Punjabi, Kannada etc version of Microsoft Windows? Linux? Office?	See Chapter 8.
21.	Can I uninstall the input languages?	Yes, anytime! But your computer must retain at least one input language, though not necessarily English!